Literacy in the Information Age

Final Report of the International Adult Literacy Survey

ORGANISATION FOR ECONOMIC CO-OPERATION AND DEVELOPMENT

STATISTICS CANADA

ORGANISATION FOR ECONOMIC CO-OPERATION AND DEVELOPMENT

Pursuant to Article 1 of the Convention signed in Paris on 14th December 1960, and which came into force on 30th September 1961, the Organisation for Economic Co-operation and Development (OECD) shall promote policies designed:

- to achieve the highest sustainable economic growth and employment and a rising standard of living in Member countries, while maintaining financial stability, and thus to contribute to the development of the world economy;
- to contribute to sound economic expansion in Member as well as non-member countries in the process of economic development; and
- to contribute to the expansion of world trade on a multilateral, non-discriminatory basis in accordance with international obligations.

The original Member countries of the OECD are Austria, Belgium, Canada, Denmark, France, Germany, Greece, Iceland, Ireland, Italy, Luxembourg, the Netherlands, Norway, Portugal, Spain, Sweden, Switzerland, Turkey, the United Kingdom and the United States. The following countries became Members subsequently through accession at the dates indicated thereafter: Japan (28th April 1964), Finland (28th January 1969), Australia (7th June 1971), New Zealand (29th May 1973), Mexico (18th May 1994), the Czech Republic (21st December 1995), Hungary (7th May 1996), Poland (22nd November 1996) and the Republic of Korea (12th December 1996). The Commission of the European Communities takes part in the work of the OECD (Article 13 of the OECD Convention).

STATISTICS CANADA

Statistics Canada, Canada's central statistical agency, has the mandate to "collect, compile, analyse, and publish statistical information relating to the commercial, industrial, financial, social, economic and general activities and condition of the people of Canada." The organization, a federal government agency, is headed by the Chief Statistician of Canada and reports to Parliament through the Minister of Industry Canada.

Statistics Canada provides information to governments at every level and is the source of statistical information for business, labour, academic and social institutions, professional associations, the international statistical community, and the general public. This information is produced at the national and provincial levels and, in some cases, for major population centres and other sub-provincial or "small" areas.

The Agency fosters relations not only within Canada but also throughout the world, by participating in a number of international meetings and professional exchanges. Statistics Canada was responsible for managing the design and implementation of the International Adult Literacy Survey in co-operation with the Educational Testing Service of Princeton, New Jersey, and national survey teams.

Foreword

As we move into the information age, policy makers in all countries are increasingly concerned about the role knowledge and skills play in enhancing productivity growth and innovation and in improving social cohesion. The data presented in this publication, drawn from 20 countries over three cycles of data collection for the International Adult Literacy Survey, provide the world's first reliable and comparable estimates of the levels and distributions of literacy skills in the adult population.

The study offers an understanding of the nature and magnitude of literacy issues faced by countries and explores new insights into the factors that influence the development of adult skills in various settings – at home, at work and across countries. The 20 countries represented account for over 50 per cent of the world's entire gross domestic product. As such, the literacy data can contribute importantly to an understanding of the demand and supply of skills in the global, knowledge-based economy.

The results confirm the importance of skills for the effective functioning of labour markets and for the economic success and social advancement of both individuals and societies. They offer policy makers a useful tool for policy analysis and for crafting policies and programmes that can contribute to economic and social progress.

The survey was made possible thanks to a unique collaboration involving international organisations, national governments and their statistical offices, educational assessment and research institutions, and experts drawn from many countries. Such co-operation is remarkable and serves as a model for future efforts to improve the availability of official and comparable statistics in key policy domains.

The report is published on the responsibility of the Secretary-General of the Organisation for Economic Co-operation and Development, the Minister of Industry of the Government of Canada and Statistics Canada.

Table of Contents

List of Figures and Tables

Chapter 1

Chapter 2

Chapter 3

Chapter 4

Chapter 5

Introduction

This section introduces the participants in the survey. It also provides, in summary form, the definition of literacy used for the assessment and the methods employed for the data collection and scaling of the results – information necessary for an understanding of the literacy levels and performance scales used in the data analysis. Finally, an overview of the key findings is presented.

The Participants

The International Adult Literacy Survey (IALS) was a large-scale co-operative effort by governments, national statistical agencies, research institutions and the Organisation for Economic Co-operation and Development (OECD). The development and management of the survey were co-ordinated by Statistics Canada and the Educational Testing Service of Princeton, New Jersey. At various survey cycles, and in different ways, substantial input was received from the National Center for Education Statistics of the United States Department of Education, input that has greatly facilitated the project and ultimately made this publication possible.

In 1994, nine countries – Canada (English and French-speaking populations), France, Germany, Ireland, the Netherlands, Poland, Sweden, Switzerland (German and French-speaking regions) and the United States – fielded the world's first large-scale, comparative assessment of adult literacy. Data for seven of these countries were published in *Literacy, Economy and Society: Results of the First International Adult Literacy Survey* in December 1995 (OECD and Statistics Canada, 1995).[1]

Encouraged by this demonstration of success, five additional countries or territories – Australia, the Flemish Community in Belgium, Great Britain, New Zealand and Northern Ireland – decided to administer the IALS instruments to samples of their adult populations in 1996. Comparative data from this round of collection were released in November 1997 in *Literacy Skills for the Knowledge Society: Further Results from the International Adult Literacy Survey* (OECD and HRDC, 1997).

Nine other countries or regions – Chile, the Czech Republic, Denmark, Finland, Hungary, Italy,[2] Norway, Slovenia and the Italian-speaking region of Switzerland – participated in a third, large-scale round of data collection in 1998. Results for most of these countries are included in this report. Limited literacy data became available for Portugal in 1998 and are reported where the sample size is sufficient to support

---

1. France decided to withdraw from the study in November 1995, citing concerns over comparability. Data processing for Ireland was unfortunately delayed and so its results were included in a subsequent IALS publication.
2. Data for Italy are forthcoming in the publication, *La competenza alfabetica in Italia : Una ricerca sulla cultura della populazione,* Centro Europeo Dell' Educazione, Frascati and F. Angeli, Milan.

the analysis.[3] Japan, Malaysia, Mexico and the Canary Islands region of Spain have also successfully experimented with IALS-derived instruments.[4]

Definition of Literacy

Many previous studies have treated literacy as a condition that adults either have or do not have. The IALS no longer defines literacy in terms of an arbitrary standard of reading performance, distinguishing the few who completely fail the test (the "illiterates") from nearly all those growing up in OECD countries who reach a minimum threshold (those who are "literate"). Rather, proficiency levels along a continuum denote how well adults use information to function in society and the economy. Thus, literacy is defined as a particular capacity and mode of behaviour:

> the ability to understand and employ printed information in daily activities, at home, at work and in the community – to achieve one's goals, and to develop one's knowledge and potential.

In denoting a broad set of information-processing competencies, this conceptual approach points to the multiplicity of skills that constitute literacy in advanced industrialized countries. The conceptual framework, the definitions of literacy and the test items used for the assessment are described in detail in Annex A. Literacy is measured operationally in terms of the three domains described in Box A, each encompassing a common set of skills relevant for diverse tasks.

Box A.   Three Domains of Literacy Skills

- *Prose literacy* – the knowledge and skills needed to understand and use information from texts including editorials, news stories, brochures and instruction manuals.

- *Document literacy* – the knowledge and skills required to locate and use information contained in various formats, including job applications, payroll forms, transportation schedules, maps, tables and charts.

- *Quantitative literacy* – the knowledge and skills required to apply arithmetic operations, either alone or sequentially, to numbers embedded in printed materials, such as balancing a chequebook, figuring out a tip, completing an order form or determining the amount of interest on a loan from an advertisement.

Measurement of Literacy

The IALS employed a sophisticated methodology developed and applied by the Educational Testing Service to measure literacy proficiency for each domain on a scale ranging from 0 to 500 points. Literacy ability in each domain is expressed by a score, defined as the point at which a person has an 80 per cent chance of successful performance from among the set of tasks of varying difficulty included in the

---

3. Results for Portugal were obtained as part of an EU-sponsored research project, co-ordinated by the Office of National Statistics of the United Kingdom.

4. Results for these countries are not included in this report because they were obtained in feasibility studies that used limited and non-representative samples.

assessment. Box B describes five levels of literacy that correspond to measured ranges of scores achieved. These levels, explained in more depth in Annex A, are used in this report for analytical purposes.

Box B. Five Levels of Literacy

- *Level* 1 indicates persons with very poor skills, where the individual may, for example, be unable to determine the correct amount of medicine to give a child from information printed on the package.

- *Level* 2 respondents can deal only with material that is simple, clearly laid out, and in which the tasks involved are not too complex. It denotes a weak level of skill, but more hidden than Level 1. It identifies people who can read, but test poorly. They may have developed coping skills to manage everyday literacy demands, but their low level of proficiency makes it difficult for them to face novel demands, such as learning new job skills.

- *Level* 3 is considered a suitable minimum for coping with the demands of everyday life and work in a complex, advanced society. It denotes roughly the skill level required for successful secondary school completion and college entry. Like higher levels, it requires the ability to integrate several sources of information and solve more complex problems.

- *Levels* **4 and 5** describe respondents who demonstrate command of higher-order information processing skills.

Data Collection

The data presented in this report were collected by the countries participating in successive cycles of data collection between 1994 and 1998, using nationally representative samples of the adult population aged 16-65. The survey was conducted in people's homes by experienced interviewers. Annex B describes in more detail the design used for the IALS. This combined educational assessment techniques with methods of household survey research. Also included in this annex is a description of the quality control measures implemented throughout the course of the IALS in order to ensure that high-quality data would be obtained. It also describes the enhanced measures taken to further improve data quality and comparability during the subsequent cycles of the survey. Specific issues concerning validity, reliability and comparability of the data are addressed in Annex C.

In brief, respondents were first asked a series of questions to obtain background information about them, *e.g.* demographic details, work history, etc. Once this background questionnaire was completed, the interviewer presented a booklet containing six simple tasks. If a respondent failed to complete at least two of these correctly, the interview was adjourned. Respondents who completed two or more tasks correctly were then given a much larger variety of tasks, printed in a separate booklet. The assessment was not timed, and respondents were urged to try each exercise. Respondents were thus given maximum opportunity to demonstrate their skills.

Highlights

Globalisation, technological change and organisational development are shaping both the supply of, and the demand for higher levels of literacy skills in the information age. As this process of upskilling unfolds, the IALS findings can provide insights for policy makers responsible for the design of lifelong learning, social and labour market policies.

The IALS data illustrate how literacy skills are distributed, internationally and nationally, what determines the attainment of higher levels of literacy, and what are its broader social and economic outcomes and benefits. The key findings are summarised below.

Population Distributions of Literacy Skills

This new report includes data for the 12 original IALS countries and compares their literacy scores with those of nine more countries or regions for which new, previously unavailable data on the extent of the literacy problem have now become available: Chile, Czech Republic, Denmark, Finland, Hungary, Norway, Portugal, Slovenia and the Italian-speaking population of Switzerland.

In 14 out of 20 countries, at least 15 per cent of all adults have literacy skills at only the most rudimentary level, making it difficult for them to cope with the rising skill demands of the information age. Countries with large numbers of citizens at the lowest level of literacy (more than 15 per cent on the prose literacy test) are: Australia, Belgium (Flanders), Canada, Chile, Czech Republic, Hungary, Ireland, New Zealand, Poland, Portugal, Slovenia, Switzerland, the United Kingdom and the United States.

In six countries less than 15 per cent of adults find themselves at the lowest level of literacy skills (Denmark, Finland, Germany, Netherlands, Norway and Sweden), but even in the country with the highest score on the test (Sweden) 8 per cent of the adult population encounters a severe literacy deficit in everyday life and at work.

Thus, low skills are found not just among marginalised groups but among significant proportions of the adult populations in all countries surveyed. Hence, even the most economically advanced societies have a literacy skills deficit. Between one-quarter and three-quarters of adults fail to attain literacy Level 3, considered by experts[1] as a suitable minimum skill level for coping with the demands of modern life and work.

---

1. Focus groups and experts engaged by the study team responsible for the 1992 US National Adult Literacy Survey.

The largest differences between countries in literacy proficiency occur for people with the least formal education. In some countries significant numbers of adults with little schooling are able to demonstrate high levels of literacy skills; in others only a small proportion of adults with little schooling has acquired the level of skills that is likely to be required in the information age.

Adults with low literacy skills do not usually consider that their lack of skills presents them with any major difficulties. Respondents replied overwhelmingly that their reading skills were sufficient to meet everyday needs regardless of tested skill levels. This may reflect the fact that many respondents have developed coping strategies or that many ordinary jobs do not require high levels of literacy, a situation that is likely to change as the knowledge economy matures.

Antecedents of Literacy Skills

The most important predictor of literacy proficiency is educational attainment. On average, people increase their literacy scores on the IALS test by about 10 points for each additional year they attend school. Further, in most countries, age is negatively correlated with literacy skills, partly because older cohorts have on average lower educational attainment. The beneficial effects of initial education on the literacy skills of young adults are particularly pronounced in emerging economies. Efforts to further raise the levels of literacy proficiency are most effective when focused on youth from lower socio-economic backgrounds.

Although the relationship between educational attainment and literacy skills is undoubtedly strong, it is also complex. First, home background and particularly the level of education of the parents influence this relationship. Further, literacy acquisition also occurs during the years beyond school.

Literacy skills are maintained and strengthened through regular use. While schooling provides an essential foundation, the evidence suggests that only through informal learning and the active use of literacy skills in daily activities – both at home and at work – will higher levels of proficiency be attained. The creation of literacy-rich environments, in the workplace and more generally, can have lasting, intergenerational effects.

The associations between literacy skills and activities such as participation in adult education and training, reading at work and at home, and participation in voluntary community activities are generally significant in a statistical sense but seem quite small from a substantive viewpoint, especially compared with the strength of the relationships between initial educational attainment, literacy skills and the labour market.

Literacy Skills and Features of the Labour Market

Across countries, higher levels of literacy skills in the workforce are associated with larger proportions of knowledge jobs in the economy.

Literacy skills influence positively the probability of being in a white-collar high-skilled position and negatively the probability of being unemployed or in a blue-collar position. Further evidence supporting this conclusion is obtained when examining occupational categories by industrial sectors.

Literacy not only enhances career prospects, but also reduces the chance of being unemployed. In most countries, low skills are associated with a higher incidence of long-term unemployment as opposed to short-term unemployment.

The impact of improved literacy, especially in white-collar high-skilled occupations, differs according to the level of educational attainment of individuals. The benefits accruing to improved literacy skills are much higher for workers with tertiary education than for those with secondary education.

Literacy, Earnings and Wage Differentials

Of the factors studied in the wage analysis, educational attainment is the most important determinant of earnings in most countries, even when variations in the other factors are held constant. But there are also major differences in the strength of this relationship across the countries investigated.

Literacy proficiency also has a substantial effect on earnings in many of the countries studied. The effect of literacy skills on earnings depends in part on differences in levels of education, but in many countries literacy also has an independent, net effect on wages.

There are large differences between countries in how much their labour markets reward education and how much they pay for skills and experience. Labour market rewards associated with education, skills and experience are amplified or attenuated by the relative conditions of supply and demand.

Wider Social Benefits of Literacy Skills

The relationship between literacy skills and macro-economic and social development is quite complex and has not been investigated in detail in this report. However, a number of non-market benefits are associated with literacy skills. It appears that countries with a more unequal distribution of income also have a more unequal distribution of literacy skills. High literacy is also associated with better health outcomes, for example, increased longevity and healthier habits and life styles. There is a further link between literacy and public and civic participation that can be seen in the increased political participation of women as the average literacy levels of countries rise.

Conclusion

Not surprisingly, the IALS reports have attracted a great deal of interest from policy makers, analysts and the popular press. The study has provided information on a number of questions of pressing interest and concern. Yet, as with any well-conceived study, it has also raised as many questions as it has answered. Key among such questions are those asking about the relationship of literacy skills to other skills thought to be important to workforce productivity and labour market success.

Note to Readers

> Throughout this report, graphs are employed to communicate study results to a broad, non-technical audience, as well as to provide a source of informative displays that policy makers and others may use for their own purposes. To satisfy the more technical reader, data tables are provided in Annex D.

Multiple sources of uncertainty and error are a fact of life in social science research. Given the comparative nature of the study, those responsible for the study's design and implementation went to great lengths to control and quantify such errors and to establish the validity and reliability of the measures. Yet subtle differences in survey design and implementation, and in the pattern of non-response across languages and cultures, do introduce some errors into the literacy estimates.

Statistics Canada, the Educational Testing Service, and the national study teams have performed exhaustive data analyses to understand the nature and extent of errors associated with the differences in design and implementation. Notes to figures and tables are used to alert readers whenever errors may have occurred that introduce bias and affect interpretation. To assist users of the data to take error into account in interpreting the statistical significance of observed differences in national means or proportions, the standard errors of most estimates are reported in Annex D.

Country Abbreviations Used in the Report [2]

OECD Countries

Australia	**AUS**	Norway	**NOR**
Belgium	**BEL**	Poland	**POL**
Canada	**CAN**	Portugal	**PRT**
Czech Republic	**CZE**	Sweden	**SWE**
Denmark	**DNK**	Switzerland	**CHE**
Finland	**FIN**	United Kingdom	**UKM**
Germany	**DEU**	United States	**USA**
Hungary	**HUN**		
Ireland	**IRL**	**Non-OECD Countries**	
Netherlands	**NLD**	Chile	**CHL**
New Zealand	**NZL**	Slovenia	**SVN**

---

2. Results are presented separately for the three Swiss language groups in Chapter 2. For the purposes of the analyses described in the other chapters, the three population groups are combined into one single estimate for the whole country of Switzerland. Because the size of the Italian-Swiss population is much smaller than the French-Swiss and German-Swiss populations, the totals for the country are included in the 1994 category in the data tables in Annex D. The data presented in this report for the United Kingdom are based on combined estimates for Great Britain and Northern Ireland, where separate surveys were conducted. Data for Belgium (Flanders) are representative of the Flemish Community excluding the population of Brussels. In Norway two separate surveys were conducted, one in Nynorsk and the other in Bokmål. Results for Norway in this report refer to Bokmål, the language most widely used in the country.

CHAPTER 1

Skills for the Twenty-first Century

1.1 Introduction

The information age has brought about major structural changes in OECD countries and is affecting international trade, labour market structures, enterprises and the way they organise production. Individuals and societies are both shaping and having to adapt to the changes. The use of new technologies in everyday life, changing demands in the labour market and participation in the globalisation process are contributing to the need for upgraded skills.

The purpose of this first chapter is to situate the debate concerning the importance of skills in the knowledge economy. It describes the processes of globalisation, technological and labour force changes and the increased use of flexible work practices in organisations. It then describes the developments that have led to the upskilling of the workforce and to higher levels of knowledge and skills for the jobs that shape the knowledge economy.

1.2 Structural Changes in the Knowledge Economy

Globalisation and the emergence of the knowledge-based society are two main features of the economic paradigm at the start of the 21st century. The two processes are taking place simultaneously. Advances in science and technology have increased the reach and speed of communication and reduced costs. In turn, the technological advances have contributed to the internationalisation of production and of financial markets and to increased competition. In combination, the two processes are driving the transformation of OECD economies in a number of dimensions, reviewed below.

GLOBALISATION

Globalisation refers to the growing economic interdependency among countries and firms through increased trade, foreign investment, international sourcing of production inputs and inter-firm alliances. Economic growth, technological change, international competition, exchange rate fluctuations, deregulation and liberalisation of foreign trade and capital movements and other related government policies are all factors in the equation. The changes in the patterns of international transactions, summarised below, have had effects on workers' skills:

- Not only world trade but also OECD trade have increased. The latter now accounts for more than 70 per cent of world trade (World Bank, 1999). At the same time, trade volume measured in gross domestic product (GDP) has increased: trade in goods and services has risen from representing 13 per cent of OECD GDP in 1970 to 21 per cent in 1997. The figure varies depending on the size of country and GDP. In countries such as Belgium, the Czech Republic, Hungary, Ireland and the Netherlands, it exceeds 50 per cent of GDP (OECD, 1999a).

- The composition of trade in goods has shifted towards high-technology industries (Figure 1.1). The share of high-technology products has increased from 13 per cent of all manufacturing trade in 1985 to 18 per cent in 1996. The three sectors with the highest growth rates have been high-technology industries: pharmaceuticals, computers and telecommunications equipment, followed by medium-high-technology industries, which together account for more than 60 per cent of OECD manufacturing trade. Meanwhile, the share of medium-low-technology industries has fallen from 22.5 per cent to 17.6 per cent of all manufactured trade (OECD, 1999a).

FIGURE 1.1

OECD MANUFACTURING TRADE BY TECHNOLOGY INTENSITY (INDEX 1985=100)

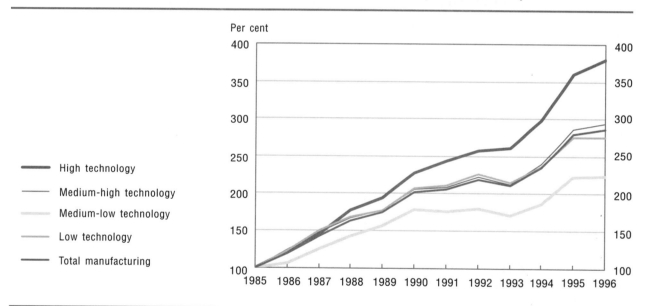

Source: OECD (1999a).

- Growth rates in technology trade have been higher than those of trade in goods and services, although their volume represents only 0.3 per cent of GDP. This form of trade includes the transfer of techniques, know-how, designs and trademarks, services with a technical content and industrial R&D.

- There has been steady growth in the trade of services. This partly represents a change in its nature towards more tradable services – software, financial services, telemarketing, transportation and accounting – and is partly a response to a shift towards the contracting-out of services in industries (OECD, 1999a).

- A shift from importing raw materials and exporting final goods towards the international sourcing of intermediate goods and intra-firm trade is taking place. These can be research and development (R&D) intensive products such as computer parts, electronics and aerospace components as well as mass-produced goods such as ferrous metals and textiles (Wyckoff, 1993).

- Patterns of intra-industry trade between countries have also changed. Trade in goods that differ in quality has risen to represent almost 40 per cent in 1996. Results for Japan and the United States show that this type of international trade is more prevalent in manufacturing industries characterised by higher R&D and/or human capital intensity (OECD, 1996a).

- Foreign investment has become a highly dynamic factor in industrial restructuring around the world. Sectors such as oil, automobile, banking and finance, telecommunications, printing and publishing, gas and electricity, business services, insurance and chemicals have attracted the highest volume of investment.

TECHNOLOGICAL CHANGE

Technological change is playing a vital role in the globalisation process. Through their effects on production methods, consumption patterns and the structure of economies, information and communication technologies (ICTs) are a key factor in the transition to the knowledge-based economy (OECD, 1998a). However, a closer look at the transition process reveals substantial differences between countries:

- Since 1985, on average, the expansion of knowledge-based industries[1] has outpaced GDP growth in developed countries (OECD, 1999d). Accounting for more than half of OECD-wide GDP, knowledge-based manufacturing companies are concentrated in larger OECD countries, such as Japan and the United States. Figure 1.2b shows that knowledge-based industries such as finance, insurance and business services have grown at a faster pace than the total business sector in most European countries.

- Investment in ICT has increased from 5.9 per cent of GDP in 1992 to 7 per cent in 1997. Much of this increase has been used to modernise telecommunications infrastructures. Although the rate of investment is highest in the English-speaking countries, Japan, the Netherlands, Sweden and Switzerland, growth has been high also in countries with a relatively low ICT intensity such as Greece, Poland and Portugal. Mediterranean and Central European countries and Mexico are the countries that spend the least as a proportion of GDP. Table 1.3 presents data on access to various technologies in the European Union.

- Infrastructure development has increased rapidly. By 1997, there was almost one fixed-access telephone line for every two inhabitants in the OECD area, and one in three households had cable access. Cellular mobile telephone networks covered 95 per cent of the total population, and subscriptions have been doubling annually between 1992 and 1997, with one of every six inhabitants owning a portable telephone by 1997.

---

1. The definition of knowledge-based industries and services includes not only high-technology industries in manufacturing but also intensive users of high technology or industries that have a highly skilled workforce, normally included in service activities such as finance, insurance and communications (OECD, 1999a).

FIGURE 1.2

KNOWLEDGE-BASED INDUSTRIES AND SERVICES

A. Share of value added in business sector, 1996 or latest available years

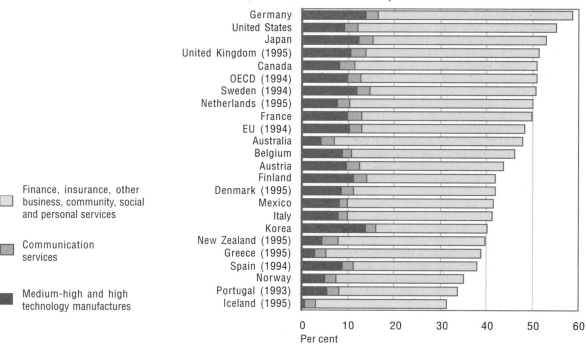

B. Real value added growth, average annual growth rate, 1985-1996 or latest available years

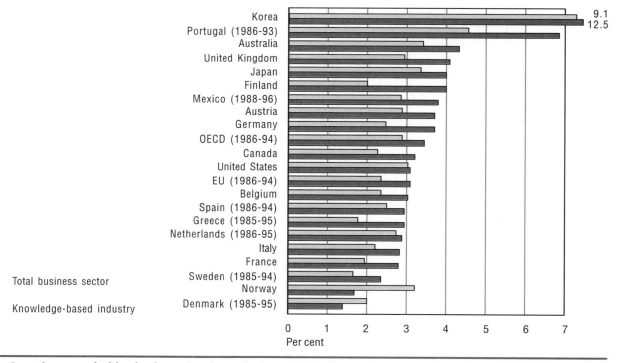

A. Countries are ranked by the decreasing share of value added in finance, insurance, other business, community, social and personal services.

B. Countries are ranked by the decrease in real value added growth in knowledge-based industry.

Source: OECD (1999a).

- The sharp reduction in computer costs during the 1990s has allowed for an increase in their use. The Internet has also grown exponentially. By January 1999 there were 40.8 million host computers in the OECD region and the number of secure web servers for e-commerce grew by 128 per cent between September 1997 and August 1998 (OECD, 1999a).

TABLE 1.3

ACCESS TO THE INFORMATION SOCIETY

Per cent use of systems of access to the information society
in the European Union, 1998

		Home	Work
1.	Personal computer	30.8	40.5
2.	Mobile telephone	30.2	23.9
3.	Cable TV	28.4	3.0
4.	Compact disk reader	20.8	24.7
5.	Satellite Dish	17.4	1.9
6.	Digital TV decoder	12.5	1.3
7.	Fax-modem	9.3	17.8
8.	Fax	7.5	33.3
9.	Connection to the Internet	8.3	13.3
10.	Minitel/vidéotexte	5.3	6.0
11.	Beeper	2.8	4.8

Source: INRA-EUROPE (1999).

CHANGES IN EMPLOYMENT

The knowledge-based economy and socio-demographic changes exert a major influence on employment and workforce skills. A general shift in labour demand from lower to higher levels of skills has led to increased unemployment among those with low skills. Although educational attainment of the population has increased concurrently, growth has not been fast enough to satisfy the demand:

- Figure 1.4 shows employment trends by industry from 1980 to 1995. Employment has fallen in agriculture in all OECD countries except Australia. The manufacturing sector has grown only in Denmark, Greece and Japan. The services sector has experienced the highest growth rates. Within services, employment has risen fastest in financial and business services, followed by community and personal services in almost all countries. By the late 1990s, two out of three jobs in the OECD area were in the services sector.

- Population ageing is another factor in employment changes. In the OECD area, by 2005, more than one worker in three will be over the age of 45. This implies that the upskilling of the workforce will have to be met partly through the continuing education and training of older workers. Training will therefore become even more important than it is today because the demand for skills cannot be met only with the supply of young and educated workers.

- The gradual rise in the level of educational attainment of the workforce is a third factor. A comparison of the population aged 55-64 with that aged 25-34 shows that almost three out of four young adults had completed upper secondary education, whereas less than half of those 55 through 64 had reached that level. For university education, the ratio is almost twice as high for the younger compared with the older group. Further, more educated adults generally evidence higher labour force participation rates. This is especially the case for women (OECD, 1998b).

FIGURE 1.4

EMPLOYMENT TRENDS BY INDUSTRY, TOTAL OECD (INDEX 1980=100)

A. Employment growth rates by industry

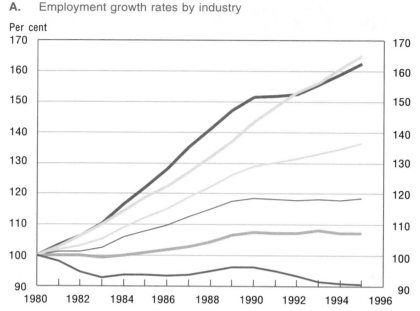

B. Employment growth rates by technology intensity

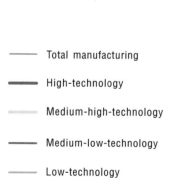

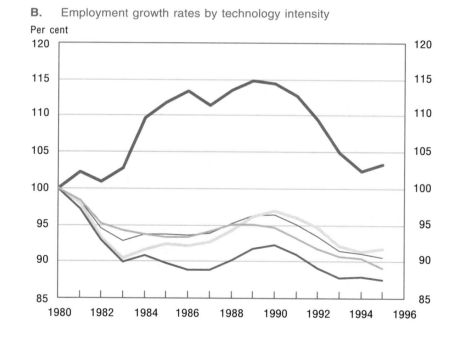

Source: OECD (1998a).

- In line with the changes mentioned, the occupational composition of the workforce has shifted towards white-collar jobs (professional, administrative and managerial, clerical and sales) and has declined for blue-collar jobs (transport and production workers and labourers) in all sectors of the economy (Section 1.3).

CHANGES IN WORK ORGANISATION

Globalisation and technological change have increased business opportunities and provided new ground for the creation of companies, while pressuring firms to become increasingly competitive. To achieve this they need appropriate organisational structures, a skilled work force and able management. Firms are responding by applying flexible management practices, such as those indicated in Table 1.5. Among the basic features are job design involving multi-skilling, extensive use of teamwork, reduced hierarchical levels and delegation of responsibility to individuals and teams. These have led firms to demand more flexibility and higher levels of skills from their work force (OECD, 1999c).

TABLE 1.5

FLEXIBLE MANAGEMENT PRACTICES

Per cent of workplaces reporting selected management initiatives
in 1996 over the past three years

	Job rotation	Team-based work organisation	Greater involvement of lower level employees	Flattening of management structures
Denmark	28	40	10	42
France	6	30	44	21
Germany	7	20	19	30
Ireland	10	27	32	23
Italy	13	28	24	10
Netherlands	9	9	46	47
Portugal	9	22	9	3
Spain	14	34	33	—
Sweden	38	29	60	46
United Kingdom	13	33	48	45
Unweighted average	**15**	**27**	**33**	**29**

Countries are ranked alphabetically.
Source: OECD (1999c).

Firm-level evidence shows that productivity is positively related to investment in education and training, and that there are tight links between organisation, skills and training on the one hand, and productivity and competitiveness on the other (OECD, 1999b). Practices such as employee involvement, pay for competence and other means of increasing worker effort, combined with training, have the greatest impact on improved productivity. Surveys of high-performance workplaces show that they have higher labour productivity, higher wages and better unit-cost performance (OECD, 1998a).

By the mid-1990s, flexible work organisation practices had been adopted by around a quarter of all enterprises in OECD countries. The manufacturing sector has been the most responsive. Assembly industries and automobile manufacturers often represent examples of high-performance workplaces, with an emphasis on quality and flexibility, reduced use of capital and horizontal supply arrangements. Flexible work organisations have been less common in the services sector with financial services and other services facing competition being most likely to adopt it.

1.3 Impact on the Demand for Skills

The changes described above are contributing to changes in the demand for workers' skills. Features such as job rotation, teamwork and total quality management imply increased employee responsibility and a higher degree of worker participation in decision-making (ILO, 1999). Research on the skills required for jobs in Australia and the United States shows that flexible work organisations have a higher educated workforce than traditional organisations. Cappelli and Rogovski (1994) concluded that teams using flexible work practices demand higher skills than those that do not. In a study of private-sector firms, Freeman *et al.* (1997) show that the likelihood of being at a firm with flexible practices increased with rising levels of education, together with the probability of participating in such practices.

Together with changes in work organisation, globalisation and technological development, more broadly, are having an impact on employment structures and on the type of labour required. To compete internationally, adapt to new technologies and attain higher levels of efficiency and productivity, firms require highly skilled employees. The increase in the level of educational attainment of the population in OECD countries is both a cause and a consequence of these changes.

The increase in the demand for highly skilled labour can be examined from various perspectives. Unemployment rates are much higher and have increased at a faster pace for people with low educational qualifications (OECD, 1997). Concurrently, their rates of participation in the labour force are lower. This suggests that people with low educational attainment face the consequences of structural changes in labour markets. The number of jobs in different sectors of the economy for the lesser skilled has decreased, while their likelihood of unemployment or inactivity has increased (Steedman, 1998).

Changes in the occupational structure of the workforce offer additional evidence. As Figure 1.6 shows, employment growth has occurred especially in white-collar high-skilled occupations. Growth has been fastest in the professional, technical, administrative and managerial occupations. In most countries growth in white-collar high-skilled occupations represented over half of total employment growth from the early 1980s until the mid-1990s.

Although total employment has decreased in the manufacturing sector, it has still experienced an increase in the number of white-collar high-skilled jobs. Growth in the services sector has been mainly driven by an increase in white-collar high-skilled positions. Finance, insurance and business services, dominated by white-collar high-skilled jobs, have grown at the fastest pace. In community, social and personal services, employment growth has been more evenly divided between jobs in high and low skill categories.

As indicated in Figure 1.7, the faster growth rate of white-collar high-skilled jobs in both manufacturing and services is not merely due to the increase in service activities (OECD, 1998a) but reflects the upskilling process. This is supported by evidence from other sources that suggests an increase in the application of skills within occupations. Two surveys conducted in the United Kingdom in 1986 and 1997 revealed a considerable increase in qualification levels of new recruits and an increase in job complexity and the use of communication skills, social skills and problem-solving skills (Green *et al.*, 1997). In the United States, job characteristics were also found to have shifted towards higher skills, especially in professional and technological occupations (Osterman, 1995).

The fall in real wages of people with low skills and widening earnings differentials since the early 1980s are also evidence of upskilling in Canada, the European Union countries and the United States (OECD, 1996b). From 1980 to 1990,

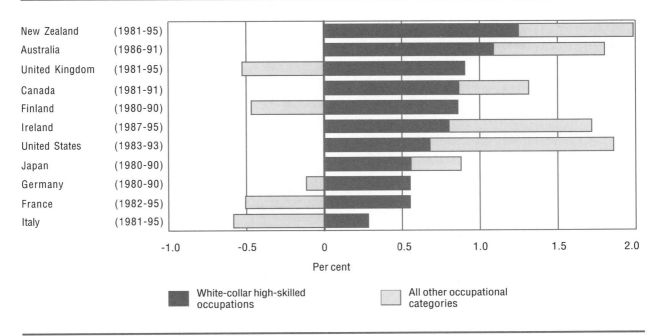

FIGURE 1.6

UPSKILLING IN TOTAL EMPLOYMENT GROWTH

Per cent contributions of occupational categories to average annual employment growth
between indicated years

New Zealand	(1981-95)
Australia	(1986-91)
United Kingdom	(1981-95)
Canada	(1981-91)
Finland	(1980-90)
Ireland	(1987-95)
United States	(1983-93)
Japan	(1980-90)
Germany	(1980-90)
France	(1982-95)
Italy	(1981-95)

Per cent

White-collar high-skilled occupations

All other occupational categories

Countries are ranked by the contribution of the white-collar high-skilled occupational category.
Source: OECD (1998a).

Canada, the United Kingdom and the United States had the highest increase in wage inequality among OECD countries, and differentials remained high throughout the 1990s. The increased premiums on education and experience indicate the worsened employment prospects of those with low educational qualifications and no experience in the labour market (ILO, 1999).

A number of studies (Berman *et al.,* 1997; Machin *et al.,* 1996; Steedman, 1998) suggest that employment shifts within industries – as opposed to between – represent a need for higher skills. Moreover, a recent study on the effects of technological change on the increase in the demand for and wages of skilled labour shows that as firms hire more skilled labour, the incentive to invest in technology rises. This leads to a complementary technological advance that further increases the demand for skilled labour (Kiley, 1999). The direct effect of technology on skill levels is another explanation for the upskilling of the workforce. OECD work also shows a positive association between technological development and skill levels. This work suggests that upskilling is not only a consequence of technological change but also of the general increase in educational attainment levels (OECD, 1996c).

Although deskilling effects can also result from technological change, as a result of an increased use of new technologies to perform a greater variety of tasks, the economy-wide diffusion and use of technologies improves productivity.

FIGURE 1.7

UPSKILLING IN MANUFACTURING AND SERVICES EMPLOYMENT GROWTH

Per cent contributions of occupational categories to average annual employment growth
in manufacturing and services between indicated years

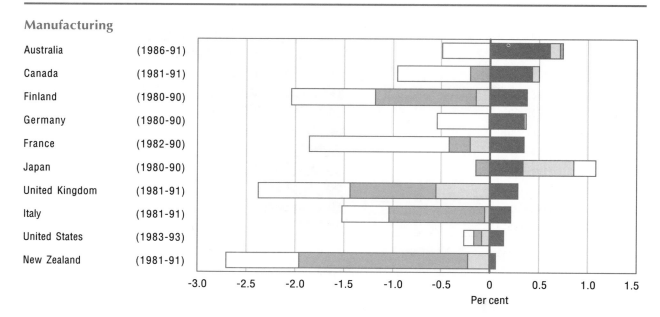

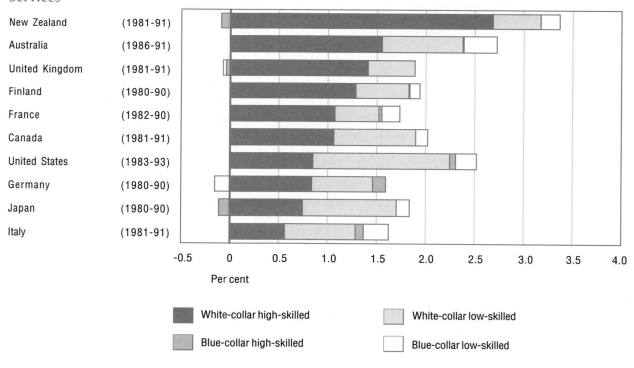

Countries are ranked by the contribution of the white-collar high-skilled occupational category.
Source: OECD (1998a).

1.4 Conclusion

Skills are becoming increasingly important in the knowledge economy, both for individuals and at the macro level. Countries with higher levels of skills will adjust more effectively to challenges and opportunities opened up by globalisation because their firms will be more flexible and better able to absorb and adapt new technologies and to work with new equipment. "The skill level and quality of the workforce will increasingly provide the cutting edge in competing in the global economy" (ILO, 1999, p. 202).

The upskilling process that is taking place is the outcome of a range of technological, organisational, institutional and societal changes that are occurring around the world. Workers are increasingly required not only to have higher levels of education, but also the capacity to adapt, learn and master the changes quickly and efficiently. They need abilities and skills that are transportable in the labour market. Thus an increased demand for and supply of high-level skills is being generated. All these changes imply that workers have to possess broad foundation skills that must be regularly updated and complemented with specific skills through training and lifelong learning processes (OECD, 1996d).

The analysis presented in Chapter 4 reveals the close association between higher literacy skills and participation in the labour force and jobs that are shaping the knowledge economy. They also highlight the conclusion that literacy skills are an essential ingredient in the process of upskilling that accompanies the economic and social transformations that are occurring in the OECD countries. While Chapter 2 provides an analysis of the overall literacy skills profiles of countries, Chapters 3 and 4 examine the interactions between literacy skills and a range of variables, linking literacy skills with participation in the labour market and in social, cultural and political life, among other characteristics.

References

BERMAN, E., BOUND, J., and MACHIN, S. (1997), "Implications of skill-biased technological change: International evidence", NBER Working Paper No. 6166, National Bureau of Economic Research, Cambridge, MA.

CAPELLI, P. and ROGOVSKI, N. (1994), "New work systems and skills requirements", *International Labour Review*, No. 2, pp. 205-220.

FREEMAN, R.B., KLEINER, M.M., and OSTROGOFF, C. (1997), "The anatomy and effects of employee involvement", Paper presented at the meeting of the American Economic Association, New Orleans, January.

GREEN, F., ASHTON, D., BURCHELL, B., DAVIES, B., and FELSTEAD, A. (1997), "An analysis of changing work skills in Britain", paper presented at the Analysis of Low Wage Employment Conference, Centre for Economic Performance, London School of Economics, 12-13 December.

ILO (1999), *World Employment Report 1998-99*, International Labour Organisation, Geneva.

INRA Europe – European Coordination Office (1999), "Measuring the information society", *Eurobarometer*, No. 50.1, Report written for DGXIII and organised by DGX, Commission of the European Communities, Brussels, 16 March.

KILEY, M. (1999), "The supply of skilled labour and skill-biased technological progress", *The Economic Journal*, No. 109, October, pp. 708-724.

MACHIN, S., RYAN, A., and van REENAN, J. (1996), "Technology and changes in skill structure: Evidence from an international panel of industries", Centre of Economic Performance Discussion Paper Series, London School of Economics and Political Science, London.

OECD (1996a), *Globalisation of Industry: Overview and Sector Reports*, Paris.

OECD (1996b), *Technology, Productivity and Job Creation. Vol. 2: Analytical Report*, Paris.

OECD (1996c), *OECD Employment Outlook,* June, Paris.

OECD (1996d), *Lifelong Learning for All*, Paris.

OECD (1997), "Policies for low paid workers and unskilled job seekers", Document DEELSA/ELSA(97)2/REV2, Paris.

OECD (1998a), *Technology, Productivity and Job Creation: Best Policy Practices*, Paris.

OECD (1998b), *Education at a Glance – OECD Indicators*, Paris.

OECD (1999a), *OECD Science, Technology and Industry Scoreboard 1999 – Benchmarking Knowledge-based Economies*, Paris.

OECD (1999b), "New enterprise work practices and their labour market implications", *Employment Outlook,* June, Paris.

OECD (1999c), *Employment Outlook*, June, Paris.

OECD (1999d), *OECD Economic Outlook,* No. 66, Paris.

OSTERMAN, P. (1995), "Skills, training, and work organisation in American establishments", *Industrial Relations*, Vol. 34, No. 2.

STEEDMAN, H. (1998), "Low skills: How the supply is changing across Europe", *Trends in the Development of Occupations and Qualifications in Europe*, CEDEFOP, Thessaloniki.

WORLD BANK (1999), *World Bank Database Compact Disk*, The World Bank Group, Washington, DC.

WYCKOFF, A. (1993), "Extension of networks of production across borders", *Science, Technology and Industry Review*, No. 13, pp. 61-87, OECD, Paris.

CHAPTER 2

Population Distributions of Adult Literacy

2.1 Introduction

Even in economically advanced countries with strong education systems, many adults have difficulties coping with the reading and numeracy activities that are common in modern life. Although adults facing serious literacy problems can be found in any country, the patterns differ greatly from one to another. The purpose of this chapter is to present an overall comparative perspective on the levels and distributions of adult literacy skills. The results clearly document the existence of significant numbers of adults with low literacy skills in all the countries surveyed. They also show how the distribution of adults with literacy difficulties varies between nations.

2.2 Patterns of Adult Literacy Skills

Figures 2.1, 2.2, and 2.3 each provide a different perspective on the distributions and levels of literacy skills in the IALS countries. Each graph is required to complete the picture presented in a previous IALS publication (OECD and HRDC, 1997). First, Figure 2.1a-c shows the mean score and scores at various percentiles, illustrating how countries differ both in the average level and in the distribution of prose, document and quantitative literacy skills. Several important observations can be drawn from this set of charts.

The average score across countries on each of the three scales shows considerable variation, with Sweden having the highest average on all three scales and Chile the lowest:

Prose:	221 to 301 points
Document:	219 to 306 points
Quantitative:	209 to 306 points

The distribution of literacy skills within a country also differs considerably on each of the three scales with a range from 0 to 500 points that are used to report the IALS results. For example, in Denmark, the range of scores from the 5th to the 95th percentile on the prose scale is around 120 points. Figure 2.1a shows that this spread is tight compared with other countries with more dispersed results. In Portugal and the United States, the other extremes, the range on the prose scale for the same two percentiles is around 231 points. Other countries fall in between.

When comparing the three scales, there is a wide variation in the results. In some cases, such as Belgium (Flanders) and Ireland, the ranges are consistently moderate among the three scales, while in others, such as Hungary or Chile, they vary from scale to scale. It is worth noting that a number of countries consistently have a small or large range between the 5th to the 95th percentile, showing the differences in the dispersion of the literacy distribution among the three scales:

Consistently small:	Consistently large:	Consistently moderate or varying:
Czech Republic	Canada	Australia
Denmark	Poland	Belgium (Flanders)
Finland	Portugal	Chile
Germany	Slovenia	Hungary
Netherlands	United Kingdom	Ireland
Norway	United States	New Zealand
Sweden		Switzerland (French, German, Italian)

FIGURE 2.1

DISTRIBUTION OF LITERACY SCORES

A. Mean scores with .95 confidence interval and scores at 5th, 25th, 75th, and 95th percentiles on the prose literacy scale, population aged 16-65, 1994-1998

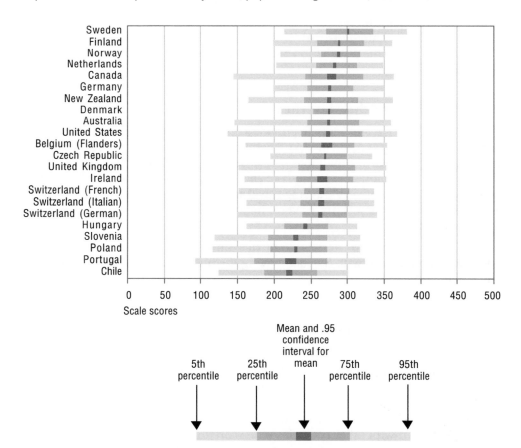

Countries are ranked by mean scores.

FIGURE 2.1 (concluded)

DISTRIBUTION OF LITERACY SCORES

B. Mean scores with .95 confidence interval and scores at 5th, 25th, 75th, and 95th percentiles on the document literacy scale, population aged 16-65, 1994-1998

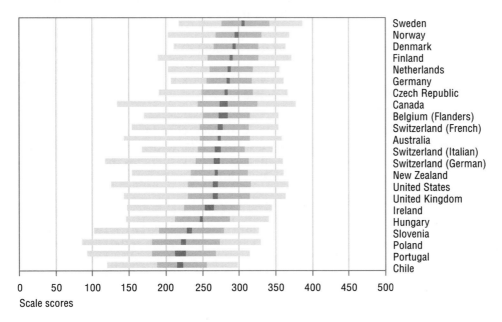

C. Mean scores with .95 confidence interval and scores at 5th, 25th, 75th, and 95th percentiles on the quantitative literacy scale, population aged 16-65, 1994-1998

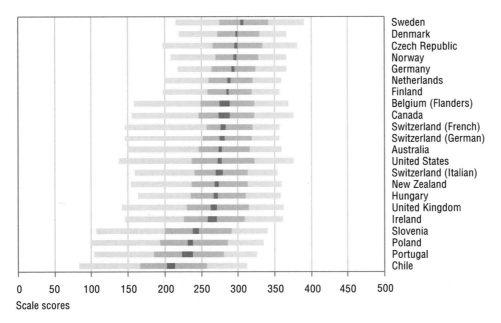

Countries are ranked by mean scores.

Source: International Adult Literacy Survey, 1994-1998.

Some countries rank similarly across the three scales in terms of their average scores. Norway and Sweden are among the four highest scoring countries on all three whereas Chile, Poland, Portugal and Slovenia score low on all three. Other countries differ in their ranking from scale to scale. The Czech Republic, for example, is in the middle of the ranking on the prose scale, but at the top on quantitative. Conversely, Canada is in the top group on the prose scale, but in the middle on the quantitative one. Hungary has a relatively higher average on quantitative than on the other two scales. Why countries differ in this way is a question addressed in the subsequent chapter.

The fact that range is somewhat independent of average can be seen in the case of Denmark: the range on the prose scale is small and the average score on prose is not high, especially compared with Denmark's average on the document and quantitative scales. Conversely, Canada has a relatively high prose average but also a very large range.

Variations in average and range are important characteristics of a country's skills profile. Issues of equity arise when there is a large discrepancy between the people with lowest and those with the highest literacy skills, as there are in many IALS countries. Questions of why countries differ in this respect ought to concern citizens and policy makers.

Figures 2.1a-c only describe where certain scores lie on a scale and what their range is, but they do not tell much about how many people fall at different places along the scale. In contrast, Figures 2.2a-c show the distribution of the adult population aged 16-65 by literacy proficiency (see Box 2A). The four levels on each of the scales are explained in detail in Annex A. These make it possible to study how countries differ in the proportions of people with different levels of literacy skills.

Box 2A. Reading the Figures

Figure 2.2 displays information in a novel way. The bars for each country are stacked; each section represents the proportion at a particular level. Rather than being stacked from the zero point, the bars are anchored between Levels 2 and 3 – allowing much readier comparison of the relative proportions of the population found to be at particular levels across countries. For example, the bars are lined up so that the proportions at Levels 1 and 2 are below the reference line and those at Levels 3 and 4/5 are above the line. The order of countries is based on the proportion of the population above the reference line. In Figure 2.2b, for example, Sweden's bar is furthest left, since that country has the largest proportion of its population at Levels 3 and 4/5 on the document scale.

As with the distribution of scores in Figure 2.1a-c, there are countries that always have large proportions of their adult population at high literacy levels. Finland, the Netherlands, Norway and Sweden typically have the largest proportions at Levels 3 and 4/5. Sweden, however, does differ from these others in having the largest proportion at Level 4/5 on all three scales.

There are also countries that just as regularly have large proportions at low levels of literacy: Chile, Poland, Portugal and Slovenia. Other countries such as New Zealand, the three language groups in Switzerland and the United States fall into the middle on each scale, although the Italian-speaking Swiss appear to do less well on the quantitative scale than the French-speaking Swiss.

It is not possible, however, to find a single literacy ranking of countries. The Czech Republic does not have comparatively large numbers at Levels 3 and 4/5 on the prose scale, but does have among the largest proportions at these levels on the quantitative scale. Denmark and Germany have prose versus quantitative distributions that are similar to that for the Czech Republic. On the other hand, Australia and Canada – which have notably similar distributions on all scales – perform relatively better on prose than on quantitative.

FIGURE 2.2

COMPARATIVE DISTRIBUTION OF LITERACY LEVELS

A. Per cent of population aged 16-65 at each prose literacy level, 1994-1998

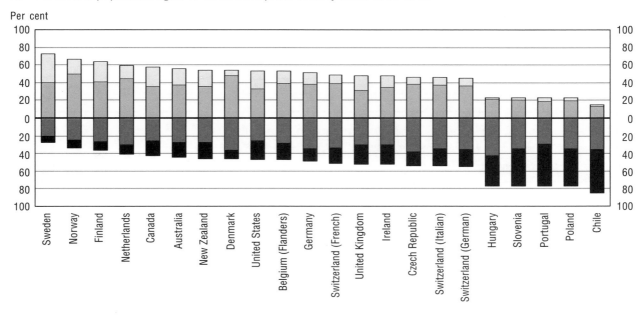

B. Per cent of population aged 16-65 at each document literacy level, 1994-1998

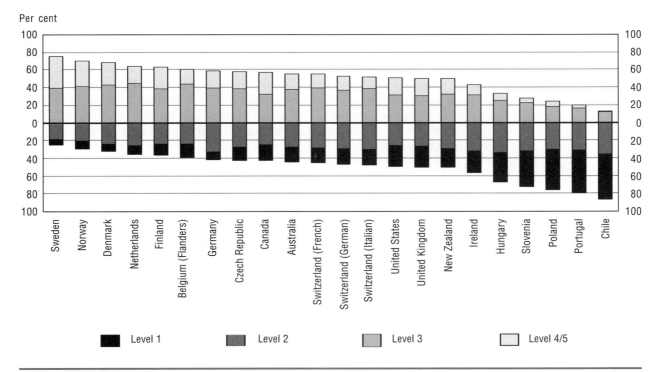

Level 1   Level 2   Level 3   Level 4/5

Countries are ranked by the proportion in Levels 3 and 4/5.

FIGURE 2.2 (concluded)

COMPARATIVE DISTRIBUTION OF LITERACY LEVELS

C. Per cent of population aged 16-65 at each quantitative literacy level, 1994-1998

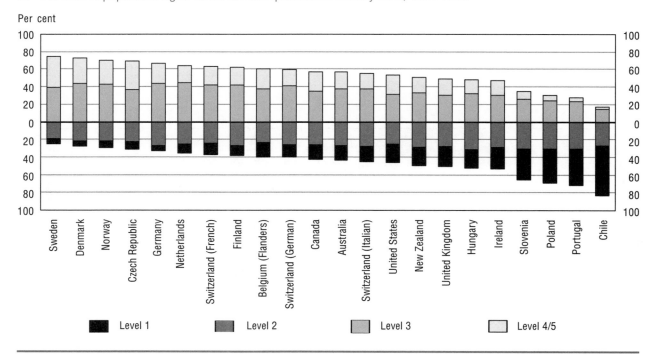

Countries are ranked by the proportion in Levels 3 and 4/5.
Source: International Adult Literacy Survey, 1994-1998.

Finally, Figure 2.3a-c provides data on just how significant the observed differences between country profiles really are. As in any household survey, some degree of sampling error and measurement error is present in the IALS data. This error must be taken into account when examining the overall differences in mean literacy scores across countries. The multiple comparisons shown in Figure 2.3a-c provide a tool for identifying those differences that are most likely to be a reflection of real differences.

As the information in Figure 2.3a-c suggests, many of the observed differences between countries are meaningful, especially those at the high and low ends of the scale. But there are other comparisons that are not really different in a statistical sense (the dot in the grey square). Thus, in terms of literacy proficiency, the three language groups in Switzerland do not differ significantly from each other on any of the scales.

The charts also reflect the different performance of some countries on each of the scales. Australia and Canada, for example, do not differ from each other on any scale. Both have significantly higher scores on prose compared with the Czech Republic, Ireland and the United Kingdom. And although the scores on the document scale for Canada are higher than those for Ireland and the United Kingdom, they are not significantly different from those for the Czech Republic. On the prose scale the Netherlands outperforms Belgium (Flanders) but the difference between the latter and Germany is not meaningful. Finally, on the quantitative scale, the Czech Republic outscores both Australia and Canada, which, in turn, outscore Ireland and the United Kingdom. However, on this scale, their scores do not differ significantly from those in the United States.

FIGURE 2.3

MULTIPLE COMPARISONS OF LITERACY PROFICIENCY

A. Comparisons of countries based on average score on the prose literacy scale, population aged 16-65, 1994-1998

COUNTRY	Sweden	Finland	Norway	Netherlands	Canada	Germany	New Zealand	Denmark	Australia	United States	Belgium (Flanders)	Czech Republic	United Kingdom	Ireland	Switzerland (French)	Switzerland (Italian)	Switzerland (German)	Hungary	Slovenia	Poland	Portugal	Chile
Sweden		▲	▲	▲	▲	▲	▲	▲	▲	▲	▲	▲	▲	▲	▲	▲	▲	▲	▲	▲	▲	▲
Finland	▼		●	▲	▲	▲	▲	▲	▲	▲	▲	▲	▲	▲	▲	▲	▲	▲	▲	▲	▲	▲
Norway	▼	●		▲	▲	▲	▲	▲	▲	▲	▲	▲	▲	▲	▲	▲	▲	▲	▲	▲	▲	▲
Netherlands	▼	▼	▼		●	▲	▲	▲	▲	▲	▲	▲	▲	▲	▲	▲	▲	▲	▲	▲	▲	▲
Canada	▼	▼	▼	●		●	●	●	●	●	●	▲	▲	▲	▲	▲	▲	▲	▲	▲	▲	▲
Germany	▼	▼	▼	▼	●		●	●	●	●	●	▲	▲	▲	▲	▲	▲	▲	▲	▲	▲	▲
New Zealand	▼	▼	▼	▼	●	●		●	●	●	●	▲	▲	▲	▲	▲	▲	▲	▲	▲	▲	▲
Denmark	▼	▼	▼	▼	●	●	●		●	●	●	▲	▲	▲	▲	▲	▲	▲	▲	▲	▲	▲
Australia	▼	▼	▼	▼	●	●	●	●		●	●	▲	▲	▲	▲	▲	▲	▲	▲	▲	▲	▲
United States	▼	▼	▼	▼	●	●	●	●	●		●	▲	▲	▲	▲	▲	▲	▲	▲	▲	▲	▲
Belgium (Flanders)	▼	▼	▼	▼	●	●	●	●	●	●		●	●	●	●	●	▲	▲	▲	▲	▲	▲
Czech Republic	▼	▼	▼	▼	▼	▼	▼	▼	▼	▼	●		●	●	▲	▲	▲	▲	▲	▲	▲	▲
United Kingdom	▼	▼	▼	▼	▼	▼	▼	▼	▼	▼	●	●		●	●	●	●	▲	▲	▲	▲	▲
Ireland	▼	▼	▼	▼	▼	▼	▼	▼	▼	▼	●	●	●		●	●	●	▲	▲	▲	▲	▲
Switzerland (French)	▼	▼	▼	▼	▼	▼	▼	▼	▼	▼	●	▼	●	●		●	●	▲	▲	▲	▲	▲
Switzerland (Italian)	▼	▼	▼	▼	▼	▼	▼	▼	▼	▼	●	▼	●	●	●		●	▲	▲	▲	▲	▲
Switzerland (German)	▼	▼	▼	▼	▼	▼	▼	▼	▼	▼	▼	▼	▼	▼	●	●		▲	▲	▲	▲	▲
Hungary	▼	▼	▼	▼	▼	▼	▼	▼	▼	▼	▼	▼	▼	▼	▼	▼	▼		▲	▲	▲	▲
Slovenia	▼	▼	▼	▼	▼	▼	▼	▼	▼	▼	▼	▼	▼	▼	▼	▼	▼	▼		●	●	▲
Poland	▼	▼	▼	▼	▼	▼	▼	▼	▼	▼	▼	▼	▼	▼	▼	▼	▼	▼	●		●	▲
Portugal	▼	▼	▼	▼	▼	▼	▼	▼	▼	▼	▼	▼	▼	▼	▼	▼	▼	▼	●	●		●
Chile	▼	▼	▼	▼	▼	▼	▼	▼	▼	▼	▼	▼	▼	▼	▼	▼	▼	▼	▼	▼	●	

Instructions: Read across the row for a country to compare performance with the countries listed in the heading of the chart. The symbols indicate whether the mean proficiency of the country in the row is significantly lower than that of the comparison country, significantly higher than that of the comparison country, or if there is no statistically significant difference between the two countries.

▲ Mean proficiency significantly* higher than comparison country

● No statistically significant* difference from comparison country

▼ Mean proficiency significantly* lower than comparison country

Countries are ranked by mean proficiency across the heading and down the rows.

* Statistically significant at 0.5 level, adjusted for multiple comparisons.

FIGURE 2.3 (continued)

MULTIPLE COMPARISONS OF LITERACY PROFICIENCY

B. Comparisons of countries based on average score on the document literacy scale, population aged 16-65, 1994-1998

COUNTRY	Sweden	Norway	Denmark	Finland	Netherlands	Germany	Czech Republic	Canada	Belgium (Flanders)	Switzerland (French)	Australia	Switzerland (Italian)	Switzerland (German)	New Zealand	United States	United Kingdom	Ireland	Hungary	Slovenia	Poland	Portugal	Chile
Sweden		▲	▲	▲	▲	▲	▲	▲	▲	▲	▲	▲	▲	▲	▲	▲	▲	▲	▲	▲	▲	▲
Norway	▼		▲	▲	▲	▲	▲	▲	▲	▲	▲	▲	▲	▲	▲	▲	▲	▲	▲	▲	▲	▲
Denmark	▼	▼		▲	▲	▲	▲	▲	▲	▲	▲	▲	▲	▲	▲	▲	▲	▲	▲	▲	▲	▲
Finland	▼	▼	▼		●	▲	▲	▲	▲	▲	▲	▲	▲	▲	▲	▲	▲	▲	▲	▲	▲	▲
Netherlands	▼	▼	▼	●		●	▲	▲	▲	▲	▲	▲	▲	▲	▲	▲	▲	▲	▲	▲	▲	▲
Germany	▼	▼	▼	▼	●		●	●	▲	▲	▲	▲	▲	▲	▲	▲	▲	▲	▲	▲	▲	▲
Czech Republic	▼	▼	▼	▼	▼	●		●	●	▲	▲	▲	▲	▲	▲	▲	▲	▲	▲	▲	▲	▲
Canada	▼	▼	▼	▼	▼	●	●		●	●	●	▲	▲	▲	▲	▲	▲	▲	▲	▲	▲	▲
Belgium (Flanders)	▼	▼	▼	▼	▼	▼	●	●		●	●	●	▲	▲	▲	▲	▲	▲	▲	▲	▲	▲
Switzerland (French)	▼	▼	▼	▼	▼	▼	▼	●	●		●	●	●	▲	▲	▲	▲	▲	▲	▲	▲	▲
Australia	▼	▼	▼	▼	▼	▼	▼	●	●	●		●	●	▲	▲	▲	▲	▲	▲	▲	▲	▲
Switzerland (Italian)	▼	▼	▼	▼	▼	▼	▼	▼	●	●	●		●	●	●	●	▲	▲	▲	▲	▲	▲
Switzerland (German)	▼	▼	▼	▼	▼	▼	▼	▼	▼	●	●	●		●	●	●	▲	▲	▲	▲	▲	▲
New Zealand	▼	▼	▼	▼	▼	▼	▼	▼	▼	▼	▼	●	●		●	●	▲	▲	▲	▲	▲	▲
United States	▼	▼	▼	▼	▼	▼	▼	▼	▼	▼	▼	●	●	●		●	▲	▲	▲	▲	▲	▲
United Kingdom	▼	▼	▼	▼	▼	▼	▼	▼	▼	▼	▼	●	●	●	●		▲	▲	▲	▲	▲	▲
Ireland	▼	▼	▼	▼	▼	▼	▼	▼	▼	▼	▼	▼	▼	▼	▼	▼		▲	▲	▲	▲	▲
Hungary	▼	▼	▼	▼	▼	▼	▼	▼	▼	▼	▼	▼	▼	▼	▼	▼	▼		▲	▲	▲	▲
Slovenia	▼	▼	▼	▼	▼	▼	▼	▼	▼	▼	▼	▼	▼	▼	▼	▼	▼	▼		▲	▲	▲
Poland	▼	▼	▼	▼	▼	▼	▼	▼	▼	▼	▼	▼	▼	▼	▼	▼	▼	▼	▼		●	●
Portugal	▼	▼	▼	▼	▼	▼	▼	▼	▼	▼	▼	▼	▼	▼	▼	▼	▼	▼	▼	●		●
Chile	▼	▼	▼	▼	▼	▼	▼	▼	▼	▼	▼	▼	▼	▼	▼	▼	▼	▼	▼	●	●	

Instructions: Read across the row for a country to compare performance with the countries listed in the heading of the chart. The symbols indicate whether the mean proficiency of the country in the row is significantly lower than that of the comparison country, significantly higher than that of the comparison country, or if there is no statistically significant difference between the two countries.

▲   Mean proficiency significantly* higher than comparison country

●   No statistically significant* difference from comparison country

▼   Mean proficiency significantly* lower than comparison country

Countries are ranked by mean proficiency across the heading and down the rows.

* Statistically significant at 0.5 level, adjusted for multiple comparisons.

FIGURE 2.3 (concluded)

MULTIPLE COMPARISONS OF LITERACY PROFICIENCY

C. Comparisons of countries based on average score on the quantitative literacy scale, population aged 16-65, 1994-1998

COUNTRY	Sweden	Denmark	Czech Republic	Norway	Germany	Netherlands	Finland	Belgium (Flanders)	Canada	Switzerland (French)	Switzerland (German)	Australia	United States	Switzerland (Italian)	New Zealand	Hungary	United Kingdom	Ireland	Slovenia	Poland	Portugal	Chile
Sweden		▲	▲	▲	▲	▲	▲	▲	▲	▲	▲	▲	▲	▲	▲	▲	▲	▲	▲	▲	▲	▲
Denmark	▼		•	•	▲	▲	▲	▲	▲	▲	▲	▲	▲	▲	▲	▲	▲	▲	▲	▲	▲	▲
Czech Republic	▼	•		•	▲	▲	▲	▲	▲	▲	▲	▲	▲	▲	▲	▲	▲	▲	▲	▲	▲	▲
Norway	▼	•	•		▲	▲	▲	▲	▲	▲	▲	▲	▲	▲	▲	▲	▲	▲	▲	▲	▲	▲
Germany	▼	▼	▼	▼		▲	▲	▲	▲	▲	▲	▲	▲	▲	▲	▲	▲	▲	▲	▲	▲	▲
Netherlands	▼	▼	▼	▼	▼		•	•	•	▲	▲	▲	▲	▲	▲	▲	▲	▲	▲	▲	▲	▲
Finland	▼	▼	▼	▼	▼	•		•	•	▲	▲	▲	▲	▲	▲	▲	▲	▲	▲	▲	▲	▲
Belgium (Flanders)	▼	▼	▼	▼	▼	•	•		•	•	•	•	•	•	▲	▲	▲	▲	▲	▲	▲	▲
Canada	▼	▼	▼	▼	▼	•	•	•		•	•	•	•	•	▲	▲	▲	▲	▲	▲	▲	▲
Switzerland (French)	▼	▼	▼	▼	▼	▼	▼	•	•		•	▲	▲	•	▲	▲	▲	▲	▲	▲	▲	▲
Switzerland (German)	▼	▼	▼	▼	▼	▼	▼	•	•	•		•	•	•	▲	▲	▲	▲	▲	▲	▲	▲
Australia	▼	▼	▼	▼	▼	▼	▼	•	•	▼	•		•	•	▲	▲	▲	▲	▲	▲	▲	▲
United States	▼	▼	▼	▼	▼	▼	▼	•	•	▼	•	•		•	▲	▲	▲	▲	▲	▲	▲	▲
Switzerland (Italian)	▼	▼	▼	▼	▼	▼	▼	•	•	•	•	•	•		•	•	▲	▲	▲	▲	▲	▲
New Zealand	▼	▼	▼	▼	▼	▼	▼	▼	▼	▼	▼	▼	▼	•		•	•	▲	▲	▲	▲	▲
Hungary	▼	▼	▼	▼	▼	▼	▼	▼	▼	▼	▼	▼	▼	•	•		•	•	▲	▲	▲	▲
United Kingdom	▼	▼	▼	▼	▼	▼	▼	▼	▼	▼	▼	▼	▼	▼	•	•		•	▲	▲	▲	▲
Ireland	▼	▼	▼	▼	▼	▼	▼	▼	▼	▼	▼	▼	▼	▼	▼	•	•		▲	▲	▲	▲
Slovenia	▼	▼	▼	▼	▼	▼	▼	▼	▼	▼	▼	▼	▼	▼	▼	▼	▼	▼		▲	▲	▲
Poland	▼	▼	▼	▼	▼	▼	▼	▼	▼	▼	▼	▼	▼	▼	▼	▼	▼	▼	▼		•	▲
Portugal	▼	▼	▼	▼	▼	▼	▼	▼	▼	▼	▼	▼	▼	▼	▼	▼	▼	▼	▼	•		▲
Chile	▼	▼	▼	▼	▼	▼	▼	▼	▼	▼	▼	▼	▼	▼	▼	▼	▼	▼	▼	▼	▼	

Instructions: Read across the row for a country to compare performance with the countries listed in the heading of the chart. The symbols indicate whether the mean proficiency of the country in the row is significantly lower than that of the comparison country, significantly higher than that of the comparison country, or if there is no statistically significant difference between the two countries.

▲ Mean proficiency significantly* higher than comparison country

• No statistically significant* difference from comparison country

▼ Mean proficiency significantly* lower than comparison country

Countries are ranked by mean proficiency across the heading and down the rows.

* Statistically significant at 0.5 level, adjusted for multiple comparisons.

Source: International Adult Literacy Survey, 1994-1998.

All three figures carry a consistent message. Variation in literacy skills is a reality within countries, across countries and between the three measures of literacy. Because such differences exist, it is important to understand what leads to them and what consequences they have, both for individuals and for economies and societies.

2.3 Literacy Skills and Education

Literacy skills are to a large extent acquired in school. Obtaining access to the instruction required to become a fluent reader, for example, is difficult outside a formal school setting. It might be expected that some of the differences observed in Figures 2.1a-c through 2.3a-c are related to cross-country differences in educational attainment, because the IALS countries differ widely in this respect (OECD, 2000). In Portugal about 80 per cent of the population aged 16-65 has not completed upper secondary school; in Sweden in contrast only 25 per cent of that population have not graduated from secondary school. To the extent that more education adds to literacy skills, one would therefore expect Sweden to have higher average scores than Portugal.

Figure 2.4a-c compares the average literacy scores of groups of individuals with different levels of educational attainment in the IALS countries. As expected, there is an association between education and literacy skills in every country. Yet countries still differ in literacy at any level of educational attainment, suggesting that there are other factors that influence literacy skills as well. Some of these are studied in the next chapter.

FIGURE 2.4

EDUCATIONAL ATTAINMENT AND LITERACY PROFICIENCY

A. Mean prose score on a scale with range 0-500 points, by level of educational attainment, population aged 16-65, 1994-1998

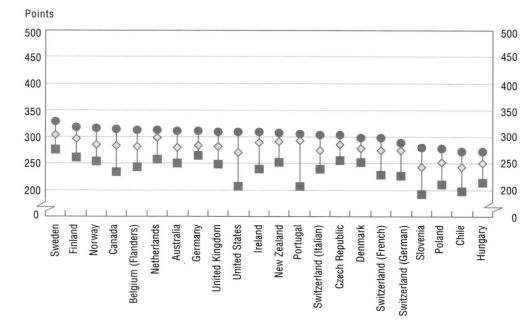

Countries are ranked by the mean score of those who have completed tertiary education.

FIGURE 2.4 (concluded)

EDUCATIONAL ATTAINMENT AND LITERACY PROFICIENCY

B. Mean document score on a scale with range 0-500 points, by level of educational attainment, population aged 16-65, 1994-1998

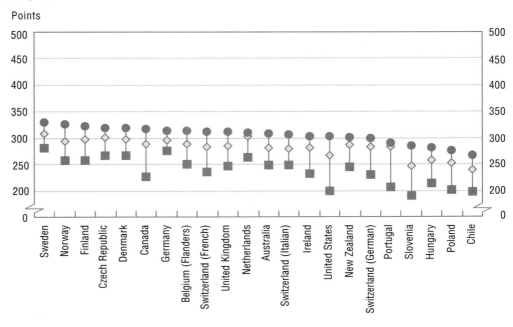

C. Mean quantitative score on a scale with range 0-500 points, by level of educational attainment, population aged 16-65, 1994-1998

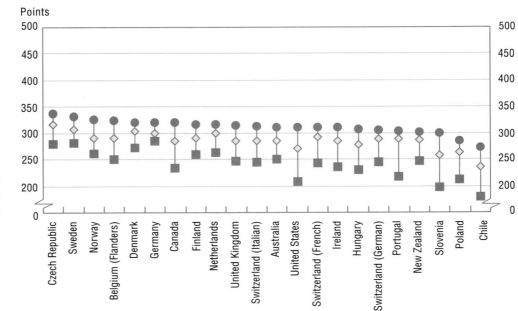

Countries are ranked by the mean score of those who have completed tertiary education.
Source: International Adult Literacy Survey, 1994-1998.

The data in Figure 2.4a-c also offer other insights into the distribution of literacy. The case of Portugal provides an example of how the level of educational attainment of the whole population has an impact on the overall literacy performance of the country measured by IALS. In relation to other countries, the Portuguese average essentially reflects lower test performance among people who have not benefited from upper secondary education, *i.e.* a large proportion of the population. Yet Portugese adults with higher levels of educational attainment score average or higher in comparison with similarly educated adults in the comparison countries.

In all countries adults with more education have, as a group, higher average literacy scores, but the benefit of a completed tertiary education compared with secondary education differs dramatically across countries. In the Netherlands, for example, the difference in scores between those with only secondary education and those with tertiary education is very small, particularly when compared with the difference between these same education groups in the United States. In Germany, the link between educational attainment and average literacy skills is weak at all levels of education. This contrasts with the pattern observed for a country such as Slovenia.

FIGURE 2.5

DOCUMENT LITERACY LEVELS AMONG LOW EDUCATED ADULTS

Per cent of population aged 16-65 who have not completed upper secondary education but who score at Levels 3 and 4/5 on the document scale, 1994-1998

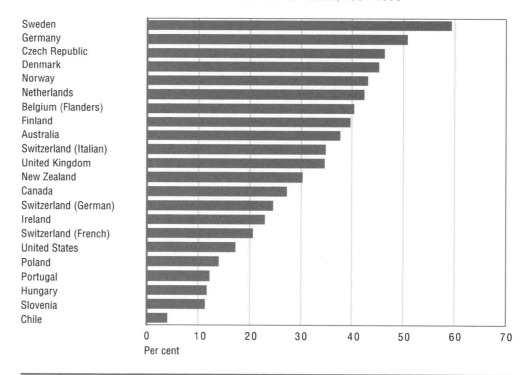

Countries are ranked by the proportion of the population without upper secondary graduation who are at Levels 3 and 4/5.

Source: International Adult Literacy Survey, 1994-1998.

It is also evident from Figure 2.4a-c that countries differ most among those who have received the least formal education. The range of country mean scores for those with the lowest level of formal education – not having completed secondary school – is about 1.5 times the range of mean scores for those with the highest level of education.

Although literacy is clearly related to educational attainment, it can be inferred from the evidence that other factors also must influence literacy skills. As the data in Figure 2.5 demonstrate, in some countries large numbers of adults with low levels of education do attain high levels of literacy. Taken together, Figures 2.4a-c and 2.5 suggest that there is not one route to attaining literacy skills. Formal schooling is a factor, probably the main factor for most adults (see conclusion of Chapter 3), but lack of initial, formal education need not inevitably consign an adult to a low level of skill. Hence it is important to understand why certain countries succeed better than others in providing high literacy skills to the least educated.

2.4   Conclusion

The findings presented in this chapter raise important issues. Countries differ markedly in the literacy attainment of their adult populations, but none does so well that it can be said that it has no literacy problem. The comparisons are also complex. That countries differ in their skill patterns from scale to scale suggests that different factors are at work in influencing literacy outcomes. Some of these factors are examined more in depth in the next chapter.

References

OECD (2000), *Education at a Glance: OECD Indicators*, Paris.

OECD and HUMAN RESOURCES DEVELOPMENT CANADA (1997), *Literacy Skills for the Knowledge Society: Further Results from the International Adult Literacy Survey,* Paris.

CHAPTER 3

How Literacy is Developed and Sustained

3.1 Introduction

The findings in the previous chapter show that countries differ in the population distribution of literacy skills. A set of variables thought to be important determinants of literacy proficiency is studied in this chapter. Among the different factors influencing literacy skills are a person's socio-economic background, educational attainment and labour force experience. Evidence on the bivariate nature of possible relationships between literacy indicators[1] and their predictor variables is presented first (Sections 3.2 to 3.7). In the concluding part (Section 3.8) an effort is made to disentangle the influences of these variables, in order to estimate how each might contribute to raising the literacy skills of populations.

3.2 Home Background and Literacy Outcomes

Comparable data on the literacy proficiency of children aged 9 and 14 were collected in the early 1990s by the International Association for the Evaluation of Educational Achievement (IEA). The results showed that there were significant differences in average literacy performance between countries already by the time children reached the ages of 9 and 14 (Elley, 1992; Postlethwaite and Ross, 1992). Within countries as well, one observes large differences in literacy proficiency among children of the same young age. These differences were attributed partly to the effects of socialisation, particularly within the family but also by peer groups.

Besides home background, education also plays a critical role in influencing literacy proficiency. In schools, for example, good teachers have high expectations of their students' ability to master the objectives of the curriculum. These expectations manifest themselves in good classroom reading practices and school routines that differ from the ordinary in terms of the effectiveness of reading instruction and the use of literacy resources. At the same time, the literacy skills acquired by children at home and at school affect their opportunities to pursue further education, as well as their transition from school to work and eventually the types of jobs they will acquire.

---

1. Each analysis was undertaken using all three literacy indicators but due to limitations of space, the results are usually reported for a single scale only. The prose scale is often used for reporting purposes but in some other cases the document or quantitative scales are employed. The choice is mostly arbitrary because of the high correlations between the three scales.

Figure 3.1a-c presents data for young adults in selected countries,[2] indicating the strength of the association between literacy proficiency and the amount and quality of initial, formal education.

There is a difference of 73 points on the prose scale between the highest and lowest country average for those young adults who have completed secondary education and of nearly 80 points for those who have not. On average, for youth and adults, each additional year of school attended corresponds to an increase of 10 points on the literacy scores on the IALS test.

In all countries, as would be expected, young adults aged 20-25 who have completed secondary school score higher, on average, than those who have not and, in turn, in many countries those who have completed tertiary education score still higher.[3] The gains from completed secondary education are often substantial, especially on the prose scale in Canada, Portugal, Slovenia and the United States. Although there is some variation across the three scales, the rank order pattern is consistent for most countries. In a few, such as Denmark, the gains of tertiary education are small relative to those for secondary. In most countries young adults with completed secondary education have average scores in the Level 3 range on the prose scale (276-325 points), though in Chile, Hungary, Poland, Slovenia and the United States this is not the case.

Mean scores vary substantially between countries and across the scales for young adults with completed tertiary education. Young tertiary graduates reach particularly high levels of literacy in the Czech Republic, Norway and Sweden on all three scales. However, for some countries and some scales, even those without completed secondary education have average scores exceeding 275 points (Sweden on three scales; Finland on prose and document; Denmark on document; Germany and the Czech Republic on document and quantitative; see Table 3.1a-c in Annex D).

FIGURE 3.1

EDUCATIONAL ATTAINMENT AND LITERACY PROFICIENCY OF YOUNG ADULTS

A. Mean prose score on a scale with range 0-500 points, by level of educational attainment, population aged 20-25, 1992-1998

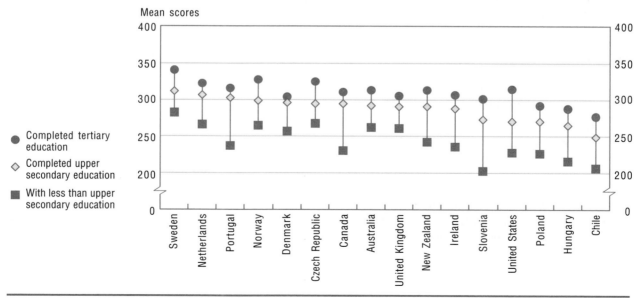

2. Not all countries had sample sizes large enough to support this particular analysis.
3. See Figure 2.5 for evidence.

FIGURE 3.1 (concluded)

EDUCATIONAL ATTAINMENT AND LITERACY PROFICIENCY OF YOUNG ADULTS

B. Mean document score on a scale with range 0-500 points, by level of educational attainment, population aged 20-25, 1992-1998

Mean scores

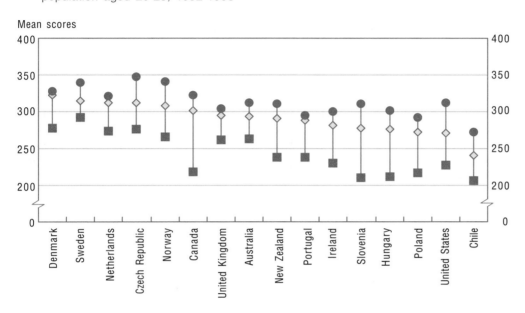

C. Mean quantitative score on a scale with range 0-500 points, by level of educational attainment, population aged 20-25, 1992-1998

Mean scores

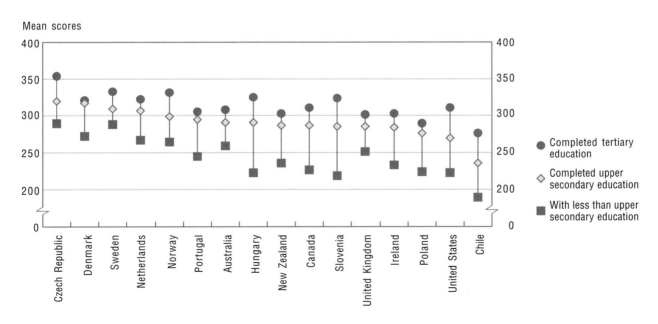

Countries are ranked by the mean scores of those who have completed upper secondary education.
Sources: International Adult Literacy Survey, 1994-1998; and US National Adult Literacy Survey, 1992.

The rank order of the countries in Figure 3.1a-c is similar to that in Figure 2.4a-c in the previous chapter, which presents mean scores for the whole population aged 16-65. It is worth noting that young secondary graduates in the Czech Republic and Denmark have the highest ranking on the quantitative scale but not on the prose scale, mirroring the performance of the adult populations as a whole in these two countries. It is also interesting to note that secondary graduates in Portugal do well on the prose and quantitative scale, but comparatively less well on the document scale. The data underlying Figure 3.1a-c thus suggest that there are differences across countries in the strength of the association between education and literacy outcomes. But, as noted above, family, and a number of other factors, also influence this relationship.

Among these other factors is education of parents. Figures 3.2a-d display, for young persons aged 16 to 25, the relationship between literacy scores and parents' education measured in years. The countries are grouped according to geographic, economic and linguistic criteria. Figures 3.3a-d show the corresponding results for the population aged 26 to 65. Each line was drawn to encompass the range of parents' education within each country from the 10th to the 90th percentiles. The lines are commonly referred to as "socio-economic gradients", and they are useful because they portray the relative level of proficiency in each country, and the extent of inequalities among people with differing socio-economic backgrounds (see Box 3A).

Box 3A. What do the Gradients Show?

Gradients are indicators of the extent of inequalities among different sub-populations. Shallow gradients indicate that there are relatively few inequalities in literacy levels among young and mature adults with differing levels of parental education. Steep gradients indicate greater inequalities.

The results for young adults show considerable differences among countries in the strength of the relationship between parents' education and respondent's levels of literacy skills, indicating substantial variation in socio-economic inequality. In the first group, which includes Australia, Canada, Ireland, New Zealand, the United Kingdom and the United States, the gradients are of similar steepness (Figure 3.2a). They suggest that a young person whose parents had eight years of schooling would on average score about 250 points, whereas someone whose parents received 12 years of schooling would on average score about 280 points. There are significant differences among these mostly English-speaking countries in their levels of performance, with a difference of about 20 points between Canada with the highest level and the United States with the lowest level. Still the gradients show that despite these overall differences, the effect of home background is similar in the six countries.

The gradients for the second group of countries, which includes Belgium (Flanders), Germany, the Netherlands, Portugal and Switzerland, are of similar steepness to those in the first group. However, the average literacy scores are on average about 20 points higher at all levels of parental education (Figure 3.2b). These countries also vary considerably among each other in their level of proficiency, with a range of about 30 points between Portugal with the lowest level and the Netherlands at the highest level.

A much different picture emerges in the results for the third group of countries, which includes Chile, the Czech Republic, Hungary, Poland and Slovenia (Figure 3.2c). The Czech Republic has a relatively high and flat gradient, similar to the gradients of the European countries displayed in Figure 3.2b. Chile also has a relatively flat gradient, but its level of proficiency is much lower, on average about 40 points lower than the Czech Republic at all levels of parental education. The levels of proficiency for the other three countries lie between Chile and the Czech Republic, but what is striking is the steepness of the gradients. In these countries, young people whose parents had eight years of education had scores similar to their counterparts in Chile, whereas youth whose parents had 14 years of education had literacy scores that approached those of their counterparts in the Czech Republic.

FIGURE 3.2

SOCIO-ECONOMIC GRADIENTS FOR DOCUMENT LITERACY SCORES

Relationship between respondent's document literacy scores and parents' education in years, population aged 16-25, 1992-1998

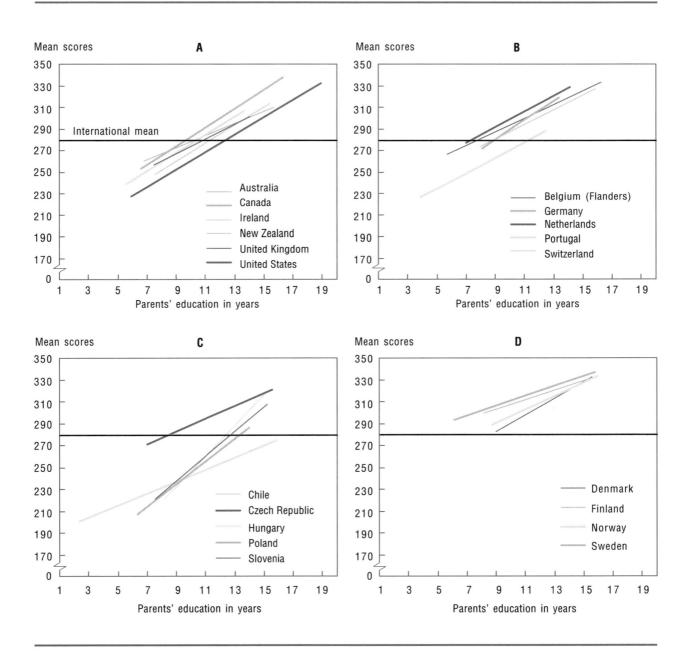

Sources: International Adult Literacy Survey, 1994-1998; US National Adult Literacy Survey, 1992.

Finally, the gradients for young people in the four Nordic countries – Denmark, Finland, Norway and Sweden – are consistently high and flat, with relatively little variation in levels of proficiency (Figure 3.2d). These results indicate not only that young people in the Nordic countries have high levels of literacy on average but also that little of the variation in skills is attributable to differing levels of parental education. The striking degree of homogeneity in these results points to the existence of a high degree of commonality in Nordic approaches to education and society.

FIGURE 3.3

SOCIO-ECONOMIC GRADIENTS FOR DOCUMENT LITERACY SCORES

Relationship between respondent's document literacy scores and parents' education in years, population aged 26-65, 1994-1998

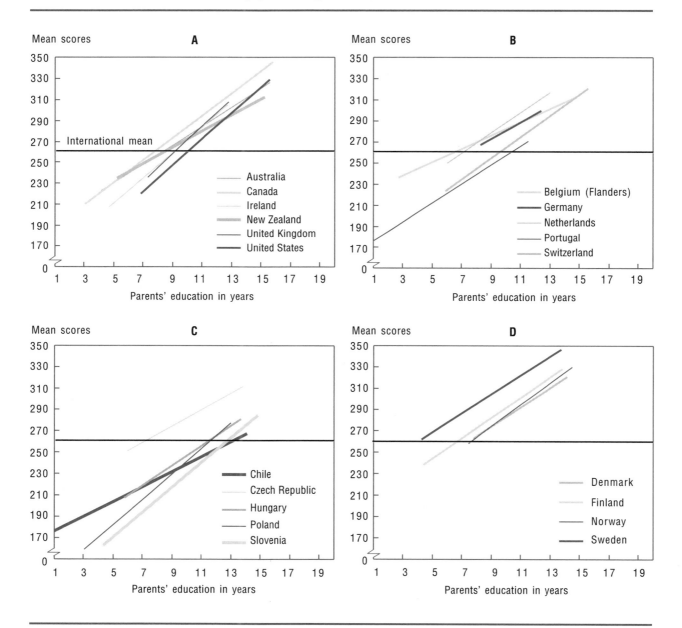

Source: International Adult Literacy Survey, 1994-1998.

Taken together, these results indicate a convergence of gradients within groups of countries, suggesting that those with the highest literacy skills are those that have been successful in bolstering the literacy levels of their least advantaged citizens. Note, however, that these gradients display the overall relationship for a country, and can mask important regional differences within a country; for example, socio-economic gradients for literacy vary considerably among provinces and states in Canada and the United States (Willms, 1999). Gradients can also vary considerably between men and women, and among different age groups. In Northern Ireland, the gap between the literacy skills of Protestants and Catholics has been steadily declining, mainly due to a raising and flattening of the gradient for Catholic women (Willms, 1998).

Figures 3.3a-d display the gradients for adults aged 26 to 65 within each country. The socio-economic gradients for adults are in most respects similar to those for youth, except that they are steeper overall, and their convergence is not as pronounced. In the first group of countries (Figure 3.3a), there is a significant gap of about 70 points between the average literacy scores of adults whose parents had 12 years of schooling (about 290) and those whose parents had only eight years of schooling (about 220). The comparable gap among the European countries displayed in Figure 3.3b is slightly less – about 60 points – attributable mainly to shallower gradients. The Czech Republic stands out in the third set of countries, shown in Figure 3.3c, with similar scores to the European countries in the second group (Figure 3.3b).

The gradients for adults in Hungary, Poland and Slovenia are similar to the Chilean gradient. A comparison of these results with those of youth in Figure 3.2c suggests that literacy skills in these countries are improving in both absolute and relative terms, owing mainly to the increase in performance by the most advantaged citizens. For their gradients to appear more like those of neighbouring European countries, policy makers in these countries will need to raise levels of proficiency of youth particularly from lower socio-economic backgrounds. The gradients for adults in the Nordic countries (Figure 3.3d) are higher than those of other European countries, but, unlike the case for the younger population, the slopes are just as steep. This suggests that the very high literacy scores of Nordic youth are largely attributable to a reduction in inequalities over the past few decades.

3.3 Literacy and Education by Age

Young adults have the benefit of more recent schooling – and as a group a larger proportion has received extended formal schooling compared with older adult groups. Older persons, on the other hand, have the benefit of more experience. Figure 3.4 shows that in every participating country when only age is considered, younger adults aged 26-35 have higher literacy scores than adults closer to retirement aged 56-65. But there are significant differences across countries: in Belgium (Flanders), Canada, Finland, Poland and Slovenia, the differences between the mean literacy scores for the two age groups are greater than 50 points. In New Zealand and the United States, on the other hand, the difference is less than 20 points.

The range of literacy scores within a country tends to be larger for older adults, although in a few countries the ranges are fairly similar for both age groups. Finland, Norway and Sweden have a comparatively high mean literacy score for both young and older adults. This finding suggests that the processes that lead to between-country differences in overall literacy attainment have a long history, confirming the finding from the gradients that Nordic countries, at all ages, have a relative literacy advantage. In some countries, such as the United States, there is a wide spread in the ranges of scores for those aged 26-35 and 56-65.

FIGURE 3.4

AGE AND LITERACY PROFICIENCY

Mean scores with .95 confidence interval and scores at 5th, 25th, 75th and 95th percentiles
on the prose literacy scale, population aged 26-35 and 56-65, 1994-1998

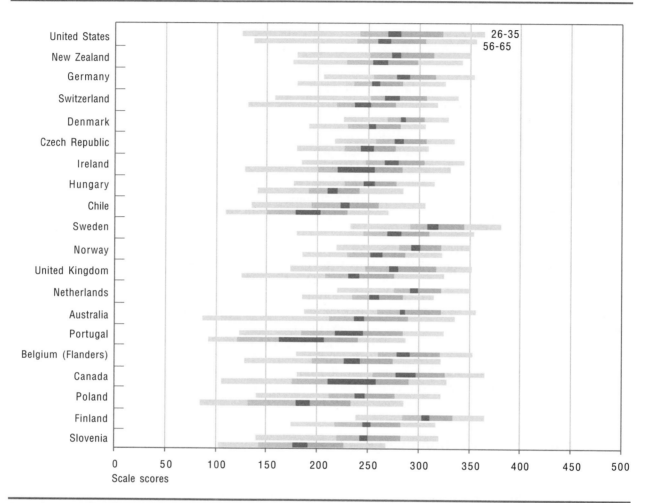

Countries are ranked by the difference in mean scores between the 26-35 and 56-65 age groups.

Source: International Adult Literacy Survey, 1994-1998.

As noted briefly in Chapter 2, education is a factor influencing the relationship between literacy and age because there are wide differences in educational attainment between age groups. However, Figure 3.5a-c shows that even when educational attainment is held constant – only adults with completed secondary education are included in this particular analysis – the skill differences among countries by age remain, even though the pattern is not the same in all countries.[4] Belgium (Flanders) is exceptional in that the literacy scores of those aged 26-35 are closer to those aged 46-65 than to those aged 16-25. In most countries – for example Poland and Switzerland – people aged 46-65 have markedly lower literacy scores than those aged 26-35.

---

4. In some countries the sample included too few adults with completed secondary education in the 46-55 and 56-65 age groups to support separate reporting. Therefore, these two age groups are combined for this particular analysis.

FIGURE 3.5

AGE AND LITERACY CONTROLLING FOR EDUCATION

A. Mean prose literacy scores for persons in different age groups with completed secondary education, 1992-1998

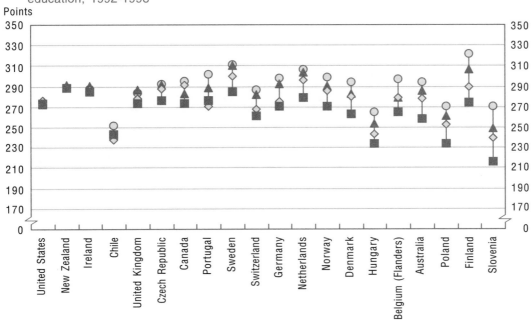

B. Mean document literacy scores for persons in different age groups with completed secondary education, 1992-1998

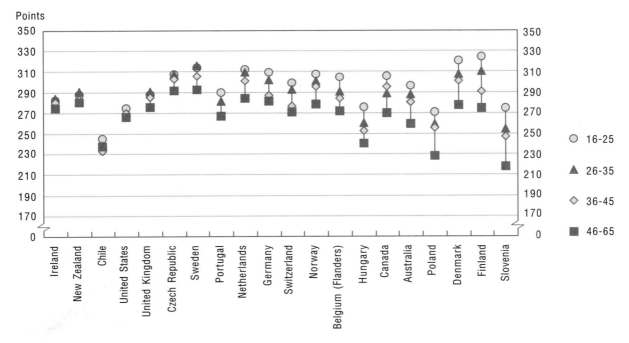

Countries are ranked by the difference in mean scores between the 16-25 and 46-65 age groups.

FIGURE 3.5 (concluded)

AGE AND LITERACY CONTROLLING FOR EDUCATION

C. Mean quantitative literacy scores for persons in different age groups with completed secondary education, 1992-1998

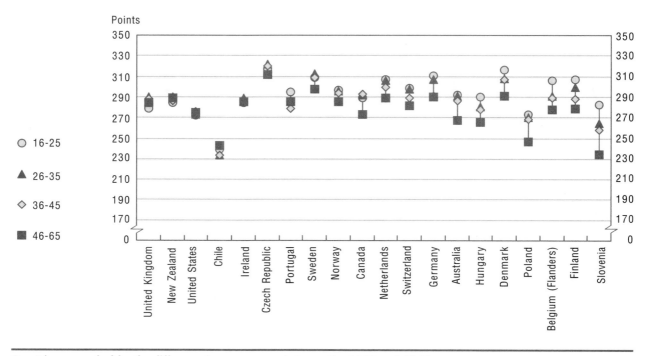

Countries are ranked by the difference in mean scores between the 16-25 and 46-65 age groups.

Sources: International Adult Literacy Survey, 1994-1998; US National Adult Literacy Survey, 1992.

3.4 Literacy and Work

Literacy skills profiles and indicators of the world of work are related in complex ways. As noted in Chapter 1, because literacy is required in many jobs, and increasingly so in knowledge economy jobs, high literacy skills are likely to lead to better employment prospects. At the same time, the workplace is a factor in literacy acquisition and maintenance, a place where a considerable amount of reading, writing and arithmetic takes place. Often these two aspects of workplace literacy reinforce each other: skills learned in schools facilitate engaging more frequently in more complex activities at the workplace that in turn build skills. The survey results confirm this dual role of workplace literacy.

As Figure 3.6 indicates, individuals who are in the labour force[5] consistently have higher literacy skills than those who are not. Whereas the size of the difference varies from country to country [relatively small in Switzerland, larger in Belgium (Flanders) and the Netherlands], the literacy skills of the reserve labour force are generally lower than those of the active labour force. Contributing to improve the skills of those not working could help them to successfully enter the labour market (compare with Figures 4.1 and 4.3a-c).

---

5. Working at the time of the interview or having worked or looked for work during the year preceding it.

FIGURE 3.6

LABOUR FORCE PARTICIPATION AND LITERACY PROFICIENCY

Rates of labour force participation by low (Levels 1 and 2) and medium to high (Levels 3 and 4/5) literacy proficiency, document scale, population aged 25-65, 1994-1998

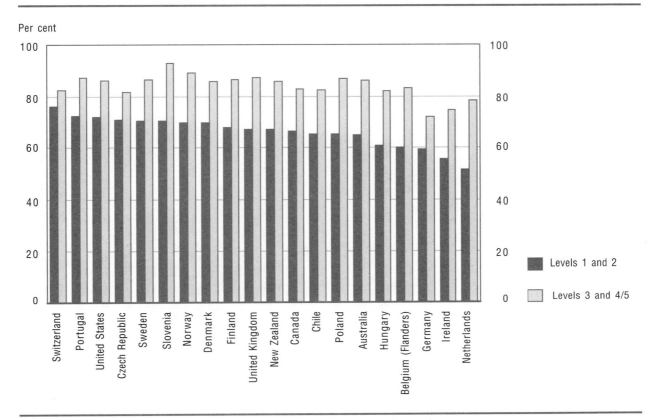

Per cent

Levels 1 and 2

Levels 3 and 4/5

Countries are ranked by the labour force participation rate of those at Levels 1 and 2.
Source: International Adult Literacy Survey, 1994-1998.

Once in the labour market, individuals with low literacy skills – those who often have a low level of initial education – face an increased likelihood of being unemployed. Figure 3.7 compares the proportion of adults with low skills – those at Levels 1 and 2 on the document scale – who were unemployed at the time of the interview with the proportion of those with medium to high skills who were without work. In many countries – Australia, Belgium (Flanders), Canada, Denmark, Germany, Ireland, Finland, New Zealand, Slovenia and the United Kingdom – the incidence of unemployment is twice as high among adults with low skills than among adults with medium to high skills. In a few countries, notably Norway, Switzerland and the United States, the overall level of unemployment is so low that low-skilled adults face only a relatively small risk of unemployment. Figure 4.4 in the next chapter suggests that literacy is related not only to unemployment incidence but also to unemployment duration.

Those with low skills find themselves without work more often even if they find some employment during the year. In some countries, those with the lowest literacy skills work fewer weeks per year. For example, Figure 3.8 shows for Canada that the difference in average weeks worked between those at Level 1 and the other groups is about seven weeks. In Finland and Norway this difference is close to four weeks and in Australia and New Zealand it is around three weeks.

FIGURE 3.7

UNEMPLOYMENT AND LITERACY

Unemployment rate by level of literacy proficiency for the labour force aged 16-65, document scale, 1994-1998

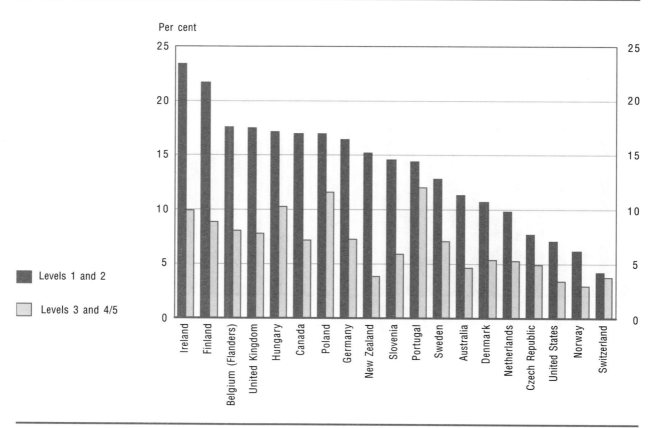

Countries are ranked by the incidence of unemployment of those at Levels 1 and 2.
Source: International Adult Literacy Survey, 1994-1998.

In summary, Figures 3.6, 3.7 and 3.8 display the significant reduction in opportunity to work for adults with low skills: they are less likely to be in employment, less likely to find work when looking for it and less likely to work regularly when a job is obtained. Because the world of work also is a significant factor in the acquisition and building of skills, adults with low skills find themselves at a distinct disadvantage.

Individuals who engage regularly in informal learning at work through activities such as reading, writing and calculation have more and better opportunities to maintain and enhance their foundation skills than people who do not use these skills regularly. Not surprisingly, the evidence from IALS indicates that people with high levels of literacy skills have more opportunities to use them in the workplace than people with low levels of skills. Figures 3.9 and 3.10[6] show just how much richer in literacy the workplace is for adults with Level 4/5 skills than it is for adults with Level 1 skills.

_____

6. Unfortunately, these questions were not included in the same format in the Swedish survey.

FIGURE 3.8

Employment Disadvantage of Low-Skilled Adults

Mean number of weeks worked by persons who were employed during the year preceding the interview, by literacy level, quantitative scale, population aged 25-65, 1994-1998

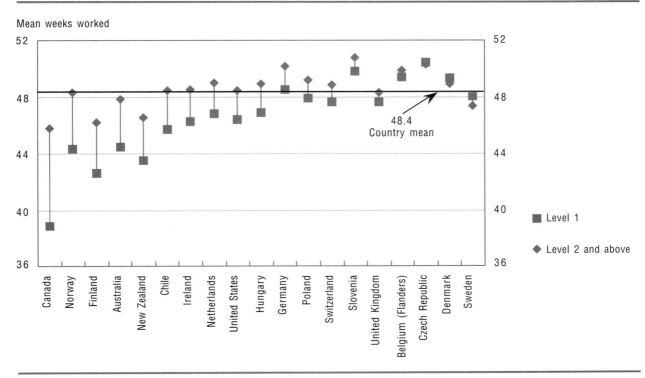

Countries are ranked by the difference in weeks worked by those in Level 1 and those in other levels.
Source: International Adult Literacy Survey, 1994-1998.

BOX 3B. What do the Reading and Writing Indices Measure?

Individuals were asked how frequently at work they engaged in literacy activities with various kinds of texts: reports, letters, schemas, manuals, invoices and instructions. The reading variety index is constructed from these responses. It records how many of the six different types of texts the respondent said that he or she read at least once a week. Thus, someone whose index is 6 would have reported using each of the six every week. Persons who said they used four of the six every week would have an index of 4. The writing index is constructed in the same way using four questions about different kinds of writing activities in the workplace: letters and memos, reports, financial documents and specifications. Thus, the indices reflect both variety and frequency. Someone with a higher index does not necessarily read more frequently but has a greater variety of literacy experiences more often.

The contrast between those with high and low scores on the reading practices index tends to be small in countries where the range of literacy is narrow: the Czech Republic, Finland, Germany and Norway. However, in countries with a greater literacy range such as the United Kingdom, there still is a relatively smaller range in workplace literacy practices. Yet, as with literacy skills, countries differ widely in the degree of literacy engagement at work. Countries that have large differences in engagement tend to be those that also have wide differences in skills, as can be seen by comparing Figures 3.9 and 3.10 with Figures 2.1a-c and 2.2a-c in the previous chapter.

FIGURE 3.9

READING AT WORK

Index scores for engagement in reading at work by literacy level, document scale,
population aged 16-65, 1994-1998

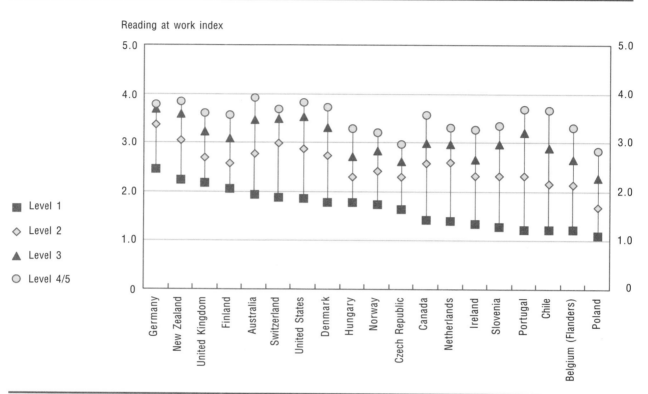

Countries are ranked by the reading engagement index of those at Level 1.
Source: International Adult Literacy Survey, 1994-1998.

The reading index in Figure 3.9 is below 2 for Level 1 respondents in almost all countries. The exceptions are Finland, Germany, New Zealand and the United Kingdom. A web of relationships is involved. On average, adults at Level 1 have few opportunities to interact with literacy materials during a working week but typically do have some opportunity to use their reading skills. At the same time, the relationship works in the opposite direction: little opportunity to practice skills at work increases the probability of being in Level 1.

Figure 3.10 presents index scores for engagement in writing at work. The results show that for most countries this index is below 1 for respondents with Level 1 skills – the exceptions are Germany, Switzerland and the United Kingdom. Hence, in the large majority of countries, individuals with poor literacy skills engage in writing at work less than once a week. Given that persons with poor skills have little exposure to literacy tasks at work, it would seem unlikely that they can develop their skills without some form of formal instruction or training. However, the evidence from IALS about participation in training, presented in the next section, suggests that in most countries, people with lower literacy skills are not having this opportunity.

FIGURE 3.10

WRITING AT WORK

Index scores for engagement in writing at work by literacy level, prose scale, population aged 16-65, 1994-1998

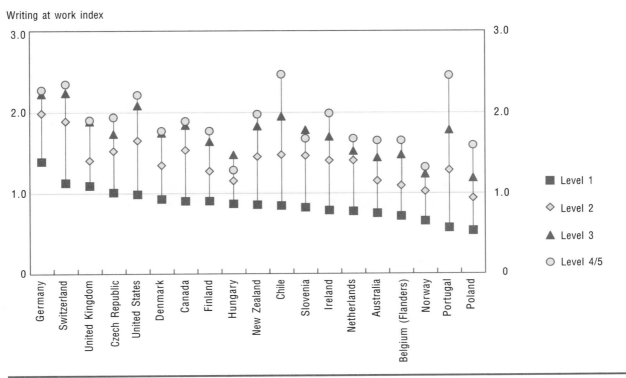

Writing at work index

Legend:
- ■ Level 1
- ◇ Level 2
- ▲ Level 3
- ○ Level 4/5

Countries are ranked by the writing engagement index of those at Level 1.

Source: International Adult Literacy Survey, 1994-1998.

3.5   Literacy and Formal Adult Education

Indicators of literacy-related, informal learning activities were examined above. Formal learning encounters are studied in this section. Figure 3.11 shows the average hours of continuing education and training per adult aged 16-65 in a range of countries, taking account both of varying participation rates and differences in the volume of adult education and training.[7] Training hours per adult provide a comprehensive measure of the overall, formal adult education effort of the countries. The data suggest that efforts vary substantially across countries. It is relatively low in Belgium (Flanders), Chile, the Czech Republic, Hungary and Poland, but high in Denmark, Finland and New Zealand. Figure 3.11 also shows the estimated hours of job-related education and training per adult. On this measure, Canada has a profile very similar to Norway, whereas the United Kingdom is more similar to Finland.

---

7. Calculated as the mean number of hours per participant multiplied by the participation rate and divided by 100, excluding full-time students and persons participating in educational activities for less than six hours.

In many countries, participation in adult education and training has become a common activity rather than an exception. Figure 3.12 suggests that the IALS countries fall broadly into three groups:

- The Nordic countries are in the first group, where lifelong learning has become a reality for a large segment of the population. Over the 12-month period preceding the survey, Denmark, Finland and Sweden have overall participation rates over 50 per cent. This might be explained by their long history of adult education and the fact that they have a large publicly-funded sector of adult popular education. New Zealand and Norway also have rates close to 50 per cent.

- The majority of the countries in IALS have a rate of participation in adult education and training of around 40 per cent.

- There is a group of countries where lifelong learning is a less common activity. Chile, Hungary, Poland and Portugal have rates below 20 per cent whereas those of Belgium (Flanders), the Czech Republic, Ireland and Slovenia are in the 20-30 per cent range.

FIGURE 3.11

HOURS OF CONTINUING EDUCATION AND TRAINING PER ADULT

Mean number of hours of continuing education and training per adult by type of training, population aged 16-65[1], 1994-1998

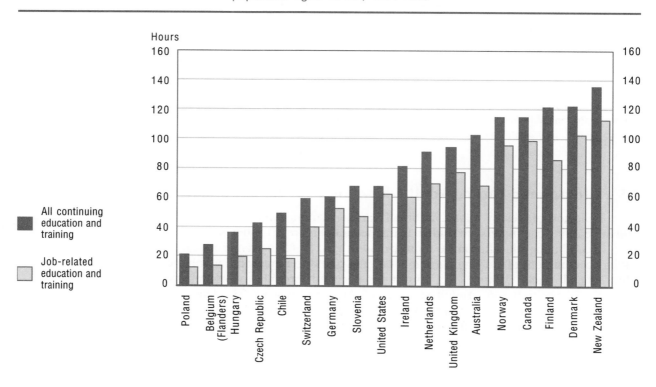

Countries are ranked by the average hours of all continuing education and training per adult.

1. Full-time students and people who received less than six hours of education or training are excluded.

Source: International Adult Literacy Survey, 1994-1998.

FIGURE 3.12

LITERACY AND ADULT EDUCATION PARTICIPATION

Per cent of population aged 16-65 participating in adult education and training during the year preceding the interview at each literacy level and in total, document scale, 1994-1998

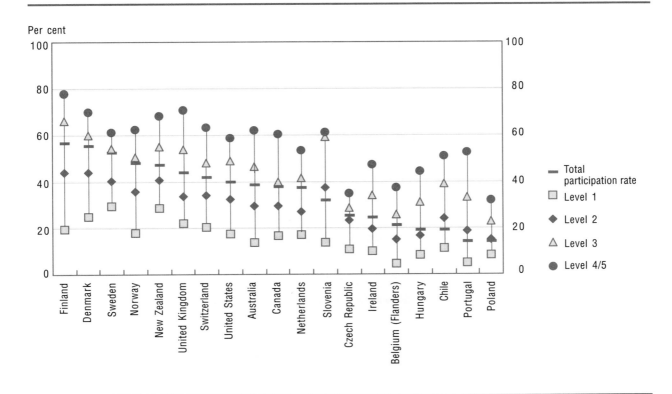

Countries are ranked by the total participation rate.

Source: International Adult Literacy Survey, 1994-1998.

While the rates vary between countries, the data show that in each country there are large groups outside the emerging learning society. Those outside are often those most in need of skills enhancement, whether through formal or informal learning. With large groups of adults possessing low literacy skills, it is particularly important from a policy perspective to look at their readiness to engage in learning. Figure 3.12 indicates that participation in adult education increases gradually by level of literacy. Those with low literacy skills receive the least adult education. The level of inequality – although large – is relatively smaller in Denmark, New Zealand and Sweden, countries with high overall participation rates.[8]

As discussed previously, much of the variation in mean literacy levels observed in Figure 3.12 can be attributed to the "literate culture" in which a person grew up, and the effect this has had on educational attainment. The "long arm of the family" is further extended through the way in which educational credentials, to a large extent, determine entry into the labour market and the early stages of a person's occupational career (Tuijnman *et al.*, 1988).

---

8. Relative inequality is lowest in the Czech Republic, a country with a relatively low participation rate.

FIGURE 3.13

LIKELIHOOD OF PARTICIPATION BY OCCUPATION

Adjusted odds of participating in employer-sponsored adult education and training,
by occupational category, population aged 16-65, 1994-1998

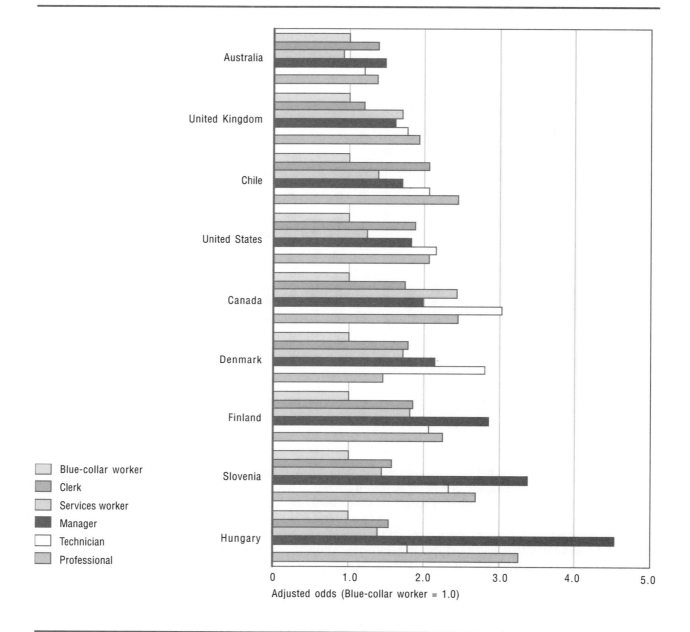

Adjusted odds (Blue-collar worker = 1.0)

- Blue-collar worker
- Clerk
- Services worker
- Manager
- Technician
- Professional

Countries are ranked by the adjusted odds of those in managerial occupations participating in employer-sponsored adult education and training.

Source: International Adult Literacy Survey, 1994-1998.

A challenge facing all countries is how to overcome the disparity between the rising demand for skills in the knowledge economy, noted in Chapter 1, and the presence in the workforce of large numbers of people with poor literacy skills. A first step is to recognise the importance of the "long arm of the job" in determining adults' frequency of engagement in both formal and informal learning. The IALS data on participation in adult education reflect the fundamental shift that has occurred over the last 15 years towards an increase in adult education provision (Bélanger and Valdivielso, 1997). This development mirrors the increased importance accorded to learning as a prerequisite for economic growth (OECD, 1996; Rubenson and Schuetze, 2000).

Figure 3.13 presents the likelihood of receiving education or training sponsored by an employer for workers in different occupational categories, with the likelihood of blue-collar workers receiving training as the baseline for the comparison. See Box 3C for an explanation of odds ratio analysis.

Box 3C. Using Odds Ratios

Differences are expressed in terms of the likelihood of various groups participating in employer-sponsored education and training. An odds ratio of 1 represents equal odds of receiving and not receiving training. Coefficients with values below 1 indicate less chance of receiving training, and coefficients larger than 1 represent an increased chance. For the purpose of this particular analysis, the likelihood of blue-collar workers being trained is set at 1 for all the countries.

The results presented in Figure 3.13 show that managers and professionals tend to receive more training than blue-collar workers. This result is not surprising in itself, and it confirms the training distributions observed in many national surveys (OECD, 1999). More striking is the extent of the differences both within and between countries. Australia shows a much more equal training pattern by occupational groups than Canada, Hungary and Slovenia. And in some countries – Canada, Denmark and the United States – technicians are the occupational group most likely to participate. Further work is needed to discover why these different patterns might have occurred.

Information on various sources of financial support for training is reported separately for men and women in Figure 3.14a-b.[9] The findings confirm the central role that employers play in training. In all countries, employers are by far the main external source of financial support for adult education for men. The proportion receiving financial support from government sources is below 10 per cent in almost all countries, except Denmark, New Zealand, Norway and Slovenia. A comparison between Figure 3.14a and Figure 3.14b indicates that men benefit more often than women from employer support for their education. The gender difference in employer support is particularly noticeable in Belgium (Flanders), the Czech Republic and the Netherlands. Consequently, as shown in Figure 3.14b, women must, to a larger extent than men rely on alternate sources – mainly, self-financing. The gender difference in the financing of training is in part a result of the lower labour market participation rate of women and the fact that they work part time more often than men.

---

9. The question asked whether the education or training was financially supported by the individual or the family, an employer, or the government. Hence the data concern the source of financial support but not the actual amount involved.

FIGURE 3.14

SOURCES OF FINANCIAL SUPPORT FOR ADULT EDUCATION AND TRAINING

A. Per cent of men participating in adult education and training who receive financial support from various sources, population aged 16-65, 1994-1998

B. Per cent of women participating in adult education and training who receive financial support from various sources, population aged 16-65, 1994-1998

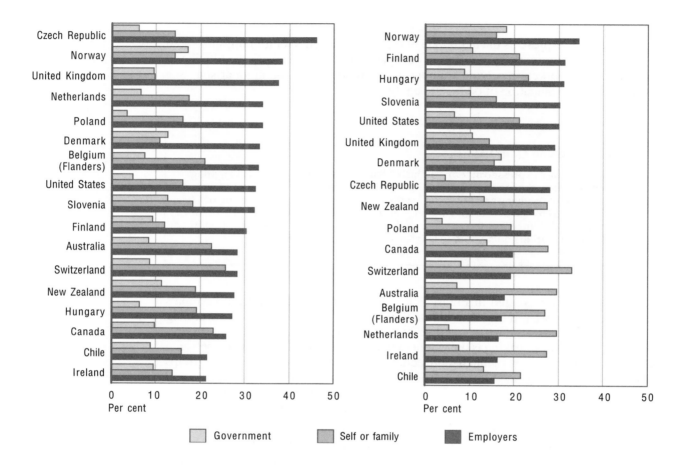

A. Countries are ranked by the share of employers in the financing of education or training for men.
B. Countries are ranked by the share of employers in the financing of education or training for women.
Source: International Adult Literacy Survey, 1994-1998.

However, despite the gender imbalance, in 9 of the 17 countries for which information was available, employers are the main source of financing training for women. In the Czech Republic, Denmark, Norway, Slovenia and the United Kingdom, about twice as many women receive financial support from the employer as rely on self-financing. In Canada, Chile, Denmark, New Zealand and Norway a substantial proportion of female participants received financial support from government sources, as is the case for men in Denmark, Norway and Slovenia. In contrast governments play a very modest role in financing in most other countries, particularly in the Czech Republic, the Netherlands, Poland and the United States.

FIGURE 3.15

LIKELIHOOD OF PARTICIPATION BY LITERACY ENGAGEMENT AT WORK

Adjusted odds of receiving employer-sponsored adult education and training by level of literacy engagement at work, employed population aged 16-65, 1994-1998

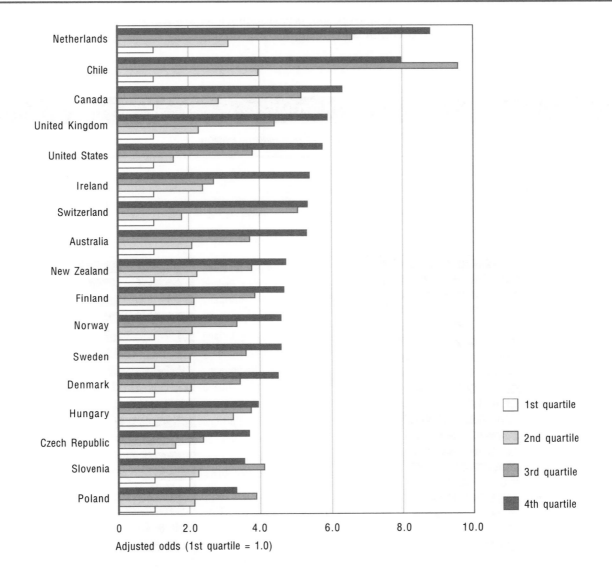

Countries are ranked by the adjusted odds of those in the 4th quartile receiving employer-sponsored adult education and training.

Source: International Adult Literacy Survey, 1994-1998.

Figure 3.15 shows the likelihood of receiving employer-sponsored education and training by literacy engagement at work, measured as described in Box 3D. This likelihood is expressed in odds ratios adjusted for industry, full-time and part-time work, company size and occupation.[10] The likelihood that workers receive training support from employers is closely connected with these workers' use of literacy skills at work. It is likely that this relationship works in both directions. In Chile and the Netherlands, workers who use workplace literacy skills the least are less likely to participate in employer-supported training than workers who use workplace literacy skills the most (eight and nine times respectively).

FIGURE 3.16

READING BOOKS AND WATCHING TELEVISION

A. Per cent of population aged 16-65 who reported reading a book at least once a month, 1994-1998

B. Per cent of population aged 16-65 who reported watching television for more than 2 hours per day, 1994-1998

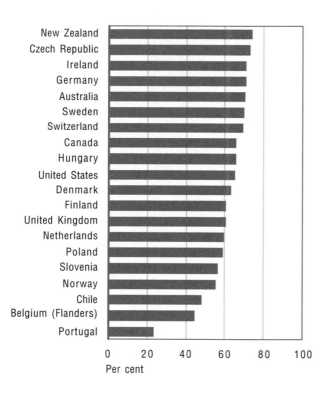

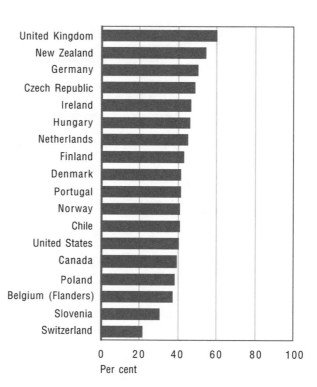

A.   Countries are ranked by the proportion of respondents reading a book at least once a month.

B.   Countries are ranked by the proportion of respondents watching television for more than two hours per day.

Source: International Adult Literacy Survey, 1994-1998.

10. Odds ratios are not adjusted for company size in the Netherlands and Sweden because this variable is not available.

> **BOX 3D. Combined Index of Literacy Engagement at Work**
>
> The combined literacy engagement at work index is constructed to study the link between the use of workplace literacy and employers' willingness to invest in the continuing education and training of the workforce. This quartile-based index combines the reading and writing indices described in Box 3B. The 1st quartile represents workers who use workplace literacy skills the least and the 4th quartile represents workers who use workplace literacy skills the most. For the purpose of the analysis reported in Figure 3.15, the likelihood that workers in the 1st quartile receive employer support for training is set at 1.

Even after controlling for full or part-time work, firm size and occupational category, workers in Canada, Chile, the United Kingdom and the United States with the highest use of literacy skills at work, are still six to eight times more likely to receive support from their employers for education and training than those who use workplace literacy skills the least. Employers' willingness to invest in the continuing education and training of their workforce is somewhat more equally distributed in the Czech Republic, Hungary, Poland and Slovenia.

3.6 Literacy, Culture and Civic Skills

The IALS findings presented so far point to the importance of broadening the discussion about the skills required for the knowledge economy from a narrow focus on the supply of skills to how the demand structure governs adults' readiness to engage in lifelong learning. The IALS background questionnaire included a few questions that address informal learning in the form of reading and writing activities at work (see Box 3B) and in daily life. To regularly engage in reading activities is important not only to learn new skills but also to maintain learning capability. Analysis of the IALS data has shown that literacy scores are positively related to peoples' daily reading practices, and negatively related to the amount of television they watch (OECD, 1997, p. 77), suggesting that if literacy skills are not used they will deteriorate. Figure 3.16a-b presents the proportions of the adult population who read a book at least once a month and who view television for more than two hours per day. There is a widespread public belief that literacy and watching television are somehow incompatible. The IALS data indicate that the link between the two varies from country to country.

Figure 3.16a suggests that the practice of book reading varies substantially across countries. In Portugal, only one in four adults reports reading a book at least once a month. In Chile this figure is one in two while close to 75 per cent of New Zealanders were regular book readers. Figure 3.16b indicates that there are substantial differences also in television viewing. Britons, New Zealanders and Germans are keen television viewers. In these countries at least half of the respondents report that they, on average, watch television two hours or more a day. The Swiss and Slovenians spend considerably less time in front of the TV set. The results also show that those most likely to watch television for significant periods of time are usually at the lower levels of literacy performance, while those at higher literacy levels tend to spend less time in front of television.[11]

---

11. Data in Figure 4.10 in *Literacy, Economy and Society* (OECD and Statistics Canada, 1995), p. 108.

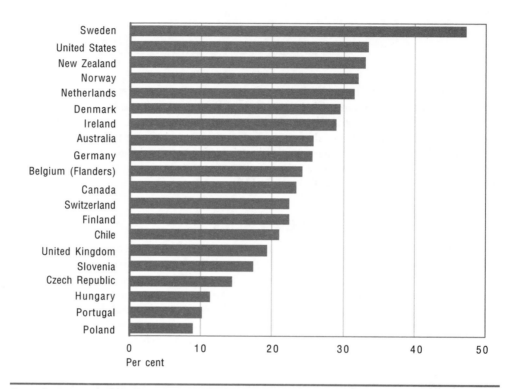

FIGURE 3.17

PARTICIPATION IN COMMUNITY ACTIVITIES

Per cent of population aged 16-65 who reported engaging in community activities at least once a month, 1994-1998

Countries are ranked by the proportion of respondents engaging in community activities at least once a month.

Source: International Adult Literacy Survey, 1994-1998.

Social capital theorists argue that participation in non-work contexts is an important determining factor of the quality of democratic life and civic society (Coleman, 1988; Ostrom, 1994). Putnam (1993) sees social capital reflected in participation in voluntary associations, norms of reciprocity and trust, and networks of civic engagement. According to its proponents, social capital enables people to achieve goals that would not have been possible in its absence. Verba *et al.* (1995) argue that certain resources including civic skills are necessary for political participation. They also point to the acquisition of civic skills that takes place in voluntary associations. Just as literacy skills are a prerequisite to learn efficiently on the job, participation in civic society is necessary for developing civic skills. Voluntary associations and community activities are therefore important arenas for informal learning that can stimulate the development of new skills as well as preventing others from being lost due to lack of use.

The IALS touches upon the issue of civic skills and social capital in a question about the extent to which the respondents participate in voluntary community activities. Figure 3.17 shows the crucial role the voluntary sector plays in Swedish society, where close to 50 per cent of the adult population participate at least once a month in voluntary associations. An investigation conducted in that country (SOU, 1996) found that these associations provide a rich environment for informal learning that fosters democratic values and helps keep individuals mentally active. Citizens of the Czech Republic, Hungary, Poland and Portugal do not seem to have access to an equivalent collectively constituted arena for informal learning. In these countries 15 per cent or less reported that they are active on a regular base in voluntary associations.

In order to assist those with low literacy skills, a strategy will have to be devised that reaches out to workplaces and also builds on the community and voluntary sector. In its *Reviews of National Policies for Education,* the OECD (1991; 1995) sends a strong message about the importance of the voluntary sector in delivering adult education and strengthening a culture of literacy and civic society. This sector is flexible and reaches out to adults who otherwise might not engage in adult learning. Promoting civic society is an important task for all OECD countries striving for social cohesion in the knowledge economy.

Policies to strengthen cohesion while capitalising on the benefits of cultural heterogeneity and linguistic diversity are being pursued throughout the OECD area. Globalisation and the increased movement of people it brings are major contributing factors. Mass tourism, for example, has created an entirely new dimension in social and cultural interaction. In addition to tourism, there are important trends in international migration. The share of foreigners, immigrants and asylum-seekers in the total population has grown markedly in many countries since the early 1980s. These migrants must somehow be accommodated in the economy and society. This implies the challenges of taking linguistic diversity and cultural barriers into account while finding a new equilibrium in accommodating new values alongside existing ones, both in workplaces and in communities. Literacy in the dominant or official languages is key to unlocking the social and economic benefits of the new country while nurturing linguistic diversity is important for safeguarding cherished cultural values.

Immigration has long been seen as a source of new workers. But immigrants can also have an impact on the distribution of literacy skills because they bring different educational experiences, may have learned an official language only as second or third language, or may be less familiar than the native-born population with the dominant literate culture of the country.

Figure 3.18 presents data on the proportions of the native-born and non-native language foreign-born populations who are at Levels 1 and 2 compared with Levels 3, 4 and 5 on the document scale. In countries in North America and Western Europe where there has been a large influx of immigrants over the years, there are larger numbers of foreign-born people whose mother tongue is not the dominant language of the new country at low levels of literacy than native-born.[12] The differences in proportions are somewhat less pronounced in Australia and New Zealand, two countries that appear to have attracted both low and high-literate non-English speaking immigrants. The skill patterns for immigrants in Norway and Sweden are consistent, with large differences between the native and second-language foreign-born at low levels of literacy, but also large numbers of immigrants at high levels of literacy.

---

12. Canada has a large number of immigrants whose mother tongue is English or French. In the country, the proportion of all immigrants at Level 4/5 is larger than the proportion of native-born at this level.

FIGURE 3.18

NATIVE-BORN VERSUS FOREIGN-BORN (SECOND LANGUAGE) POPULATION AND LITERACY

Per cent of native-born and second-language foreign-born population aged 16-65
at each literacy level, document scale, 1994-1998

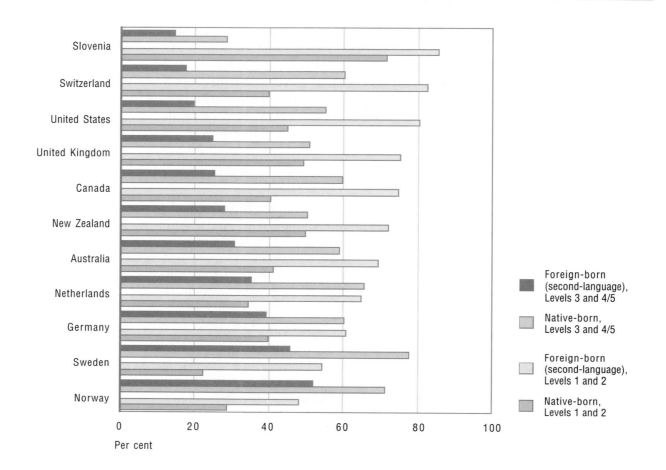

Countries are ranked by the proportion of foreign-born (second-language) persons at Levels 3 and 4/5.
Source: International Adult Literacy Survey, 1994-1998.

3.7 Self-assessed Literacy Skills

Another perspective on skills comes from adults' subjective judgements about the adequacy of their own skills. As Figure 3.19 shows, adults at low levels of skills in different countries offer different self-assessments of how well they read. In most countries fewer than half of those at Level 1 think that their skills are less than good. Because respondents to this question may not all share the same concept of "moderate" reading skills, some of the differences may be due to different expectations about skills, among other reasons.

Figure 3.20 provides data on a somewhat less subjective self-assessment of skills, one that asks respondents how well their skills meet changing workplace demands. Here, too, there is considerable variation. Though it may be expected that the extent of experience with skills demand might be a factor in how individuals reach their judgements on these questions, there is no simple relationship between the measures of experience offered by the reading and writing indices presented previously in Figures 3.9 and 3.10 and the self-assessments of skills reflected in Figures 3.19 and 3.20. Adults with Level 1 skills in Canada and Ireland have very similar average reading index scores, but offer very different reports about how they rate their skills and how limiting they find them relative to workplace demand for skills.

These observations about self-assessed skills sufficiency are relevant to policy. Many adults who score poorly on the literacy test do not themselves consider this to be a problem. A number of studies have investigated how low-skilled adults cope with literacy demands at work (Fingeret, 1983). These find that such adults develop different coping strategies to deal with or mask their skills deficit and to enable them to manage their daily lives. Nonetheless, the data on the relationship between literacy skills and labour market activity, reviewed in Section 3.4 and elaborated in Chapter 4, point to the real limitations low levels of skills bring – regardless of whether these limits are acknowledged by those with low skills.

FIGURE 3.19

SELF-ASSESSMENT OF READING SKILLS

Per cent of population aged 16-65 who rate their reading skills as either poor or moderate and are at literacy Level 1, prose scale, 1994-1998

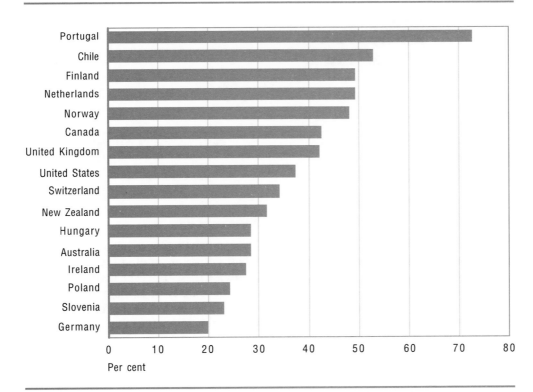

Countries are ranked by the proportion of the population who report their skills as either poor or moderate.

Source: International Adult Literacy Survey, 1994-1998.

FIGURE 3.20

HANDICAPS IMPOSED BY LOW READING SKILLS

Per cent of population aged 16-65 who report that their reading skills limit their opportunities at work and are at literacy Level 1, document scale, 1994-1998

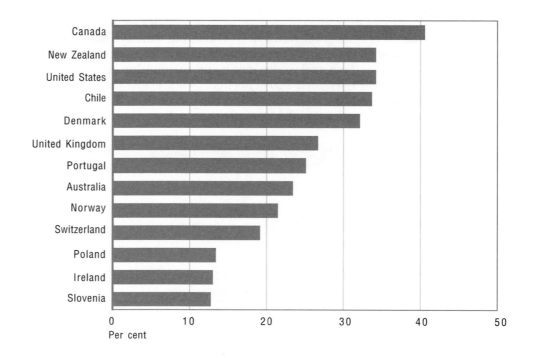

Per cent

Countries are ranked by the proportion of the population with reading skills that limit the opportunities at work.

Source: International Adult Literacy Survey, 1994-1998.

3.8 Factors Explaining Literacy Proficiency

So far in this chapter a large number of variables thought to be associated with literacy performance have been examined. The variables studied were suggested either by theory or were chosen on the basis of previous research. The mainly bivariate analytical techniques used generally confirm that there are close associations between the predictor variables and the outcome, literacy proficiency. While the results indicate significant correlations, they do not provide information about the relative importance of the different factors in predicting literacy.

It is not possible to make strong causal inferences from bivariate relationships among variables because the predictor variables themselves are probably interrelated. For example, people with high occupational status are likely to read more often at work. In such cases, the strength of the bivariate relationship between the outcome and the predictor variable does not necessarily reflect the true influence of the predictor, because it partially reflects the influences of other unobserved variables.

In this concluding part a more sophisticated multivariate method was used to determine the relative contribution of 12 different factors in explaining the observed literacy proficiency data in 20 countries. The purpose of the data analysis was to find out, first, how much of the variance in the outcome variable could be explained by the predictor variables in each country, and second, how much of that explained variance could be attributed to each of the predictors while holding the other factors constant. The methodology is described in Box 3E.

The bars in Figure 3.21 indicate how well the 12 antecedent variables explain the variance observed in literacy proficiency. In Canada, Chile, Portugal, Slovenia and the United States, more than 50 per cent of the variance in literacy performance is accounted for – mainly by a small subset of the predictor variables. In Australia and Finland that amount is between 45 and 49 per cent. As can be seen from Figure 3.21, most countries fall in the 40-44 per cent range. The model explains much less of the variance in literacy proficiency in the Czech Republic, Germany and Sweden, a finding which deserves further investigation. A good part of the unexplained variance can likely be attributed to quality differences in the experience of initial education, but other factors no doubt play a role as well.

A summary of the main results is presented in Table 3.22 page 57. Four variables are listed for each country. Given the amount of explained variance in literacy, these variables have the highest weight in the regression equation and therefore can be interpreted as exerting the most important influences on the dependent variable, literacy proficiency.

FIGURE 3.21

Variance explained in literacy proficiency

Per cent of variance (R^2) in literacy proficiency accounted for by 12 predictor variables, measured as a latent construct combining three scales, population aged 25-65, 1994-1998

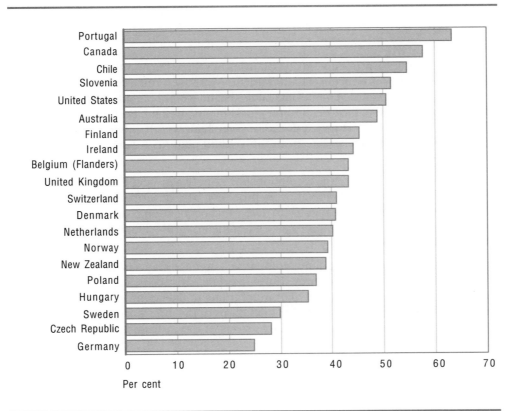

Countries are ranked by the per cent of variance explained in literacy proficiency.

Source: International Adult Literacy Survey, 1994-1998.

> **BOX 3E. How the LISREL Parameters are Obtained**
>
> The outcome variable, literacy proficiency, is measured as a latent construct based on the prose, document and quantitative scales. The model includes 12 predictor variables, entered in sequence: (1) gender; (2) age; (3) non-native language status; (4) parents' education; (5) respondent's own educational level measured in years and levels; (6) labour force participation; (7) industry sector; (8) occupational status; (9) frequency reading memos at work; (10) participation in adult education and training; (11) frequency reading books at home; and (12) frequency participating in voluntary or community-based activities. All variables had identical measurement properties across countries.
>
> The effects on literacy proficiency are estimated in Linear Structural Relations (LISREL) path models. See Jöreskog and Sörbom (1996a; 1996b) and Tuijnman and Keeves (1994) for an explanation of the method. The analysis is based on the population aged 25-65.
>
> In the first step coefficients of correlation are computed using the population weights and different methods depending on variable type. Several variables are measured on dichotomous scales with two response categories, for example, gender or participation in adult education. In such cases polychoric and polyserial estimation functions are used, in addition to the product-moment fit function employed in other cases.
>
> The correlation coefficients provide the basis for a regression analysis that in a first step employs the two-stage least-squares method to obtain starting values for the subsequent linear structural equations estimation under the maximum likelihood fit function. The regression weights presented in Table 3.21 in Annex D are standardised coefficients that allow meaningful comparisons to be made across the models even though the countries used different designs to collect the data.
>
> Table 3.21 in Annex D and Table 3.22 next page shows the regression weight of each variable and its associated standard error. Also shown are the R^2 values which indicate the total amount of variance explained in literacy. The residuals are small and the goodness of fit indices high, demonstrating acceptable model fit.

Perhaps not surprisingly, in all countries but three the number one predictor of literacy proficiency is educational attainment. Moreover, relative to the importance of the other factors included in the data analysis, the weight of education is especially strong in Canada, Chile, the Czech Republic, Hungary, Ireland, Portugal and Slovenia. In fact, in Chile and Portugal, education overshadows all other variables in the analysis. Three countries deviate from this overall pattern: Australia, Germany and Switzerland.

In Germany, the strongest relationship is between occupation category and literacy proficiency. This association is probably best described as non-recursive, since literacy proficiency is expected to determine occupational status and *vice versa*. Age and non-native language status also exert meaningful – albeit for age negative – effects on literacy in Germany.

In Australia and Switzerland, non-native language status is the most important determinant of literacy proficiency. In Switzerland this result is probably not only attributable to the literacy handicap of immigrants in the country. The Swiss survey employed a complex design since the populations of the different cantons were tested either using German, French or Italian versions of the instruments.[13]

---

13. Because in each canton only one test language was administered, the Swiss survey required an unknown number of people to take the test in a language other than their native one. The analysis suggests that this field practice has had an impact on the Swiss literacy results.

TABLE 3.22

MAJOR DETERMINANTS OF LITERACY PROFICIENCY

The four most important determinants of literacy proficiency and their standardised regression weights, out of 12 factors, population aged 25-65, 1994-1998

Per cent of explained variance	Countries	Factors
>50	Canada	Respondent's education (0.47); Native versus foreign language (0.18); Occupational category (0.15); Participation in voluntary activities (0.09)
	Chile	Respondent's education (0.57); Parents' education (0.10); Reading at work (0.08); Native versus foreign language (0.07)
	Portugal	Respondent's education (0.80); Gender (0.15); Industrial sector (-0.09); Native versus foreign language (0.08)
	Slovenia	Respondent's education (0.40); Age (-0.18); Parents' education (0.09); Labour force participation (0.08)
	United States	Respondent's education (0.39); Native versus foreign language (0.25); Occupational category (0.13); Labour force participation (0.10)
45-49	Australia	Native versus foreign language (0.30); Respondent's education (0.29); Occupational category (0.16); Age (-0.13)
	Finland	Respondent's education (0.32); Age (-0.18); Parents' education (0.16); Occupational category (0.14)
40-44	Belgium (Flanders)	Respondent's education (0.38); Native versus foreign language (0.15); Age (-0.15); Reading at home (0.13)
	Denmark	Respondent's education (0.33); Age (-0.24); Occupational category (0.18); Gender (0.11)
	Ireland	Respondent's education (0.49); Labour force participation (0.10); Participation in voluntary activities (0.10); Occupational category (0.07)
	Netherlands	Respondent's education (0.35); Age (-0.16); Labour force participation (0.11); Occupational category (0.11)
	Switzerland	Native versus foreign language (0.23); Respondent's education (0.20); Occupational category (0.17); Parents' education (0.16)
	United Kingdom	Respondent's education (0.29); Native versus foreign language (0.18); Occupational category (0.18); Labour force participation (0.13)
35-39	Hungary	Respondent's education (0.43); Age (-0.11); Labour force participation (0.08); Parents' education (0.07)
	New Zealand	Respondent's education (0.34); Native versus foreign language (0.24); Occupational category (0.14); Labour force participation (0.11)
	Norway	Respondent's education (0.33); Age (-0.20); Native versus foreign language (0.14); Occupational category (0.14)
	Poland	Respondent's education (0.39); Age (-0.16); Gender (0.13); Participation in voluntary activities (0.12)
<35	Czech Republic	Respondent's education (0.42); Participation in voluntary activities (0.09); Age (-0.08); Parents' education (0.07)
	Germany	Occupational category (0.20); Respondent's education (0.18); Age (-0.17); Native versus foreign language (0.10)
	Sweden	Respondent's education (0.24); Native versus foreign language (0.18); Parents' education (0.15); Age (-0.12)

Source: International Adult Literacy Survey, 1994-1998.

Educational attainment aside, the results present a complex picture. In all countries except Chile, Portugal and the United States, age has a substantial and negative influence on literacy proficiency, net of the variance attributable to the differences in educational levels between generations. Gender, parents' education, labour force participation and occupational category are among the other variables that show meaningful relationships with literacy in a range of countries.

Non-native language status is a significant factor in all English-speaking countries: Australia, Canada, New Zealand, the United Kingdom and the United States. It also exerts an effect in the smaller European countries with large immigrant populations, for example Belgium (Flanders), Finland, Norway, Sweden and Switzerland.

Parents' education is a major predictor of literacy proficiency in Finland, Sweden and Switzerland. Although for labour force participation and occupational status the direction of causality is less certain than it would be for home background measured by parents' education, the variables are clearly important, especially in Australia, Canada, the Netherlands, New Zealand and the United Kingdom.

Important is the observation that the combined effect on literacy of the four labour-market variables – labour force participation, occupation, industry, and frequency of reading memos at work – is substantial in most countries. Literacy clearly is a factor in the likelihood of securing employment and pursuing a career, but the reverse is probably also true. Interestingly, industry does not exert a meaningful influence on literacy proficiency in any of the countries once labour force participation and occupation category are held constant in the model.

The effects on literacy associated with participation in adult education, reading at work and at home, and participation in voluntary activities are significant in a statistical sense but seem quite small from a substantive viewpoint and in comparison with the magnitude of the effect of initial, formal education.

3.9   Conclusion

Associations between literacy indicators and a number of predictor variables were studied in this chapter. In the preceding section structural equation models were used to examine the relative weights of these determinants in explaining literacy proficiency. The relationships between literacy skills and several social and economic outcomes are examined in the next chapter. The following conclusions can be drawn from the analysis of determinants of literacy:

- Formal educational attainment is the main determinant of literacy proficiency. For 17 out of 20 countries it is both the first and the strongest predictor. There is a difference of 73 points on the prose scale between the highest and lowest country average for those who have completed secondary education and of nearly 80 points for those who have not. On average, youth and adults increase their literacy scores on the prose scale by about 10 points for each additional year they attend school.

- Age and occupation are also major determinants. White-collar high-skilled occupational categories correspond with high literacy, but the higher the age of the respondent, other variables equal, the lower the level of literacy.

- Using a language other than the one used for testing is as important a determinant of literacy proficiency as occupational category and age. This is especially true for the English-speaking countries in the survey (with the exception of Ireland, which has had a relatively smaller immigrant population) but also for smaller European countries that have either two or more official languages (Belgium, Finland, Norway and Switzerland) or that traditionally have been open to immigration (Sweden).

- Labour force participation, formal adult education and informal learning at work measured by reading practices show significant associations with literacy proficiency in most countries. But compared with the other variables mentioned previously, their role is relatively modest. To an extent this result is attributable to the strength of the relationship between literacy and occupation.

- High literacy scores of Nordic and Czech youth are in large part attributable to a reduction, accumulated over decades, in socio-economic inequality measured by the effect of parents' education on the mean level and range of literacy scores.

- Literacy skills in the IALS countries with emerging economies are improving in both absolute and relative terms, owing mainly to high proficiency by citizens with high levels of formal education.
- Countries striving to reach the same mean literacy level as the Nordic countries could focus on efforts to reduce inequality in the range of literacy scores, for example, by raising the level of literacy of adults with a brief formal education and, particularly, of youth from lower socio-economic backgrounds.

References

BÉLANGER, P. and VALDIVIELSO, S. (1997), *The Emergence of Learning Societies: Who Participates in Adult Learning?,* Pergamon Press, Oxford.

COLEMAN, J.S. (1988), "Social capital in the creation of human capital", *American Journal of Sociology,* Vol. 94 (Supplement), pp. 95-120.

ELLEY, W.B. (1992), *How in the World do Students Read?,* IEA Secretariat, The Hague.

FINGERET, H.A. (1983), "Social network: A new perspective on independence and illiterate adults", *Adult Education Quarterly,* Vol. 33(3), pp. 133-146.

JÖRESKOG, K.G., and SÖRBOM, D. (1996a), *PRELIS 2: User's Reference Guide*, Scientific Software International, Chicago.

JÖRESKOG, K.G., and SÖRBOM, D. (1996b), *LISREL 8: User's Reference Guide*, Scientific Software International, Chicago.

OECD (1991), *Reviews of National Policies for Education: Norway*, Paris.

OECD (1995), *Reviews of National Policies for Education: Hungary*, Paris.

OECD (1996), *Lifelong Learning for All*, Paris.

OECD (1997), *Education Policy Analysis*, Paris.

OECD (1999), *Employment Outlook,* June, Paris.

OSTROM, E. (1994), "Constituting social capital and collective action", *Journal of Theoretical Politics,* Vol. 6(4), pp. 527-562.

POSTLETHWAITE, T.N. and ROSS, K.N. (1992), *Effective Schools in Reading: Implications for Educational Planners,* IEA Secretariat, The Hague.

PUTNAM, R.D. (1993), *Making Democracy Work: Civic Traditions in Modern Italy,* Princeton University Press, Princeton, NJ.

RUBENSON, K. and SCHUETZE, H. (Eds.) (2000), *Transitions to the Knowledge Economy*, University of British Columbia Press, Vancouver, BC.

SOU (1996), *Cirkelsamhället. Studiecirklars betydelse för individ och lokalsamhälle,* Statens Offentliga Utredningar, SOU 1996:47, Ministry of Education and Science, Stockholm.

TUIJNMAN, A.C., CHINAPAH, V., and FÄGERLIND, I. (1988), "Adult education and earnings: A 45-year longitudinal study of 834 Swedish men", *Economics of Education Review,* Vol. 7(4), pp. 423-437.

TUIJNMAN, A.C. and KEEVES, J.P. (1994), "Path analysis and linear structural relations analysis", *International Encyclopedia of Education, Second Edition,* Pergamon Press, Oxford, pp. 4339-4352.

VERBA, D., LEHMAN, K., SCHOLZMAN, E., and BRADY, H. (1995), *Voice and Equality: Civic Voluntarism in American Politics*, Harvard University Press, Cambridge, MA.

WILLMS, J.D. (1998), "Community differentials in adult literacy skills in Northern Ireland", in K. Sweeney (Ed.), *Adult Literacy in Northern Ireland,* Northern Ireland Statistics and Research Agency, Belfast.

WILLMS, J.D. (1999), "Inequalities in literacy skills among youth in Canada and the United States", *International Adult Literacy Survey, Monograph No. 6,* Human Resources Development Canada and National Literacy Secretariat, Ottawa, ON.

CHAPTER 4

Outcomes and Benefits of Literacy

4.1 Introduction

The benefits of human capital have been examined in different contexts, and individuals, organisations and countries have recognised the need to strengthen it as one of the means of achieving high rates of employment, economic growth and social progress. Lifelong learning and human capital investment have been at the heart of education and labour market policies in recent years. This has contributed to an increase in the level of educational attainment of populations, growth in workforce training rates and increased spending on research and development. In this chapter, literacy is considered as constituting one component of the broader human capital equation. When referring to more specific literacy skills it implies those measured by IALS.

The stock of skills held by the population is important for the economic development of a country. From the 1960s until the present, different theories have linked human capital with economic growth. From Schultz (1960), Becker (1964) and Mincer (1974) through Barro (1996) and De la Fuente and Domenech (2000), the debate on the effects of education, skills and experience on economic growth has continued. Research has shown that growth in developing countries is faster when educational attainment is higher and where literacy is more pervasive (Mingat and Tan, 1996). Based on a large body of accumulated evidence, most analysts now agree that the stock of human capital present in the population is an important factor in economic growth. However, there is disagreement on which indicators to use for measuring human capital, and on the degree to which they can explain growth, although work in this direction is being undertaken. Under a mandate of the 1999 Ministerial Council, the OECD is currently examining the factors that underlie the differences in economic growth among the Member countries.

Literacy skills are an element of human capital. At an individual level, literacy contributes to personal development, through improved participation in society and in relation to labour market outcomes and earnings. Literacy can also contribute to aggregate economic and social performance but the relationship between literacy and these variables is complex. The large number of variables that affect growth and social outcomes, the inadequacies of data and the theories that have been developed to explain the contribution of human and social capital to development, among other reasons, render the disentangling of this complex relationship extremely difficult – a task that goes beyond this publication.

The purpose of this chapter is more modest. It is to describe the relationships between literacy proficiency and a number of socio-economic variables at an aggregate and individual level, taken one at a time. This bivariate approach is a first attempt to study the associations that might exist between measures of literacy and important socio-economic factors. However, the aim is not to attempt to disentangle causal relationships by isolating the impact of individual variables from a set of interrelated factors that can affect literacy attainment or its impact on other variables. The chapter begins with an analysis of literacy and labour market outcomes, focusing on individuals and their labour market experiences, and on the functioning of labour markets in relation to the knowledge economy. The next section presents the results of several exploratory analyses in which the impact of literacy proficiency and educational attainment, among other variables, is related to labour market outcomes. The purpose is to contribute to the debate on the measurement of human capital indicators. The last section offers a brief overview of some possible wider social and economic benefits of literacy.

4.2 Literacy and the Labour Force

This section examines possible links between literacy skills and a number of labour market variables. Skills and competencies not only affect the performance of an individual in the labour force, but also contribute to shape the structure of the labour force of a country, through higher participation rates, lower unemployment probabilities or higher skilled employment. The association between literacy skills and socio-occupational categories is shown in Figure 4.1.

FIGURE 4.1

LITERACY LEVELS BY SOCIO-OCCUPATIONAL CATEGORIES

Per cent of each socio-occupational category at each literacy level, prose scale, population aged 16-65, 1994-1998

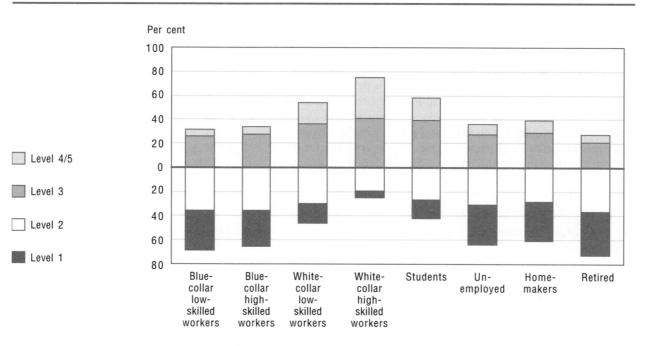

Source: International Adult Literacy Survey, 1994-1998.

The higher the level of education, the higher is participation in the labour force. This relationship is well documented both at the individual and at the aggregate country level. The evidence from IALS presented in Chapter 3 shows that labour force participation also is related to literacy proficiency. People with high skills tend to participate more in the labour force than people with low skills, as Figure 3.6 shows. Higher expected returns for the high-skilled and lower unemployment probabilities act as incentives for participation. This interpretation is supported by the data on the wage distribution of the population by skills levels presented in Figure 4.9a-b, where lower wages are associated with lower levels on the prose and document scales.

Annual hours worked is another dimension of participation in the labour force. There is an intriguing relationship between the aggregate number of hours worked by the labour force and a country's literacy skills. The data in Figure 4.2 suggest that workers in countries with high mean literacy skills (document scale) work fewer hours than those in countries with lower literacy skills, with the exception of the Czech Republic. Persons in countries with a lower GDP per capita work longer hours than persons in countries with higher GDP per capita. Typically, in a labour market, persons with a higher level of skills, and therefore a higher level of wages, work longer hours than others. The association in Figure 4.2 is based on a comparison of different countries and therefore different types of labour markets. Further analyses are needed to explain the processes that may lie behind this finding.

FIGURE 4.2

LABOUR VOLUME BY DOCUMENT LITERACY

Average annual hours worked per person in employment and mean literacy proficiency, document scale, population aged 16-65,1994-1998

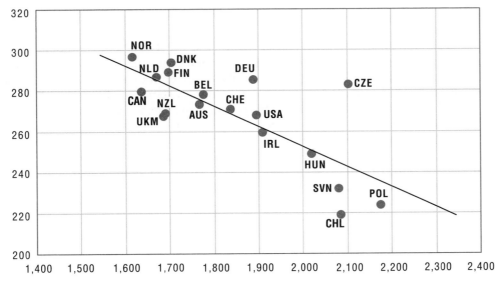

Mean document literacy

Source: International Adult Literacy Survey, 1994-1998.

The relationship between literacy and unemployment can be viewed in various ways. The data presented previously in Figure 3.7 indicate that the incidence of unemployment decreases as the level of literacy proficiency of workers increases. The proportion of individuals at prose Level 1 who are without work is consistently higher than that of persons at higher levels of literacy. Other factors, such as work experience, educational attainment and other personal characteristics influence unemployment but studies that control for these influences still find a strong association between lower levels of literacy and unemployment (Berlin and Sum, 1988; Raudenbush and Kasim, 1998; NCES, 2000). As described in Chapter 1, the availability of skilled labour is in itself a factor in attracting investment in physical capital and technology, which in turn influences the demand for labour.

Box 4A.   The Logit Model

The models estimated for Figures 4.3a-c, 4.7a-b and 4.8 consist of a dependent dichotomous variable explained by a set of co-variates. They use a logistic function that yields predicted values ranging from 0 to 1, corresponding to the probability of being in Category 1 of the dependent variable.

In Figure 4.3a-c, the dependent variable is "to be unemployed (1) or not (0)". The explanatory variables are literacy proficiency on the prose scale, gender, age and educational attainment. The results in Figures 4.3a-c are obtained by holding the values of all the explanatory variables constant while allowing prose to vary between 0 and 500 points. For this particular analysis, three graphs are shown. The clustering of the countries in these graphs is based on the differences in the shape of the curves.

In Figures 4.7a-b and 4.8, the dependent variable is being in the categories "white-collar high-skilled occupation", "white-collar low-skilled occupation", "blue-collar high-skilled occupation" or "blue-collar low-skilled occupation". Thus four equations are estimated; the reference category in each equation consists of the three other alternatives combined. The set of explanatory variables is the same as the one used for the analysis shown in Figure 4.3a-c and also includes industry. This model is more complex because it adds to the main equation the predicted value of being occupied, estimated in a first step. This is to ensure that unbiased regression estimates are obtained. The analyses allow prose scores to vary from 0 to 500 for occupational profiles.

The relationship is illustrated in Figure 4.3a-c.[1] It shows the probability of being unemployed by a range of prose scores when controlling for gender, age and educational attainment. In all countries analysed except Poland and Portugal,[2] the probability of being unemployed decreases as literacy scores increase from 0 to 500 points. Further information on where efforts to improve literacy levels can be focused can be inferred from the shape of each country's curve. The probability decreases at a faster rate in the range from 0 to 300 points in almost all countries, as shown in Figure 4.3a-c, suggesting that efforts directed at people with lower literacy scores will be more effective in reducing the probability of being unemployed than efforts directed at people who are at the high end of the scale range. Figure 4.3a shows that in Australia, Finland, the Netherlands, New Zealand and Norway, interventions are likely to be even more effective for persons in the range of prose scores from 100 to 300 points. The considerable diversity across groups of countries is however noteworthy. In Hungary, for example, the returns are the same across the whole scale. The shape of the curves shown in Figures 4.3b and 4.3c are flatter, and the deceleration rate is somewhat more apparent in Figure 4.3c.

---

1. The reader is advised to focus first on the overall shape of the curve, which shows the variation in the probability of being in the categories according to increases in prose literacy scores, and then on possible changes in the slope of the curves, which indicate different returns to increasing levels of literacy skills. A flat curve indicates no impact of increasing prose scores.

2. For both countries the prose scale was not statistically significant in the model.

FIGURE 4.3

PROBABILITY OF UNEMPLOYMENT AND LITERACY PROFICIENCY

Probability of being unemployed according to prose literacy score,
for men aged 16-25 with less than upper secondary education, 1994-1998

Probability x 100

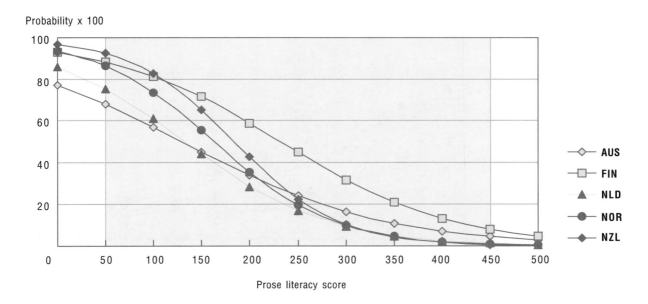

Prose literacy score

Probability x 100

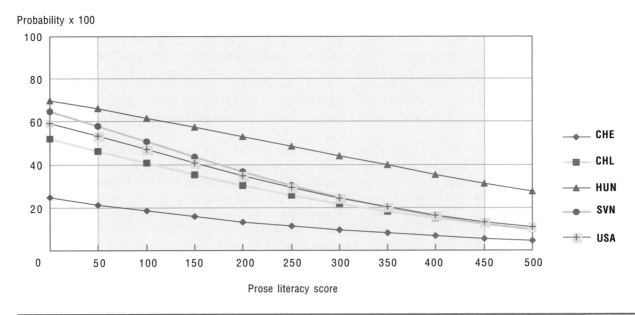

Prose literacy score

Note: Probability values in blue-shaded ranges are based on observed scale scores with sufficient effective sample sizes.
Source: International Adult Literacy Survey, 1994-1998.

FIGURE 4.3 (concluded)

PROBABILITY OF UNEMPLOYMENT AND LITERACY PROFICIENCY

Probability of being unemployed according to prose literacy score,
for men aged 16-25 with less than upper secondary education, 1994-1998

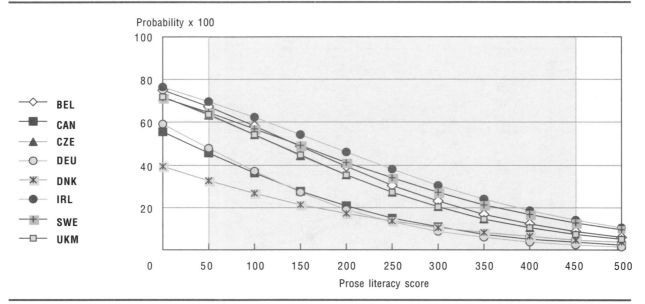

Note: Probability values in blue-shaded ranges are based on observed scale scores with sufficient effective sample sizes.
Source: International Adult Literacy Survey, 1994-1998.

Overall, there is a large difference in the literacy skills of persons experiencing short or long spells of unemployment, especially in Ireland, the Netherlands, New Zealand, Norway, Switzerland and the United States (Figure 4.4). People who have been unemployed for more than 12 months have lower literacy levels in almost all countries except Chile, Germany, Poland and Portugal, where both the short-term and long-term unemployed have similar proportions at low and high levels of literacy skills.

Chapter 3 has already shown that persons with low literacy skills have higher unemployment and find themselves without work more often than persons with higher skill levels. The analysis presented in Figure 4.4 complements these findings by breaking down both short-term and long-term unemployment by levels of literacy skills (prose scale). Figure 4.4 indicates that compared with the overall population, both short-term and long-term unemployment are dominated by people with lower literacy levels in most of the countries. A comparison of the proportions of unemployed at Levels 1 and 2 with the proportions of the overall population at these levels (see Table 2.2 in Annex D) shows that the shares at low levels of literacy are higher for the unemployed, with the exception of Hungary, Ireland, the Netherlands and the United States. In these countries, the short-term unemployed have higher literacy levels than the overall population.

The benefits of literacy can also be viewed from the perspective of the knowledge economy. The relationship between workforce skills and the growth of knowledge jobs explored in Chapter 1 is illustrated in Figure 4.5. Not surprisingly, the data reveal, across countries, a positive association between literacy skills (prose scale scores) and the proportion of workers employed in the white-collar high-skilled occupational category. This finding is supported by the individual-level data reported in Figures 4.7a-b. These show that higher levels of prose scores are associated with higher probabilities of being in a white-collar high-skilled category.

FIGURE 4.4

LITERACY AND SHORT- AND LONG-TERM UNEMPLOYMENT

Per cent of adults at prose literacy Levels 1 and 2, being short-term (less than 12 months)
and long-term (more than 12 months) unemployed, population aged 16-65, 1994-1998

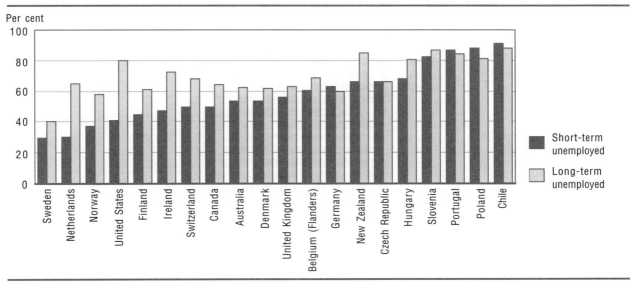

Countries are ranked according to the per cent of people at Levels 1 and 2 in short-term unemployment.
Source: International Adult Literacy Survey, 1994-1998.

FIGURE 4.5

EMPLOYMENT IN THE KNOWLEDGE ECONOMY AND LITERACY PROFICIENCY

Per cent of workers in the white-collar high-skilled occupational category[1]
and mean prose literacy proficiency, employed population 16-65, 1994-1998

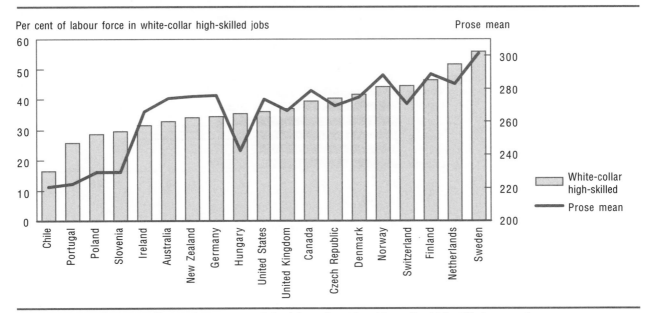

Countries are ranked according to the per cent of the labour force in white-collar high-skilled occupations.
1. According to ISCO 1988, includes legislators, senior officials and managers, professionals, technicians and associate professionals.
Source: International Adult Literacy Survey, 1994-1998.

FIGURE 4.6

LITERACY AND OCCUPATIONAL CATEGORIES

A. Per cent of managers and professionals who are at literacy Level 3 or above, document scale, population aged 16-65, 1994-1998

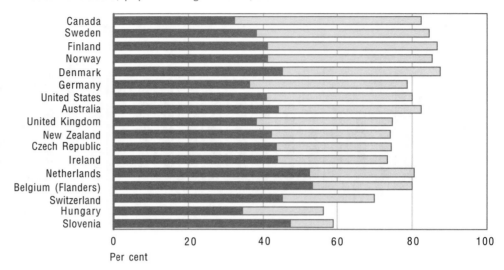

Countries are ranked by the per cent of managers and professionals at literacy Levels 4/5.

B. Per cent of technicians who are at literacy Level 3 or above, document scale, population aged 16-65, 1994-1998

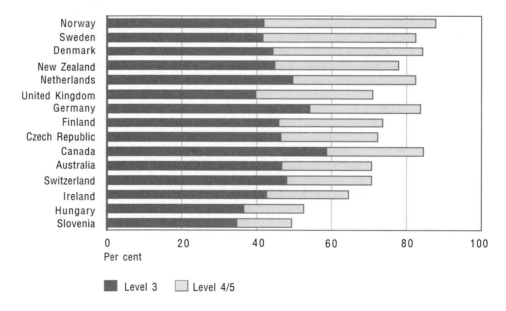

Countries are ranked by the per cent of technicians at literacy Levels 4/5.

FIGURE 4.6 (concluded)

LITERACY AND OCCUPATIONAL CATEGORIES

C. Per cent of skilled craft workers and machine operators who are at literacy
Level 3 or above, document scale, population aged 16-65, 1994-1998

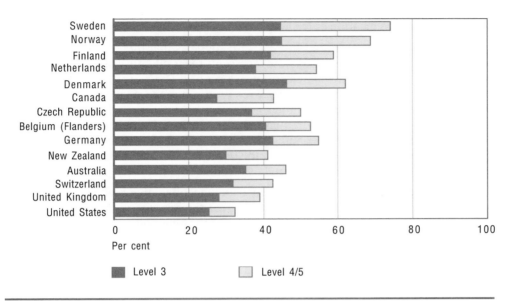

Countries are ranked by the per cent of blue-collar workers at literacy Level 4/5.
Source: International Adult Literacy Survey, 1994-1998.

The literacy profile of a country is expected to have implications for the occupational distribution of the country's labour force. Furthermore, in the knowledge economy, it is thought that workers with higher levels of skills will tend to be represented more than proportionately in occupations requiring higher levels of skills. These expectations are supported by evidence, presented in Figures 4.6a-c, on occupational categories based on groupings that depend on educational qualifications or skills. Figure 4.6a portrays the situation for managers and professionals. This occupational category is clearly dominated by persons who are at medium to high levels of literacy (document scale, Levels 3 and 4/5). In the Netherlands, for example, 80 per cent of managers and professionals are at literacy Level 3 or above and only 20 per cent are at a low skill level. Figure 4.6b shows quite similar proportions at high and low skill levels for technicians. In contrast, around 55 per cent of skilled crafts workers and machine operators are at Level 3 or above in the Netherlands (Figure 4.6c).

Comparisons among countries show how the skills profile of a country can affect the distribution of skills among occupations. In Figure 4.6a, for example, whereas 65 per cent or more of Swiss managers and professionals are at literacy Level 3 or above, in Chile the proportion is 40 per cent or less. Moreover, the data show that in some countries over half of all skilled craft workers and machine operators are at Level 1 on the document scale.

Occupational choice is, of course, a complex matter and a number of variables are related to the probability of being in one or another of the occupational categories mentioned above. Age, gender, educational attainment, literacy proficiency, adult education and training, and industry sector are all relevant predictors of the probability of being in a certain occupation. The analysis presented in Figure 4.7a-b shows that persons with an upper secondary education and high prose literacy scores have a lower probability of being in blue-collar occupational categories than upper secondary graduates with low or medium prose scores. The latter also have lower probabilities of receiving adult education or training.

The analysis reported in Figure 4.7a-b suggests that literacy skills can play a role in the upskilling process. Each line represents the probability of being in a certain occupational category with increasing prose scores. The probability of being in a white-collar high-skilled position increases with prose scores increasing from 0 to 500 points, when education level and training are held constant. The pattern is clear for the two sectors shown, services and manufacturing. There is also a clear effect of higher literacy skills on the declining probability of being in a blue-collar low-skilled position in both sectors. The effects on the white-collar low-skilled and blue-collar high-skilled occupations are similar in both sectors.

In the services sector, the probability of being white-collar high-skilled increases at a faster pace between 0 to 350 points, whereas the increase in the marginal return to literacy slows down from 350 to 500 points. For the blue-collar low-skilled category, the impact of literacy skills is the strongest when increasing the skills of a person with low initial prose levels. This finding is important in a lifelong-learning perspective. Training that results in the upgrading of the literacy skills of less-advantaged workers can help them to improve their position in the labour market. In the manufacturing sector, the impact of increasing prose scores affects all categories except the white-collar low-skilled one, for which the probability is low across the entire scale range. Higher literacy scores lower the probability of being in the blue-collar categories and raise the chance of being in a white-collar high-skilled position.

4.3 Education, Literacy and Experience

A major issue in the debate on the effects of human capital is the use of different indicators to explain economic and social development. Educational attainment is commonly used as a proxy measure for skills in growth equations (see Box 4B). In this section literacy skills and educational attainment, among other variables, are used as inputs into explaining different labour market outcomes. The analysis of the effects of different variables such as age, gender, educational attainment and literacy skills, among others, on unemployment, occupations and wages can shed further light on this debate.

The analysis of the probabilities of being unemployed, presented in the previous section, used both literacy skills and educational attainment as predictor variables. The preliminary findings indicate that literacy proficiency (prose scale) is more often significant than educational attainment in explaining the probability of being unemployed. In the logit model (see Box 4A) that underpins Figure 4.3a-c, the effects of gender, age, prose literacy and educational attainment on the probability of being unemployed are estimated. The effects of literacy skills are significant in all countries except Poland and Portugal. Age is also a significant factor in all but Germany and Portugal, whereas the impact of educational attainment is significant only in half of the countries. In Chile, the Czech Republic, the Netherlands, New Zealand, Norway, Slovenia, Sweden and Switzerland, prose literacy and age have significant effects on the probability of being unemployed but educational attainment does not.

FIGURE 4.7

PROBABILITY OF BEING IN AN OCCUPATIONAL CATEGORY BY INCREASING LITERACY SCORES

A. Probability of being in an occupational category by increasing literacy scores for men with upper secondary education, working in the services sector, and having received adult education or training, prose scale, population aged 36-45, 1994-1998

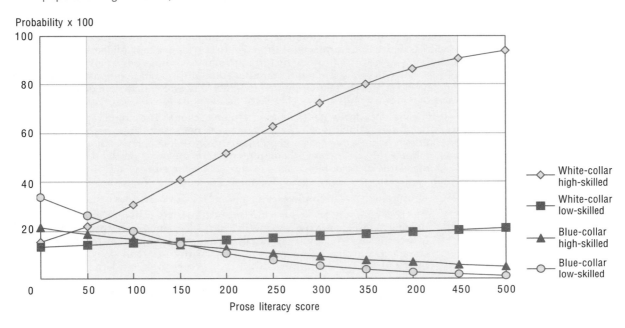

B. Probability of being in an occupational category by increasing literacy scores for men with upper secondary education, working in the manufacturing sector, and having received adult education or training, prose scale, population aged 36-45, 1994-1998

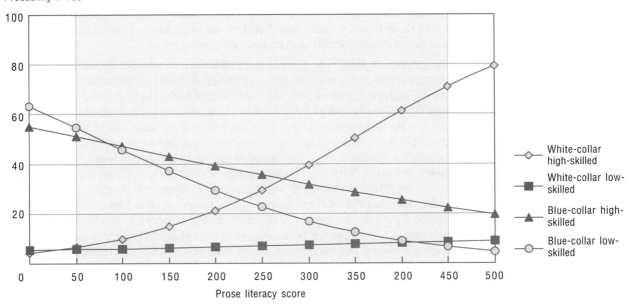

Note: Probability values in blue-shaded ranges are based on observed scale scores with sufficient effective sample sizes.
Source: International Adult Literacy Survey, 1994-1998.

BOX 4B.   Skills and Wages: An Ongoing Debate

Work on the impact of human capital – "the diverse knowledge, skills, competencies and other attributes embodied in individuals that are relevant to economic activity" (OECD, 1998a, p. 9) – has established a close connection between education, productivity and earnings. Cross-sectional studies of average age-earnings profiles in the OECD countries show that the relationship between formal education and earned income increases in strength up to about age 40 and then levels off (OECD, 1998b). The age at which this peak occurs tends to be higher the higher the level of initial education. This is often interpreted as a sign of decreasing marginal productivity, with depreciation setting in earlier for individuals with a brief formal education. There is evidence that adult education and training are also implicated: the turning point in earnings power arrives at a later age for workers with additional education and training compared with workers who lack such training (Tuijnman, 1989; Mincer, 1991). Recent evidence shows that literacy skills are another factor in the equation (Bloom *et al.,* 1997).

There are different approaches to measuring human capital. The indirect approach takes educational attainment as a proxy measure because of an expected high correlation between education and skills, on the one hand, and skills and wages on the other. There are, however, a number of factors that can render it difficult to use measures of completed years or levels of education as substitutes for human capital stock (OECD, 1998a; Tuijnman, 2000):

- Requirements for completed educational levels vary across countries.
- People who enter the labour market with similar educational qualifications have not necessarily mastered the same level of proficiency in assorted skills. Countries differ in the degree to which they produce a standard, and thus comparable, product with respect to skills, judged by the standard deviations in literacy scores observed for recent graduates.
- The acquisition of new skills does not end upon leaving school.
- Skills acquired through formal schooling can be lost through obsolescence and disuse.
- Qualification and skill levels are not static but gradually increase over time.

In Australia, Belgium (Flanders), Canada, Denmark, Finland, Hungary, Ireland, the United Kingdom and the United States both literacy proficiency and educational attainment are relevant in combating unemployment but the effect of age is insignificant. Strategies to raise literacy skills can therefore be one element in the mix of policies required to boost employability and counter unemployment.

The impact of skills and educational attainment can also be traced through a logistic regression developed for assessing the probability of being in a white-collar high-skilled category. Figure 4.8 shows the effect of both education and literacy skills (prose scale) on the probability of employment in the white-collar high-skilled category. For a person who is between 26 and 35 years old and working in the business sector (finance and business services and community, social and personal services sectors), the probabilities increase at a fast pace with an increase in literacy skills. The probabilities, however, vary widely depending on the educational level of the worker, although the patterns for workers with lower and upper secondary education are more similar than that for workers with tertiary education. The higher the educational attainment of a person, the higher is the probability of being in a white-collar high-skilled occupation. However, it is important to note that the differences between the levels of education are the least pronounced both at low and at extremely high prose levels. This may imply that people at the highest literacy levels have similar chances of being in the white-collar high-skilled category, and that skills diminish the importance of educational attainment. In contrast, the differences between the curves in the scale range from 200 to 300 points show that educational attainment is a relevant factor at low to medium skill levels. The evidence therefore suggests that education and skills are complementary.

Different studies have demonstrated a positive correlation between individuals' educational attainment and their earnings from work (Psacharopoulos, 1994). However, questions about how to interpret these findings still arise. How much of the observed returns can be attributed to initial as opposed to further education, how much to skill, and how does experience factor in? These relationships would be further attenuated by structural features of the labour market, such as collective bargaining agreements that influence the experience and earnings profiles of countries.

The impact of skill-biased technological change on the returns to skills can also be considered. Evidence from the United States, based on an analysis of the National Adult Literacy Survey (NALS), suggests that economic returns to literacy skill increase with the knowledge intensity of jobs (Raudenbush and Kasim, 1998). Given the fact that most employment creation in the OECD area is concentrated in job areas with high knowledge intensity, skills can be expected to play an increasingly important role in determining the wage structure in OECD economies.

Figure 4.9a-b shows the relationship between literacy proficiency and earnings for two scales, prose and quantitative. The graphs present the proportions of people aged 25-65 at each literacy level who are in the top 60 per cent of wage earners, expressed in per cent difference from Level 3. The data in Figures 4.9a and 4.9b clearly indicate that the percentage of people with relatively high incomes increases with increasing levels of proficiency. It is generally believed that this earnings gain arises in part because people with higher skills are more productive on the job and are therefore paid a wage premium. The wage premium related to literacy appears to be comparatively high in the Czech Republic, Ireland, the United Kingdom and the United States. Conversely, the lower wages associated with Level 1 proficiency are consistently larger across all countries and more variable.

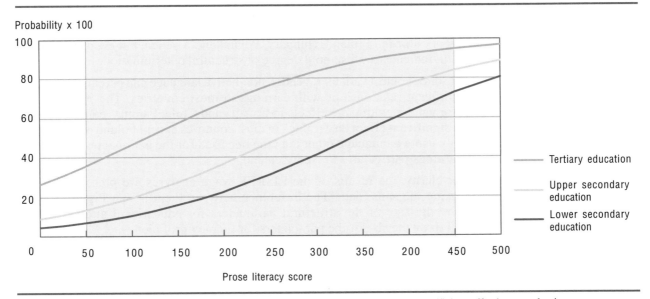

FIGURE 4.8

PROBABILITY OF BEING WHITE-COLLAR HIGH-SKILLED BY EDUCATION LEVELS AND LITERACY SKILLS

Probability of being white-collar high-skilled by increasing literacy scores for men working in the transport, storage and communications sectors and who have not received adult education or training, prose scale, population aged 26-35, 1994-1998

Note: Probability values in blue-shaded ranges are based on observed scale scores with sufficient effective sample sizes.
Source: International Adult Literacy Survey, 1994-1998.

Another interesting finding is that there appears to be more dispersion and a larger return to quantitative skills compared with prose skills in some countries, notably Canada, the United Kingdom and the United States. This finding is consistent with the emerging research literature on differential returns to different types of skills as an explanation for growing wage gaps (see *e.g.* Carliner, 1996; Rivera-Batiz, 1994).

The data presented in Figure 4.9a-b cannot offer an approximation of the relationship between literacy skills and earnings because there are a number of other variables that are not accounted for. Clearly, the discussion in Box 4B precludes a simple interpretation of the association between educational attainment, skills and earnings. The issue can be addressed only if both educational attainment and direct measures of skills are included in the earnings equation.

Figure 4.10 and Figure 4.11a-b present the results of a multivariate analysis that aims to estimate the magnitude of the influences of educational attainment, literacy proficiency and experience[3] on earnings for a group of countries, while controlling for the effects of gender, parents' education and non-native language. The methodology is explained in Box 4C.

BOX 4C.   Interpreting the Regression Coefficients

The results in Figures 4.10 and 4.11a-b are obtained in linear structural relations models (see Box 3E). Educational attainment is a latent construct measured by years and levels of schooling. Literacy proficiency is a latent construct based on the three scales. Experience is a derived variable measured by the natural logarithm of (age minus years of schooling minus 5). Earnings are measured on an interval scale using quintiles because continuous wage data are not available for all countries. The models control for the variance associated with gender, parents' education and non-native language. Regression estimates are standardised regression weights obtained under the maximum likelihood fit function.

The results should *not* be compared to those presented in Table 2.10 in *Literacy Skills for the Knowledge Society* (OECD and HRDC, 1997) because of differences in the applied methodology.

Figure 4.10 presents the estimated amount of variance explained in the dependent variable, earnings quintiles, by the predictor variables specified in the wage equation. Chile stands out with over 50 per cent of the variance accounted for by the predictor variables. Over 45 per cent of the variance in the wage quintiles is explained in Belgium (Flanders), Canada, New Zealand and the United Kingdom. The amounts are below one-third in Finland, Hungary, Poland and Sweden, but even this smaller amount still indicates a substantial degree of structural determination.

The three control variables, gender, non-native language and parents' education, show significant relationships with earnings in most countries. The pattern is the clearest for gender, with large effects in Canada and Chile. Parents' education has a weak but significant effect on earnings in most countries except Poland and Portugal. Commonly using a language other than the one used for the national test negatively affects earnings particularly in New Zealand.

For clarity, the results of the LISREL wage analyses are presented in two graphs, using the same data. The difference between them is that Figure 4.11a is ordered by the size of the structural parameters for educational attainment and Figure 4.11b by the size of the parameters for literacy proficiency.

---

3. Information on cumulative labour force experience is not available from IALS. Experience is therefore a derived variable that mostly reflects age and does not take into account the various interruptions men and especially women may have encountered over the course of their working lives.

FIGURE 4.9

ADULT LITERACY AND EARNINGS QUINTILES

A. Per cent of population aged 25-65 at each literacy level who are in the top 60 per cent of earners: percentage points difference from Level 3, prose scale, 1994-1998

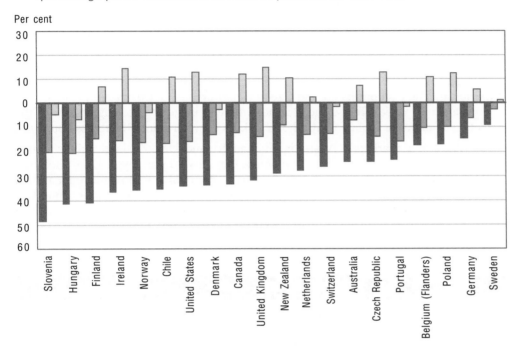

B. Per cent of people aged 25-65 at each literacy level who are in the top 60 per cent of earners: percentage points difference from Level 3, quantitative scale, 1994-1998

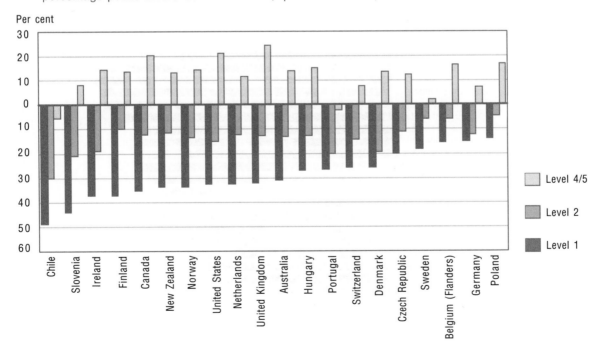

Coutries are ranked by the relative income disadvantage of workers with Level 1 skills.
Source: International Adult Literacy Survey, 1994-1998.

As expected given theory and previous research findings, the standardised regression weights presented in Figure 4.11a indicate that educational attainment is the most important determinant of earnings in almost all countries, even if the variation in the other factors is held constant. But there also are major differences in the strength of this relationship across the countries investigated. The effects are very strong in Belgium (Flanders) and Slovenia. In Norway, Portugal and Sweden, the effect of education on earnings while controlling for the variation in literacy skills and experience is much weaker than in the comparison countries.

Figure 4.11b shows that literacy proficiency is a somewhat stronger determinant of earnings than educational attainment in two countries, Canada and Norway. But literacy proficiency has a substantial effect on earnings in most of the countries studied, an effect that is independent of the influences of educational attainment and experience. The exceptions are the Czech Republic and Germany with statistically significant but weak effects, and Poland, where it is zero. The magnitudes of the effect coefficients associated with literacy skills vary substantially across countries.

The labour markets in Australia, Finland, Ireland, New Zealand and the United Kingdom reward education about as much as they reward literacy skills. In Belgium (Flanders), Denmark, Hungary, the Netherlands, Portugal and Slovenia, educational attainment and literacy skills are both rewarded substantially in the labour market, although the return to education is the larger of the two. Thus, the results of the data analysis, and particularly the indicators of the goodness of fit of the models to the data

---

FIGURE 4.10

AMOUNT OF VARIANCE EXPLAINED IN EARNINGS

Per cent of variance (R^2) in earnings accounted for by six predictor variables: gender, parents' education, non-native language, respondent's education, literacy proficiency, and experience, population aged 25-55, 1994-1998

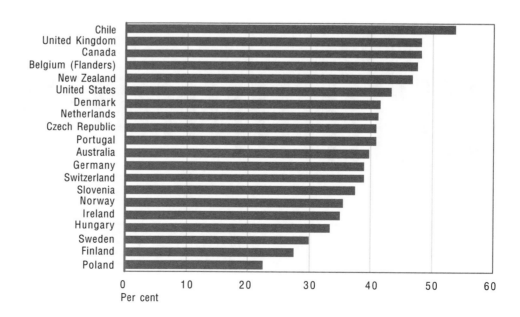

Countries are ranked by the per cent of variance explained in earnings.
Source: International Adult Literacy Survey, 1994-1998.

presented in Table 4.10-11 in Annex D, support the notion – still rather new in the economic literature – that there is a measurable, net return to literacy skills in OECD societies.[4] Poland appears to be the only exception.

In every country except Slovenia, experience has a positive and significant effect on earnings, with standardised regression coefficients ranging from 0.37 in Sweden to 0.05 in Slovenia. The effect of experience on earnings is large in Finland, Portugal and Sweden, where it exceeds the impact of educational attainment and literacy proficiency. The Czech Republic, Denmark, Norway and Switzerland also demonstrate relatively large effects of experience on earnings. The effects of experience on earnings are rather small – albeit statistically significant – in Australia (0.12), Chile (0.13), Hungary (0.08), Ireland (0.11), New Zealand (0.16), Poland (0.16) and the United States (0.12).

4.4 Windows into the Socio-economic Benefits of Literacy

The preceding sections have focused on literacy impacts of a mainly economic nature. This section looks at some of the broader social dimensions of literacy skills. It begins with an exploration of whether there is an association between literacy, overall levels of GDP per capita and income inequality. This is followed by an analysis of the broader issues related to possible positive externalities of literacy, such as health outcomes and political participation. The IALS data can make a useful contribution to this analysis by helping to better measure some aspects of human capital.

Figure 4.12a-b shows that, across countries, literacy and gross domestic product (GDP) per capita go hand in hand. The higher the proportion of adults with low prose skills in a country, the lower that country's income per capita (Figure 4.12a). Conversely, the higher the proportion of adults with high prose skills (Level 4/5), the higher is the GDP per capita (Figure 4.12b). Although the countries cluster in two main groups – Chile, Hungary, Poland, Portugal and Slovenia being at the lower end, and the rest at the higher end – both clusters show an association between literacy and GDP per capita. There is a two-way relationship between these two variables: countries with higher per capita income can devote more resources to literacy development. Conversely, literacy skills can contribute to economic growth and productivity per capita.

Literacy profiles may also be related to measures of inequality. Income inequality, which has increased in a number of OECD countries from the mid-1980s to the mid-1990s, has been caused by several factors. Increased income differentials between households according to type of employment (part-time, temporary, etc.) have led to a simultaneous increase in work-rich and work-poor shares of households (OECD, 1999b). Other factors can also have indirect effects: Benabou (1996) and Alesina and Rodrik (1992) show an indirect link between education and the distribution of income. They provide evidence that the distribution of income can affect education or political and economic mechanisms, among other factors, which can have an indirect effect on economic growth. In this context it is worth inquiring whether there is any association between income inequality and literacy inequality. As can be seen in Figure 4.13, higher levels of prose inequality across IALS countries are associated with greater inequality in distribution of income (see Box 4D for notes on methodology).

---

4. In the absence of reliable data on the relationship between earnings and skill domains other than literacy, it remains an open question how much of this return falls to literacy and how much to other, as yet unobserved skill domains.

FIGURE 4.11

EARNINGS, EDUCATION AND LITERACY

A. Earnings and education, controlling for literacy proficiency and experience, population aged 25-55, 1994-1998

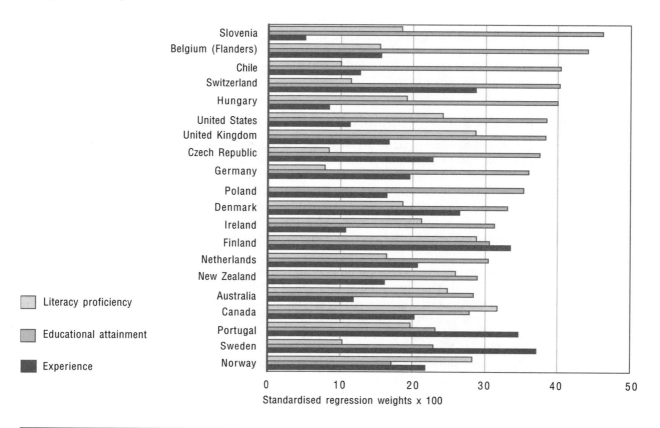

Countries are ranked by the magnitude of the effect parameter associated with educational attainment.

BOX 4D.   The Measurement of Inequality

The Gini coefficient as a measure of income inequality reflects the distribution of income in a population. The closer the coefficient is to 0, the more equal the distribution of income across the population, whereas the closer it is to 1, the higher the inequality. For the presentation in Figure 4.13, the Gini coefficient has been multiplied by 100.

Inequality in the distribution of literacy in Figure 4.13 is expressed as the ratio between those in the top 10 per cent in prose literacy scores (D9) and the bottom 10 per cent (D1). The closer the index is to 1, the more inequality in literacy scores within the population.

There is a vast literature that tackles the issue of economic inequality and the different factors that may cause it. The factors that have been analysed include, among others, earnings distribution, education policies, social and labour market policies and labour force structure (Osberg, 2000). The information in Figure 4.13 is not presented as evidence of a direct causal relationship. To the extent that the distribution of human capital in a population is a factor in income inequality of that population,

FIGURE 4.11 (concluded)

EARNINGS, EDUCATION AND LITERACY

B. Earnings and literacy proficiency, controlling for educational attainment and experience, population aged 25-55, 1994-1998

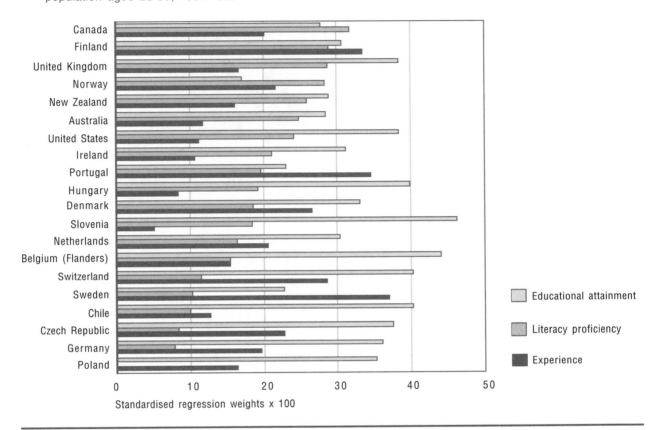

Standardised regression weights x 100

Countries are ranked by the magnitude of the effect parameter associated with literacy proficiency.
Source: International Adult Literacy Survey, 1994-1998.

literacy distribution has a role to play. However, there can be a causal relationship in the other direction: higher degrees of income inequality can cause unequal investment in education and literacy skills. In addition, there can be other variables that produce both inequalities simultaneously. It is clear that these relationships, which are important for social cohesion, deserve further research and analyses, and the IALS data can be of use in this regard.

Literacy has other direct and indirect returns for societies. There are relationships between high literacy, greater social cohesion and better health, while literacy is also a factor in the wider social outcomes analysed below.

Studies on the social and non-market effects of education have been undertaken by a number of authors. Wolfe and Haveman (2000) argue that the non-market effects of education can be as large as the market effects of education. The positive relationships found between schooling and health status of family members, of education and efficiency of consumption choices, and of schooling and fertility choices or non-participation in criminal activities can all be listed as non-market effects of education. Particularly, in terms of a person's success in making personal choices, more schooling is indicated to have a positive influence, probably through gaining information that promotes more efficient decisions. Part of it may be the ability to

FIGURE 4.12

GDP PER CAPITA AND LITERACY

A. Relationship between GDP per capita[1] and per cent at prose literacy Levels 1 and 2, population aged 16-65, 1994-1998

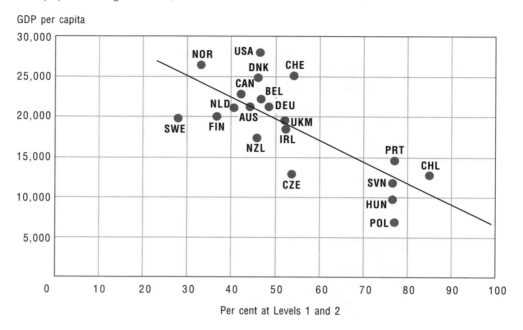

GDP per capita

Per cent at Levels 1 and 2

B. Relationship between GDP per capita[1] and per cent at prose literacy Level 4/5, population aged 16-65, 1994-1998

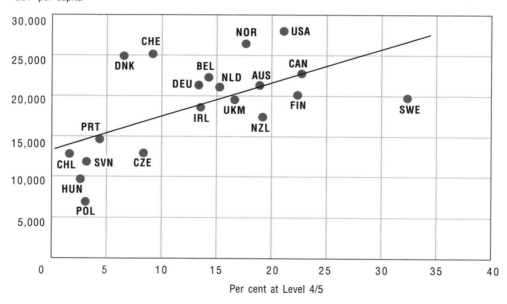

GDP per capita

Per cent at Level 4/5

1. In current prices, equivalent US dollars converted using Purchasing Power Parities.
Sources: International Adult Literacy Survey, 1994-1998; OECD database; and economic data for Chile and Slovenia from UNDP, *Human Development Report 1999.*

accomplish better matches, while another part may be in the reduction of time spent in the search for information for making better choices.

As stated in the previous paragraph, literacy can be linked to better health. Figure 4.14a-b shows that life expectancy at birth is higher in countries that have a higher proportion of people at higher levels of prose literacy. Although it is not possible to say whether longevity is a cause or an effect of higher literacy, there is a relationship between the two. Previous findings have shown that people with higher educational attainment have healthier habits and life styles, and are more educated towards the management of their own health through access and understanding of information and preventive health practices. For example, in Canada and the United States, people with more years of education are less likely to smoke (Health Canada, 1999; USDHS, 1998). In the United States, data show that the likelihood of being overweight is related to years of education: being overweight is more prevalent among people who are less educated (USDHS, 1998). Both are risk factors that can have a strong impact on health outcomes and are influenced by literacy. Furthermore, there is a link between perceived health status and education level that shows that adults with more schooling report having better health. And previous findings have shown that higher levels of education are associated with higher rates of longevity.

Evidence has also been found concerning the broader gains to society. People with more schooling are likely to make more informed choices when voting and to participate more actively in their communities. Evidence has shown that schooling is positively associated with both voting behaviour (Campbell *et al.*, 1976) and social inequalities (Comer, 1988). Research has also established that education levels are

---

FIGURE 4.13

ECONOMIC INEQUALITY AND LITERACY INEQUALITY

Relationship between economic inequality (Gini coefficient) and inequality in the distribution of literacy (9th decile/1st decile) within countries, prose scale, 1994-1998

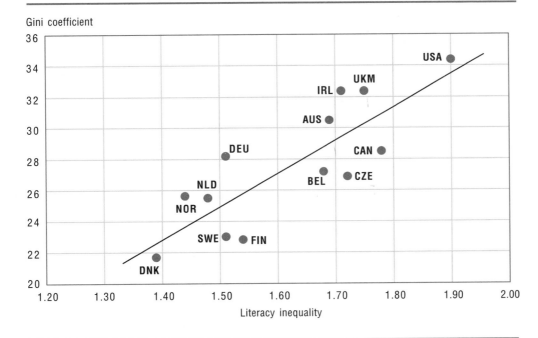

Sources: International Adult Literacy Survey, 1994-1998; OECD, *Trends in Income Distribution and Poverty in OECD Area 1999.*

FIGURE 4.14

LIFE EXPECTANCY AT BIRTH AND LITERACY PROFICIENCY

A. Relationship between life expectancy at birth in 1997 and per cent of adults aged 16-65 at literacy Levels 1 and 2, prose scale, 1994-1998

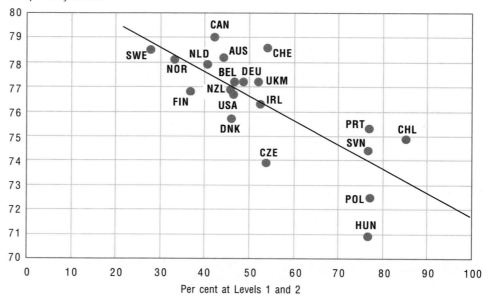

B. Relationship between life expectancy at birth in 1997 and per cent of adults aged 16-65 at literacy Level 4/5, prose scale, 1994-1998

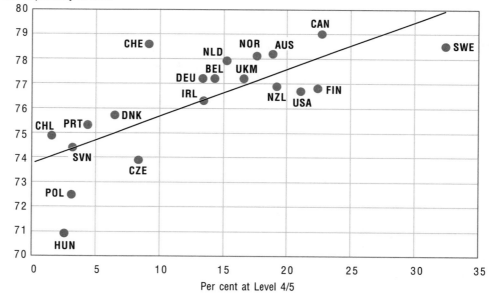

Sources: International Adult Literacy Survey, 1994-1998; UNDP, *Human Development Report 1999.*

important determinants of people's trust in others and that these outcomes produce positive externalities to societies as a whole (Temple, 2000; Knack, 2000). Literacy has also been reviewed to have a bearing on social participation. A positive relationship between participation in voluntary community activities and higher literacy is shown for a number of countries, for example Ireland, Norway and the United Kingdom in Table 3.22 page 57.

Moreover, Figure 4.15 shows the strong association between the number of women in parliament and the literacy level of a country. The greater the mean prose score of a country, the greater is the political participation of women. This relationship can be viewed in two ways, either as literacy contributing to greater gender equality or as an effect of high female literacy. The direction of the relationship is influenced by many other factors, and indeed there could be different causes that produce both higher literacy and higher female political participation. However, the statistical correlation between the two is strong, suggesting that the higher the level of literacy the more women participate in the civic realm of society.

FIGURE 4.15

WOMEN IN PARLIAMENT AND LITERACY PROFICIENCY

Relationship between the proportion of seats in parliament held by women and mean literacy proficiency, prose scale, population aged 16-65, 1994-1998

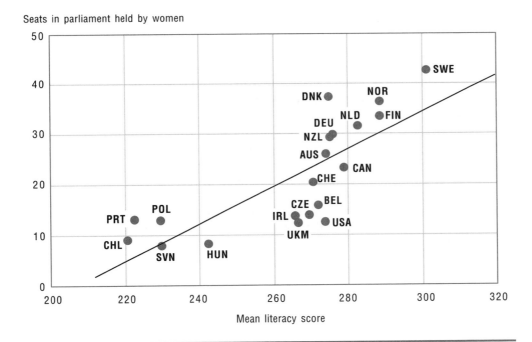

Seats in parliament held by women

Mean literacy score

Sources: International Adult Literacy Survey, 1994-1998; UNDP, *Human Development Report 1999.*

4.5 Conclusion

Societies consider high levels of literacy to be desirable for all of their members to sustain widespread participation in economic, social, cultural, and political life. Literacy is important for communication and making informed decisions. It is a necessary ingredient for citizenship, community participation and a sense of belonging. Literacy is also a tool for efficient learning, particularly self-directed learning of the sort that is enabled by information and communication technologies.

The association between human capital and labour market outcomes has commonly been explored using indicators of initial educational attainment. This chapter has made a contribution by including more variables thought to be important determinants of both human capital and labour market outcomes. Several interesting findings have emerged from this analysis.

First, literacy skills are related to various labour market outcomes – for example, increased employability, reduced unemployment probabilities and increased earnings – even when educational attainment is held constant. Literacy skills are therefore a factor of importance in the move towards the knowledge economy. At the same time, the analysis shows how educational attainment and literacy skills are complementary.

Second, for workers in blue-collar low-skilled occupations, the benefits will be the largest when increasing the skills of those with low initial prose levels. This finding is important in a lifelong learning perspective. Training that results in upgrading the literacy levels of less-advantaged workers can help them to improve their position in the labour market.

Third, increasing the literacy skills of the labour force will have beneficial effects on the upskilling of the workforce by increasing the probability of being in white-collar high-skilled occupations.

Fourth, separate analyses have provided evidence for the existence of a relationship between economic inequality and literacy inequality. Future analysis could look into the issue of the direction of cause and effect and whether there are other intermediate variables that influence both outcomes.

Fifth, strategies to raise literacy skills can therefore be one element in the mix of policies required to boost employability and counter unemployment.

Sixth, education attainment is the most important determinant of earnings among the factors studied. But in many of the countries literacy proficiency also has a substantial effect on earnings, a net effect that is independent of the effects of education. Thus, the analysis supports the conclusion that there is a net, measurable return to literacy skills in many countries.

Finally, there are substantial non-market benefits that accrue to literacy skills. Greater social cohesion, political participation of women and improved health are among the associations that have been explored in this chapter. It is likely that these benefits offer an incomplete picture of the range of effects literacy has on living conditions and the quality of life in OECD societies. It is hoped that the IALS data studied in this report will prove useful in advancing policy analysis and research currently underway to decipher the complex relationships between human capital, economic outcomes and social benefits.

References

ALESINA, A. and RODRIK, D. (1992), "Income distribution and economic growth: A simple theory and empirical evidence", in A. Cukierman, Z. Hercowitz and L. Leiderman (Eds.), *The Political Economy of Business Cycles and Growth*, MIT Press, Cambridge, MA.

BARRO, R.J. (1996), "Determinants of economic growth: A cross-country empirical study", NBER Working Paper No. 5698, National Bureau of Economic Research, Cambridge, MA.

BECKER, G. (1993), *Human Capital: A Theoretical and Empirical Analysis with Special Reference to Education* (Third Edition), University of Chicago Press, Chicago.

BENABOU, R. (1996), "Inequality and growth", *NBER Macroeconomics Annual 1996*, pp. 11-92.

BERLIN, G. and SUM, A. (1988), "Toward a more perfect union: Basic skills, poor families", Occasional Paper No. 3, Ford Foundation Project on Social Welfare and the American Future, The Ford Foundation, New York.

BLOOM, M.R., BURROWS, M., LAFLEUR, B., and SQUIRES, R. (1997), "The economic benefits of improving literacy skills in the workplace", mimeo, The Conference Board of Canada, Ottawa, Ontario.

CAMPBELL, A., CONVERSE, P.E., MILLER, W.E. and STOKES, D.E. (1976), *The American Voter*, University of Chicago Press, Chicago.

CARLINER, G. (1996, September), "The wages and language skills of US immigrants", NBER Working Paper No. 5763, National Bureau of Economic Research, Cambridge, MA.

COMER, J.P. (1988), "Educating poor minority children", *Scientific American*, Vol. 29(5), pp. 42-48.

DE LA FUENTE, A. and DOMENECH, R. (2000), "Human capital in growth regressions: How much difference does data quality make?", Paper presented at an OECD-HRDC Conference, The Contribution of Human and Social Capital to Sustained Economic Growth and Well-Being, March 19-21, 2000, Quebec City, PQ.

GRILICHES, Z. (1996), "Education, human capital and growth: A personal perspective", NBER Working Paper No. 5426, National Bureau of Economic Research, Cambridge, MA.

HEALTH CANADA (1999), *Statistical Report on the Health of Canadians*, Ottawa.

KNACK, S. (2000), "Trust, associational life and economic performance in the OECD", Paper presented at an OECD-HRDC Conference, The Contribution of Human and Social Capital to Sustained Economic Growth and Well-Being, March 19-21, 2000, Quebec City, PQ.

MINCER, J. (1974), *Schooling, Experience and Earnings*, Columbia University Press, New York.

MINCER, J. (1991), "Job training: Costs, returns and wage profiles", in D. Stern and J.M.M. Ritzen (Eds.), *Market Failure in Training? New Economic Analysis and Evidence on Training of Adult Employees*, Springer-Verlag, Berlin.

MINGAT, A. and TAN, J. (1996), "The full social returns to education: Estimates based on countries' economic growth performance", *Human Capital Development Working Papers*, The World Bank Group, Washington, DC.

NCES (2000), *Literacy in the Labor Force: Results from the National Adult Literacy Survey*, National Center for Education Statistics, US Department of Education, Washington, DC.

OECD (1998a), *Human Capital Investment: An International Comparison*, Paris.

OECD (1998b), *Education at a Glance: OECD Indicators*, Paris.

OECD (1999a), *Employment Outlook*, June, Paris.

OECD (1999b), "Trends in income distribution and poverty in the OECD area", Document DEELSA/ELSA/WP1(99)15, Paris.

OECD and HUMAN RESOURCES DEVELOPMENT CANADA (1997), *Literacy Skills for the Knowledge Society: Further Results from the International Adult Literacy Survey*, Paris.

OECD and STATISTICS CANADA (1995), *Literacy, Economy and Society: Results of the First International Adult Literacy Survey*, Paris and Ottawa.

OSBERG, L. (2000), "Long run trends in economic inequality in five countries – A birth cohort view", Revised version of paper presented at CRESP Workshop on "Equality, Security and Community", Vancouver, October 21, 1999. (http://www.is.dal.ca)

PSACHAROPOULOS, G. (1994), "Returns to investment in education: A global update", *World Development,* Vol. 22(9), pp. 1325-1343.

RAUDENBUSH, S.W. and KASIM, R.M. (1998), "Cognitive skill and economic inequality: Findings from the National Adult Literacy Survey", *Harvard Educational Review*, Vol. 68 (1), pp. 33-79.

RIVERA-BATIZ, F.L. (1994), "Quantitative literacy and the likelihood of employment among young adults in the United States", *Journal of Human Resources,* Vol. XXVII, No. 2, pp. 313-328.

SCHULTZ, T.W. (1960), "Capital formation by education", *Journal of Political Economy*, Vol. 68, pp. 571-583.

TEMPLE, J. (2000), "Growth effects of education and social capital in the OECD", Paper presented at an OECD-HRDC Conference, The Contribution of Human and Social Capital to Sustained Economic Growth and Well-Being, March 19-21, 2000, Quebec City, PQ.

TUIJNMAN, A.C. (1989), *Recurrent Education, Earnings, and Well-being: A 50-year Longitudinal Study of a Cohort of Swedish Men,* Almqvist and Wiksell International, Stockholm.

TUIJNMAN, A.C. (2000), "Measuring human capital: Data gaps and survey requirements", in K. Rubenson and H. Schuetze (Eds.), *Transitions to the Knowledge Economy*, University of British Columbia Press, Vancouver, BC.

UNDP (1999), *Human Development Report 1999*, Geneva and New York.

UNITED STATES DEPARTMENT OF HEALTH and HUMAN SERVICES (1998), *Health, United States 1998*, Hyattsville, Maryland.

WOLFE, B. and HAVEMAN, R. (2000), "Accounting for the social and non-market effects of education", Paper presented at OECD-HRDC Conference, The Contribution of Human and Social Capital to Sustained Economic Growth and Well-Being, March 19-21, 2000, Quebec City, PQ.

CHAPTER 5

Future Developments

5.1 Introduction

The IALS has, for the first time, collected reliable and internationally comparable data on the levels and distributions of broadly defined literacy skills in the adult population. The main purpose of this report has been to make this new information available to a broad audience. It brings together results for 20 countries and populations, shown in Figure 5.1. By 1998, the survey covered 10.3 per cent of world population (United Nations, 1998) and 51.6 per cent of world GDP (World Bank, 1999).[1]

The purpose of this concluding chapter is to describe briefly the innovative nature of the applied methodology and review some of the priorities in regard to further data development. The conclusions raise a number of important issues for policy. This report has not addressed them, but the new data sets can be used with advantage for secondary policy analysis involving multivariate and multi-level modelling.

Previously, the possibility to study the fundamental relationships in the IALS data has been constrained by limited heterogeneity across countries and by limitations imposed on statistical modelling by insufficient cases. Now that the IALS has a total of 68,755 individual respondents and more than 25 distinct populations in its sample of primary strata, an extensive programme of study aimed at revealing the determinants and consequences of the observed skills distributions can be launched.

5.2 Methodological Advances

The IALS has served to advance international comparative assessment. The survey represents the world's first attempt at employing, in combination, the tools of educational assessment and household survey techniques to profile the skill levels of adult populations in a diverse range of countries and across various languages. Considerable difficulties in management, funding, staffing and quality assurance had to be overcome in making it happen. Despite the obvious difficulties encountered during the course of this challenging undertaking, the IALS has made a contribution in setting a new quality standard for measurement in several respects.

---

1. Excluding France and Italy.

FIGURE 5.1

WORLD MAP SHOWING THE COUNTRY POPULATIONS COVERED BY THE INTERNATIONAL ADULT LITERACY SURVEY

First, the study has set a new standard for providing a theoretical basis for its measurement framework that explicitly identifies the factors that explain the relative difficulty of the texts and tasks representing the skills needed by adults in confronting the complexity of their daily lives (Annex A).

Second, the survey employed an advanced psychometric approach, one that uses strict empirical criteria for establishing common performance scales for participating countries. This approach is useful in determining more precisely the degree to which international comparisons of proficiency levels are valid and reliable – information that tended to be unavailable for previous comparative studies of student achievement (Annex C).

Third, the IALS has, through the application of rigorous procedures for statistical quality control, achieved unprecedented levels of reliability in scoring open-ended items across cultures and languages. With average inter-rater reliabilities approaching 90 per cent both within and between countries, the possibility that observed cross-country variations in skill levels are attributable to differences in the ways in which the scorers judged responses is minimal, something that few assessment studies can claim (Annex B).

Fourth, owing in large measure to the advanced methods it applied in the scaling of the assessment results, the IALS has taken great care to explicitly test psychometric assumptions that can have an impact on the accuracy and comparability of findings within and between countries. For example, the fit of each test item to the underlying statistical model is empirically tested rather than presumed (Annex A), improving upon the practice hitherto employed in international studies of student achievement.

Finally, the quality assurance protocol employed in each successive round of data collection has been improved significantly by taking into account the weaknesses exposed in earlier rounds (examples are provided in Annex B). Recently conducted evaluation studies have also contributed new knowledge about the efficacy of the applied methodology (Annex C). Given the novelty of household survey assessment, such continual improvement is critical to meeting the scientific objectives and supporting the comparative aspirations of the study. This suggests the importance of undertaking new work to further improve skills assessment methodology.

A step of crucial importance involves the replication of the IALS study in additional countries and over time. Policy makers want to know how the distributions of skills observed in the IALS will evolve with time. Ideally, longitudinal data on the development of individual skills over the life course are needed to answer this issue. But because longitudinal surveys of the same individuals over time are difficult and costly to develop, a second-best approach would involve undertaking periodic cross-sectional assessments. Providing that care is taken to properly link the data to the original IALS scales, repeated cohort analysis could then be used to study how literacy skills evolve over time in relation to changes in underlying variables. It is for this reason that the planned Adult Literacy and Lifeskills (ALL) survey, which is scheduled to move into the field in 2002, has chosen to replicate all aspects of the prose and document literacy scales carried as part of the IALS, including the linking to the original IALS scales.

Another priority for a future assessment is to extend the coverage of the study to include additional skill domains. For this reason, the ALL survey will replace the quantitative literacy scale with a broader measure of numeracy skill and aims to assess certain aspects of performance in problem-solving, team work and the capacity to use information and communication technologies.[2]

The OECD education work programme is dedicated to improving the availability of international indicators of education systems. As part of this programme, the OECD has agreed to extend and formalise work on the definition and measurement of adult competencies. Further advances in this area will involve using the instrument of household survey assessment. This will require a concerted effort and substantial investment on the part of interested countries. This work would build upon the success already achieved in IALS and will consolidate the on-going work on the ALL survey and the project on Definition and Selection of Competencies (DeSeCo), currently supported by Switzerland and the United States.

5.3 Main Findings

There is considerable variation between countries in the extent of inequality in the population distribution of literacy skills. The results indicate that the countries with the highest levels of skills have been successful in bolstering the literacy levels of their least advantaged citizens. Initial education is the main factor in improving the levels of literacy, particularly of youth from lower socio-economic backgrounds.

The principal finding of this report is that all countries have a significant skills deficit in older compared with younger population cohorts. After controlling for age-related variation in educational attainment, the deficit appears to be much larger in some countries than in others. Thus countries vary in how well they succeed in updating and refreshing the stock of skills the population has acquired through initial education and by other means. This finding suggests that investment in the initial education of youth will not be enough to address the problem of skills deficits for adults in a timely manner. Special measures for improving and replenishing the skills among adults are also needed.

---

2. Information about the ALL survey can be retrieved on the World Wide Web from NCES (2000), International Adult Literacy and Lifeskills survey: http://www.nces.ed.gov/ilss

An alternative hypothesis is that younger, more educated age groups will resist the processes of skills attrition. If this were to be the case, the proportions of adults at low levels of skills would continue to decline, a fact that would change the focus of policy considerably.

Analysis of the IALS data suggests that four factors work to modify the skills of adults after the completion of the initial cycle of education and training. First, labour force participation, and especially occupational status, are associated with literacy outcomes. Second, differences in the use of literacy skills in the workplace, related to underlying differences in industrial and occupational structures and in the organisation of work, serve to support or undermine literacy acquisition. Third, differing rates of participation in formal adult education and training seem to contribute to processes of skills acquisition, maintenance and loss in adulthood. Fourth, differences in the social demand for the use of literacy skills at home serve either to support or to detract from literacy acquisition and maintenance.

These findings, observed in the data for the countries participating in the first round of collection, are also supported by the evidence gathered in countries that participated in subsequent rounds of data collection. Because the new data sets bring greater heterogeneity, they help researchers in undertaking more robust analyses. For example, the analyses contained in this volume confirm the fundamental importance of the quality and quantity of initial education for raising the overall literacy level of nations. The greater heterogeneity in data coming from the newly emerging economies (Chile, the Czech Republic, Hungary and Slovenia) shows that the relationship between educational attainment and literacy proficiency is even stronger than previously believed.

5.4 Issues for Further Analysis

The data provide important insights into the factors that underlie differences in skills across and within countries. They also provide reliable information on the factors that influence skill levels in adulthood, information that is key to understanding how the current skills distributions are likely to evolve in the information age. They help in better understanding the relationships between education, skills, economic success and social outcomes at the level of the individual and of the nation. Such insights are crucial to the efficient design and targeting of programmes, both preventive and remedial, and in judging the relative urgency of such interventions.

The new data can be used to study the underlying processes that explain the phenomenon of literacy acquisition and development. In particular, the newly available data can be employed to help examine:

- the contribution of socio-economic and family factors, workplace practices, and cultural variables in determining literacy skills and their social distribution within countries;
- the role of literacy skills in the processes of human and social capital investment and their impact on economic growth and social equity;
- the relative effectiveness of schooling in raising literacy outcomes for youth in different countries;
- the factors that underlie the social distribution of literacy skills and how policy interventions can modify them;
- the functioning of the markets for skills, education and learning, for example by studying the relative importance of education, skills and wage differentials as explanations of between-country differences in labour market outcomes.

To enable such policy analysis and thereby ensure a good return on the substantial investment already made by countries in collecting the IALS data, Statistics Canada, the OECD and most of the participating countries have agreed to make the micro data sets and associated documentation available to interested analysts and researchers.[3] The national survey teams and the organisations and agencies that have facilitated the design and implementation of the survey since its early days in 1992 expect that much new knowledge will be gained from further work on the determinants and outcomes of literacy skills in the information age.

References

UNITED NATIONS SECRETARIAT (1998), *World Population Prospects: The 1998 Revision,* United Nations Population Division, New York.

WORLD BANK (1999), *Country at a Glance Tables*, World Bank Group Homepage, Washington, DC.

---

3. The micro data sets for the countries that collected data in 1998 will become available to researchers interested in secondary analysis subsequent to the publication of the results. Requests for access to the data sets for countries that participated in the several rounds of data collection can be addressed in writing to: The Director-General, Institutions and Social Statistics, Statistics Canada, Tunney's Pasture, Ottawa, K1A 0T6, Canada.

ANNEX A

Definitions of Literacy Performance on Three Scales

Introduction

The results of the International Adult Literacy Survey (IALS) are reported on three scales – prose, document and quantitative – rather than on a single scale. Each scale ranges from 0 to 500. Scale scores have, in turn, been grouped into five empirically determined literacy levels. As mentioned in the introduction to this report, each of these levels implies an ability to cope with a particular subset of reading tasks. This annex explains in more detail how the proficiency scores can be interpreted, by describing the scales and the kinds of tasks that were used in the test, and the literacy levels that have been adopted.

While the literacy scales make it possible to compare the prose, document and quantitative skills of different populations and to study the relationships between literacy skills and various factors, the scale scores by themselves carry little or no meaning. In other words, whereas most people have a practical understanding of what it means when the temperature outside reaches 0°C, it is not intuitively clear what it means when a particular population group is at 287 points on the prose scale, or 250 points on the document scale, or at Level 2 on the quantitative scale.

One way to gain some understanding about what it means to perform at a given point along a literacy scale is to identify a set of variables that can be shown to underlie performance on these tasks. Collectively, these variables provide a framework for understanding what is being measured in a particular assessment, and what knowledge and skills are demonstrated at various levels of proficiency.

Toward this end, the text below begins by describing how the literacy scale scores were defined. Detailed descriptions of the prose, document and quantitative scales are then provided, along with definitions of the five levels. Sample tasks are presented to illustrate the types of materials and demands that characterise the levels.

Defining the Literacy Levels

The Item Response Theory (IRT) scaling procedures that were used in the IALS constitute a statistical solution to the challenge of establishing one or more scales for a set of tasks with an ordering of difficulty that is essentially the same for everyone. First, the difficulty of tasks is ranked on the scale according to how well respondents actually perform them. Next, individuals are assigned scores according to how well they do on a number of tasks of varying difficulty.

The scale point assigned to each task is the point at which individuals with that proficiency score have a given probability of responding correctly. In the IALS, an 80 per cent probability of correct response was the criterion used. This means that individuals estimated to have a particular scale score perform tasks at that point on the scale with an 80 per cent probability of a correct response. It also means they will have a greater than 80 per cent chance of performing tasks that are lower on the scale. It does not mean, however, that individuals with given proficiencies can never succeed at tasks with higher difficulty values; they may do so some of the time. It does suggest that their probability of success is "relatively" low – *i.e.* the more difficult the task relative to their proficiency, the lower the likelihood of a correct response.

An analogy might help clarify this point. The relationship between task difficulty and individual proficiency is much like the high jump event in track and field, in which an athlete tries to jump over a bar that is placed at increasing heights. Each high jumper has a height at which he or she is proficient – that is, the jumper can clear the bar at that height with a high probability of success, and can clear the bar at lower heights almost every time. When the bar is higher than the athlete's level of proficiency, however, it is expected that the athlete will be unable to clear the bar consistently.

Once the literacy tasks are placed along each of the scales using the criterion of 80 per cent, it is possible to see to what extent the interactions among various task characteristics capture the placement of tasks along the scales. Analyses of the task characteristics – which include the materials being read and the type of questions asked about these materials – reveal that ordered sets of information-processing skills appear to be called into play to successfully perform the various tasks displayed along each scale (Kirsch and Mosenthal, 1993).

To capture this order, each scale is divided into five levels reflecting the empirically determined progression of information-processing skills and strategies. While some of the tasks were at the low end of a scale and some at the very high end, most had values in the range 200-400. It is important to recognise that these levels were selected not as a result of any inherent statistical property of the scales, but rather as the result of shifts in the skills and strategies required to succeed at various tasks along the scales, ranging from simple to complex.

The remainder of this annex describes each scale in terms of the nature of task demands at each of the five levels. Sample tasks are presented and the factors contributing to their difficulty discussed. The aim is to facilitate interpretation of the results and data analyses presented in the main body of the report.

Interpreting the Literacy Levels

PROSE LITERACY

The ability to understand and use information contained in various kinds of text is an important aspect of literacy. The study therefore included an array of prose selections, including text from newspapers, magazines and brochures. The material varied in length, density of text, content, and the use of structural or organisational aids such as headings, bullets and special typefaces. All prose samples were reprinted in their entirety with the original layout and typography unchanged.

Each prose selection was accompanied by one or more questions asking the reader to perform specific tasks. These tasks represent three major aspects of information-processing: locating, integrating and generating. Locating tasks require the reader to find information in the text based on conditions or features specified in the question or directive. The match may be literal or synonymous, or the reader may need to make an inference in order to perform successfully. Integrating tasks ask the reader to pull together two or more pieces of information in the text. The information could be found in a single paragraph, or in different paragraphs or sections. With the generating tasks, readers must produce a written response by processing information from the text and by making text-based inferences or drawing on their own background knowledge.

In all, the prose literacy scale includes 34 tasks with difficulty values ranging from 188 to 377. These tasks are distributed by level as follows: Level 1, 5 tasks; Level 2, 9 tasks; Level 3, 14 tasks; Level 4, 5 tasks; and Level 5, 1 task. It is important to remember that the tasks requiring the reader to locate, integrate and generate information extend over a range of difficulty as a result of combining other variables, including:

- the number of categories or features of information the reader must process;
- the extent to which information given in the question or directive is obviously related to the information contained in the text;
- the amount and location of information in the text that shares some of the features with the information being requested and thus appears relevant, but that in fact does not fully answer the question (these are called "distractors"); and
- the length and density of the text.

The five levels of prose literacy are defined as follows.

Prose Level 1   Score range: 0 to 225

Most of the tasks at this level require the reader to locate one piece of information in the text that is identical to or synonymous with the information given in the directive. If a plausible incorrect answer is present in the text, it tends not to be near the correct information.

Typically the match between the task and the text is literal, although sometimes a low-level inference may be necessary. The text is usually brief or has organisational aids such as paragraph headings or italics that suggest where the reader can find the specified information. Generally, the target word or phrase appears only once in the text.

The easiest task in Level 1 (difficulty value of 188) directs respondents to look at a medicine label to determine the "maximum number of days you should take this medicine". The label contains only one reference to number of days and this information is located under the heading "DOSAGE". The reader must go to this part of the label and locate the phrase "not longer than 7 days".

Prose Level 2   Score range: 226 to 275

Tasks at this level generally require the reader to locate one or more pieces of information in the text, but several "distractors" may be present, or low-level inferences may be required. Tasks at this level also begin to ask readers to integrate two or more pieces of information, or to compare and contrast information.

As with Level 1, most of the tasks at Level 2 ask the reader to locate information. However, more varied demands are made in terms of the number of responses the question requires, or in terms of the distracting information that may be present. For example, a task based on an article about the impatiens plant asks the reader to determine what happens when the plant is exposed to temperatures of 14°C or lower. A sentence under the section "General care" states "When the plant is exposed to temperatures of 12-14°C, it loses its leaves and won't bloom anymore". This task received a difficulty value of 230, just in the Level 2 range.

What made this task somewhat more difficult than those identified at Level 1 is that the previous sentence in the text contains information about the requirements of the impatiens plant in various temperatures. This information could have distracted some readers, making the task slightly more difficult. A similar task involving the same text asks the reader to identify "what the smooth leaf and stem suggest about the plant". The second paragraph of the article is labelled "Appearance" and contains a sentence that states, "... stems are branched and very juicy, which means, because of the tropical origin, that the plant is sensitive to cold". This sentence distracted some readers from the last sentence in that same paragraph: "The smooth leaf surfaces and the stems indicate a great need of water". This task received a difficulty value of 254, placing it in the middle of Level 2.

Prose Level 3   **Score range: 276 to 325**

Tasks at this level generally direct readers to locate information that requires low-level inferences or that meets specified conditions. Sometimes the reader is required to identify several pieces of information that are located in different sentences or paragraphs rather than in a single sentence. Readers may also be asked to integrate or to compare and contrast information across paragraphs or sections of text.

One Level 3 task (with a difficulty value of 281) refers the reader to a page from a bicycle owner's manual to determine how to ensure the seat is in the proper position. The reader must locate the section labelled "Fitting the bicycle" and then identify and summarise the correct information in writing, making sure the conditions stated are contained in the summary. A second Level 3 task, receiving a difficulty value of 310, directs the reader to look at a set of four film reviews to determine which review was least favourable. Some reviews rate films using points or some graphic such as stars; these reviews contain no such indicators. The reader needs to glance at the text of each review to compare what is said in order to judge which film received the worst rating.

Another Level 3 question involves an article about cotton diapers. Here readers are asked to write three reasons why the author prefers to use cotton diapers rather than disposable ones. This task is relatively difficult (318) because of several variables. First, the reader has to provide several answers requiring text-based inferences. Nowhere in the text does the author say, "I prefer cotton diapers because ...". These inferences are made somewhat more difficult because the type of information requested is a "reason" rather than something more concrete such as a date or person. And finally, the text contains information that may distract the reader.

Prose Level 4   **Score range: 326 to 375**

These tasks require readers to perform multiple-feature matching or to provide several responses where the requested information must be identified through text-based inferences. Tasks at this level may also require the reader to integrate or contrast pieces of information, sometimes presented in relatively lengthy texts. Typically, these texts contain more distracting information, and the information requested is more abstract.

One task falling within Level 4 (338) directs readers to use the information from a pamphlet about hiring interviews to "write in your own words one difference between the panel interview and the group interview". Here readers are presented with brief descriptions of each type of interview; then, rather than merely locating a fact about each or identifying a similarity, they need to integrate what they have read to infer a characteristic on which the two types of interviews differ. Experience from other large-scale assessments reveals that tasks in which readers are asked to contrast information are more difficult, on average, than tasks in which they are asked to find similarities.

Prose Level 5   **Score range: 376 to 500**

Tasks at this level typically require the reader to search for information in dense text that contains a number of plausible distractors. Some require readers to make high-level inferences or to use specialised knowledge.

There is one Level 5 task in this assessment, with a difficulty value of 377. Readers are required to look at an announcement from a personnel department and "list two ways in which CIEM (an employee support initiative within a company) helps people who will lose their jobs because of a departmental reorganisation". Responding correctly requires readers to search through this text to locate the embedded sentence "CIEM acts as a mediator for employees who are threatened with dismissal resulting from reorganisation, and assists with finding new positions when necessary". This task is difficult because the announcement is organised around information that is different from what is being requested in the question. Thus, while the correct information is located in a single sentence, this information is embedded under a list of headings describing CIEM's activities for employees looking for other work. This list of headings serves as an excellent set of distractors for the reader who does not search for or locate the phrase containing the conditional information stated in the directive – that is, those who lose their jobs because of a departmental reorganisation.

DOCUMENT LITERACY

Adults often encounter materials such as schedules, charts, graphs, tables, maps and forms at home, at work, or when travelling in their communities. The knowledge and skills needed to process information contained in these documents is therefore an important aspect of literacy in a modern society. Success in processing documents appears to depend at least in part on the ability to locate information in a variety of displays, and to use this information in a number of ways. Sometimes procedural knowledge may be required to transfer information from one source to another, as is necessary in completing applications or order forms.

Thirty-four tasks are ordered along the IALS document literacy scale from 182 to 408, as the result of responses of adults from each of the participating countries. These tasks are distributed as follows: Level 1, 6 tasks; Level 2 , 12 tasks; Level 3, 13 tasks; Level 4, 2 tasks; and Level 5, 1 task. By examining tasks associated with these proficiency levels, characteristics that are likely to make particular document tasks more or less difficult can be identified. There are basically four types of questions associated with document tasks: locating, cycling, integrating and generating. Locating tasks require the reader to match one or more features of information stated in the question to either identical or synonymous information given in the document. Cycling tasks require the reader to locate and match one or more features of information, but differ from locating tasks in that they require the reader to engage in a series of feature matches to satisfy conditions given in the question. The integrating tasks typically require the reader to compare and contrast information in adjacent parts of the document. In the generating tasks, readers must produce a written response by processing information found in the document and by making text-based inferences or drawing on their own background knowledge.

As with the prose tasks, each type of question extends over a range of difficulty as a result of combining other variables:

- the number of categories or features of information in the question the reader must process or match;
- the number of categories or features of information in the document that seem plausible or correct because they share some but not all of the information with the correct answer;

- the extent to which the information asked for in the question is clearly related to the information stated in the document; and
- the structure and content of the document.

A more detailed discussion of the five levels of document literacy follows.

Document Level 1   **Score range: 0 to 225**

Most of the tasks at this level require the reader to locate a single piece of information based on a literal match. Distracting information, if present, is typically located away from the correct answer. Some tasks may direct the reader to enter personal information onto a form.

One document task at this level (with a difficulty value of 188) directs the reader to identify from a chart the per cent of teachers from Greece who are women. The chart displays the per cent of women teachers from various countries. Only one number appears on the chart for each country.

A similar task involves a chart from a newspaper showing the expected amounts of radioactive waste by country. This task, which has a difficulty value of 218, directs the reader to identify the country that is projected to have the smallest amount of waste by the year 2000. Again, there is only one percentage associated with each country; however, the reader must first identify the per cent associated with the smallest amount of waste, and then match it to the country.

Document Level 2   **Score range: 226 to 275**

Document tasks at this level are a bit more varied. While some still require the reader to match a single feature, more distracting information may be present or the match may require a low-level inference. Some tasks at this level may require the reader to enter information onto a form or to cycle through information in a document.

One Level 2 task on the document scale (242) directs the reader to look at a chart to identify the year in which the fewest people were injured by fireworks in the Netherlands. Part of what perhaps makes this task somewhat more difficult than those in Level 1 is that two charts are presented instead of just one. One, labelled "Fireworks in the Netherlands", depicts years and numbers representing funds spent in millions of Canadian dollars, whereas the other, "Victims of fireworks", uses a line to show numbers of people treated in hospitals. It is worth noting that in a second version of the assessment this label was changed to read "Number injured".

Several other tasks falling within Level 2 direct the reader to use information given to complete a form. In one case they are asked to fill out an order form to purchase tickets to see a play on a particular day and at a particular time. In another, readers are asked to complete the availability section of an employment application based on information provided that included: the total number of hours they are willing to work; the hours they are available; how they heard about the job; and the availability of transportation.

Document Level 3   **Score range: 276 to 325**

Tasks at this level are varied. Some require the reader to make literal or synonymous matches, but usually the reader must take conditional information into account or match on the basis of multiple features of information. Some require the reader to integrate information from one or more displays of information. Others ask the reader to cycle through a document to provide multiple responses.

One task falling around the middle of Level 3 in difficulty (with a value of 295) involves the fireworks charts shown earlier (see *Document level 2*). This task directs the reader to write a brief description of the relationship between sales and injuries based on the information shown in the two graphs. A second task, falling at the high end of Level 3 (321), involves the use of a quick copy printing requisition form that might be found in the workplace. The task asks the reader to state whether or not the quick copy centre would make 300 copies of a statement that is 105 pages long. In responding to this directive, the reader must determine whether conditions stated in the question meet those provided in the requisition form.

Document Level 4 Score range: 326 to 375

Tasks at this level, like those at the previous levels, ask the reader to match on the basis of multiple features of information, to cycle through documents, and to integrate information; frequently, however, these tasks require the reader to make higher-order inferences to arrive at the correct answer. Sometimes the document contains conditional information that must be taken into account by the reader.

One of the two tasks falling within this level (341) asks the reader to look at two pie charts showing oil use for 1970 and 1989. The question directs the reader to summarise how the percentages of oil used for different purposes changed over the specified period. Here the reader must cycle through the two charts, comparing and contrasting the percentages for each of the four stated purposes, and then generate a statement that captures these changes.

Document Level 5 Score range: 376 to 500

Tasks at this level require the reader to search through complex displays of information that contain multiple distractors, to make high-level inferences, process conditional information, or use specialised knowledge.

The only Level 5 task in this international assessment (with a difficulty value of 408) involves a page taken from a consumer magazine rating clock radios. The reader is asked for the average advertised price for the "basic" clock radio receiving the highest overall score. This task requires readers to process two types of conditional information. First, they need to identify the clock radio receiving the highest overall score while distinguishing among the three types reviewed: "full-featured", "basic" and those "with cassette player". Second, they need to locate a price. In making this final match, they need to notice that two are given: the suggested retail price, followed by the average advertised price.

The same document is used for a second and considerably easier task that falls at the low end of Level 4 (327). The reader is asked "which full-featured radio is rated the highest on performance". Again, it is necessary to find the correct category of clock radio, but the reader needs to process fewer conditions. All that is required is to distinguish between the rating for "Overall Score" and that for "Performance". It is possible that some adults note the distractor ("Overall Score") rather than the criterion specified in the question, "Performance". Another factor that likely contributes to this task's difficulty is that "Overall Score" is given a numerical value while the other features are rated by a symbol. Also, some adults may find the correct category ("Performance") but select the first radio listed, assuming it performed best. The text accompanying the table indicates that the radios are rated within a category by an overall score; it is easy to imagine that some people may have equated overall score with overall performance.

QUANTITATIVE LITERACY

Since adults are frequently required to perform arithmetic operations in everyday life, the ability to perform quantitative tasks is another important aspect of literacy. These skills may at first seem to differ fundamentally from those associated with prose and document literacy, and therefore to extend the concept of literacy beyond its traditional limits. Experience in North America with large-scale assessments of adults indicates that the processing of printed information plays an important role in affecting the difficulty of tasks along the quantitative scale (Montigny *et al.*, 1991; Kirsh *et al.*, 1993).

In general, it appears that many individuals can perform single arithmetic operations when both the numbers and operations are made explicit. However, when the numbers to be used must be located in and extracted from different types of documents that contain other similar but irrelevant information, when the operations to be used must be inferred from printed directions, and when multiple operations must be performed, the tasks become increasingly difficult.

The IALS quantitative literacy scale contains 33 tasks ranging from 225 to 409 in difficulty. These tasks are distributed as follows: Level 1, 1 task; Level 2, 9 tasks; Level 3, 16 tasks; Level 4, 5 tasks; and Level 5, 2 tasks. The difficulty of these tasks – and therefore, their placement along the scale – appears to be a function of several factors including:

- the particular arithmetic operation the task requires;
- the number of operations needed to perform the task successfully;
- the extent to which the numbers are embedded in printed materials; and
- the extent to which an inference must be made to identify the type of operation to be performed.

The five levels of quantitative literacy are described in detail below.

Quantitative Level 1   **Score range: 0 to 225**

Although no quantitative tasks used in the assessment fall below the score value of 225, experience suggests that such tasks would require the reader to perform a single, relatively simple operation (usually addition) for which either the numbers are clearly noted in the given document and the operation is stipulated, or the numbers are provided and the operation does not require the reader to find the numbers.

The easiest quantitative task (225) directs the reader to complete an order form. The last line on this form reads: "Total with Handling". The line above it says: "Handling Charge $2.00". The reader simply has to add the $2.00 to the $50.00 entered on a previous line to indicate the cost of the tickets. In this task, one of the numbers is stipulated; the operation is easily identified from the word "total"; and the operation does not require the reader to perform the "borrow" or "carry-over" function of addition. Moreover, the form itself features a simple column format, further facilitating the task for the reader.

Quantitative Level 2   **Score range: 226 to 275**

Tasks at this level typically require readers to perform a single arithmetic operation (frequently addition or subtraction), using numbers that are easily located in the text or document. The operation to be performed may be easily inferred from the wording of the question or the format of the material (for example, a bank deposit or order form).

A typical Level 2 task on the quantitative scale directs the reader to use a weather chart in a newspaper to determine how many degrees warmer today's high temperature is expected to be in Bangkok than in Seoul. Here the reader must cycle through the table to locate the two temperatures and then subtract one from the other to determine the difference. This task received a difficulty value of 255.

A similar but slightly more difficult task (268) requires the reader to use the chart about women in the teaching profession that is displayed in Level 1 for the document scale. This task directs the reader to calculate the percentage of men in the teaching profession in Italy. Both this task and the one just mentioned involve calculating the difference between two numbers. In the former, however, both temperatures could be identified in the table from the newspaper. For the task involving male teachers in Italy, the reader needs to make the inference that the percentage is equal to 100 per cent minus the percentage of female teachers.

Quantitative Level 3   Score range: 276 to 325

Tasks at this level typically require the reader to perform a single operation. However, the operations become more varied – some multiplication and division tasks are included. Sometimes the reader needs to identify two or more numbers from various places in the document, and the numbers are frequently embedded in complex displays. While semantic relation terms such as "how many" or "calculate the difference" are often used, some of the tasks require the reader to make higher-order inferences to determine the appropriate operation.

One task located at 302 on the quantitative scale directs the reader to look at two graphs containing information about consumers and producers of primary energy. The reader is asked to calculate how much more energy Canada produces than it consumes. Here the operation is not facilitated by the format of the document; the reader must locate the information using both bar graphs. Another task involving this document directs the reader to calculate the total amount of energy in quadrillion (10^{15}) BTU (British Thermal Unit) consumed by Canada, Mexico and the United States. This task, which falls at 300 on the scale, requires the reader to add three numbers. Presenting two graphs likely increases the difficulty; some respondents may perform the appropriate calculation for the three countries specified using the producer energy chart rather than the consumer energy chart.

Another task at this level involves the fireworks chart shown previously for the document scale. The reader is asked to calculate how many more people were injured in 1989 than in 1988. What contributes to this task receiving a difficulty value of 293 is that one of the numbers is not given in the line graph; the reader needs to interpolate the number from information provided along the vertical axis.

A task located at 280 on the scale asks readers to look at a recipe for scrambled eggs with tomatoes. The recipe gives the ingredients for four servings: 3 tablespoons of oil, 1 garlic clove, 1 teaspoon of sugar, 500 grams of fresh red tomatoes and 6 eggs. They are then asked to determine the number of eggs they will need if they are using the recipe for six people. Here they must know how to calculate or determine the ratio needed. This task is somewhat easier than might be expected given others at the same level, perhaps because people are familiar with recipes and with manipulating them to fit a particular situation.

Another question using this recipe asks the reader to determine the amount of oil that would be needed if the recipe were being used for two people. This task received a value of 253 on the scale; a larger percentage of respondents found it easier to halve an ingredient than to increase one by 50 per cent. It is not clear why this is so. It may be that some of the respondents have an algorithm for responding to certain familiar tasks that does not require them to apply general arithmetic principles.

Quantitative Level 4   **Score range: 326 to 375**

With one exception, the tasks at this level require the reader to perform a single arithmetic operation where typically either the quantities or the operation are not easily determined. That is, for most of the tasks at this level, the question or directive does not provide a semantic relation term such as "how many" or "calculate the difference" to help the reader.

One task at this level involves a compound interest table. It directs the reader to "calculate the total amount of money you will have if you invest $100 at a rate of 6 per cent for 10 years". This task received a difficulty value of 348, in part because many people treated this as a document rather than a quantitative task and simply looked up the amount of interest that would be earned. They likely forgot to add the interest to their $100 investment.

Another task at this level requires respondents to read a newspaper article describing a research finding linking allergies to a particular genetic mutation. The question directs the reader to calculate the number of people studied who were found to have the mutant gene. To answer the question correctly, readers must know how to convert the phrase "64 per cent" to a decimal number and then multiply it by the number of patients studied (400). The text provides no clues on how to tackle this problem.

A third task involves a distance chart. Readers are asked to "calculate the total number of kilometres travelled in a trip from Guadalajara to Tecomán and then to Zamora". Here a semantic relation term is provided, but the format is difficult and the quantities are not easily identified. As a result, this task received a difficulty value of 335. In a Level 3 task using the same chart, respondents are asked to determine how much less the distance from Guadalajara to Tecomán is than the distance from Guadalajara to Puerto Vallarta. In that task (308), the quantities are relatively easy to locate.

Quantitative Level 5   **Score range: 376 to 500**

These tasks require readers to perform multiple operations sequentially, and they must locate features of the problem embedded in the material or rely on background knowledge to determine the quantities or operations needed.

One of the most difficult tasks on the quantitative scale (381) requires readers to look at a table providing nutritional analysis of food and then, using the information given, determine the percentage of calories in a Big Mac® that comes from total fat. To answer this question, readers must first recognise that the information about total fat provided is given in grams. In the question, they are told that a gram of fat has 9 calories. Therefore, they must convert the number of fat grams to calories. Then, they need to calculate this number of calories as a percentage of the total calories given for a Big Mac®. Only one other item on this scale received a higher score.

Estimating Literacy Performance Across the Levels

The literacy levels not only provide a means for exploring the progression of information-processing demands across each of the scales, but also can be used to help explain how the proficiencies individuals demonstrate reflect the likelihood they will respond correctly to the broad range of tasks used in this assessment as well as to any task that has the same characteristics. In practical terms, this means that individuals performing at 250 on each scale are expected to be able to perform the average Level 1 and Level 2 tasks with a high degree of proficiency – *i.e.* with an average probability of a correct response at 80 per cent or higher. It does not mean that they will not be able to perform tasks in Levels 3 or higher. They would be expected to do so some of the time, but not consistently.

Tables A.1 to A.3 display the probability that individuals performing at selected points on each of the scales will give a correct response to tasks of varying difficulty. For example, a reader whose prose proficiency is at 150 points has less than a 50 per cent chance of giving a correct response to the Level 1 tasks. Individuals whose proficiency score is 200, in contrast, have about an 80 per cent probability of responding correctly to these tasks.

TABLE A.1

AVERAGE PROBABILITIES OF SUCCESSFUL PERFORMANCE, IN PER CENT, PROSE SCALE

Prose level	Selected proficiency scores				
	150	200	250	300	350
1	48	81	95	99	100
2	14	40	76	94	99
3	6	18	46	78	93
4	2	7	21	50	80
5*	2	6	18	40	68

* Based on one task.

TABLE A.2

AVERAGE PROBABILITIES OF SUCCESSFUL PERFORMANCE, IN PER CENT, DOCUMENT SCALE

Document level	Selected proficiency scores				
	150	200	250	300	350
1	40	72	94	99	100
2	20	51	82	95	99
3	7	21	50	80	94
4	4	13	34	64	85
5*	< 1	1	3	13	41

* Based on one task.

TABLE A.3

AVERAGE PROBABILITIES OF SUCCESSFUL PERFORMANCE, IN PER CENT, QUANTITATIVE SCALE

Quantitative level	Selected proficiency scores				
	150	200	250	300	350
1*	34	67	89	97	99
2	21	47	76	92	98
3	7	21	51	81	94
4	1	6	22	57	86
5	1	2	7	20	53

* Based on one task.

In terms of task demands, it can be inferred that adults performing at 200 on the prose scale are likely to be able to locate a single piece of information in a brief text when there is no distracting information, or if plausible but incorrect information is present but located away from the correct answer. However, these individuals are likely to encounter far more difficulty with tasks in Levels 2 through 5. For example, they would have only a 40 per cent chance of performing the average Level 2 task correctly, an 18 per cent chance of success with tasks in Level 3, and no more than a 7 per cent chance with tasks in Levels 4 and 5.

In contrast, respondents demonstrating a proficiency of 300 on the prose scale have about an 80 per cent chance or higher of succeeding with tasks in Levels 1, 2 and 3. This means that they demonstrate success with tasks that require them to make low-level inferences and with those that entail taking some conditional information into account. They can also integrate or compare and contrast information that is easily identified in the text. On the other hand, they are likely to encounter difficulty with tasks where they must make more sophisticated text-based inferences, or where they need to process more abstract types of information. These more difficult tasks may also require them to draw on less familiar or more specialised types of knowledge beyond that given in the text. On average, they have about a 50 per cent probability of performing Level 4 tasks correctly; with Level 5 tasks, their likelihood of responding correctly decreases to 40 per cent.

Similar kinds of interpretations can be made using the information presented for the document and quantitative literacy scales. For example, someone who is at 200 on the quantitative scale has, on average, a 67 per cent chance of responding correctly to Level 1 tasks. His or her likelihood of responding correctly decreases to 47 per cent for Level 2 tasks, 21 per cent for Level 3 tasks, 6 per cent for Level 4 tasks and a mere 2 per cent for Level 5 tasks. Similarly, readers with a proficiency of 300 on the quantitative scale would have a probability of 92 per cent or higher of responding correctly to tasks in Levels 1 and 2. Their average probability would decrease to 81 per cent for Level 3 tasks, 57 per cent for Level 4 and 20 per cent for Level 5.

Estimating the Variability of Literacy Tasks Across the Participating Countries

One of the goals in conducting international surveys is to be able to compare populations on common scales. In this study, three literacy scales were used to compare both the distributions of literacy skills and the relationships between literacy skills and a variety of social, educational and labour market variables. The literacy tasks received item parameters that define its difficulty and how well it discriminates among populations of adults. These parameters were determined on the basis of how adults within and across participating countries responded to each task.

Under standard assumptions of IRT, item parameters are thought to be invariant among respondents and among countries as well as subgroups within countries. However, it has been discovered through performing large-scale assessments that this assumption is not always true. Yamamoto (1997) notes that some language/ country populations do respond differently to a subset of literacy tasks. As described in the IALS Technical Report (Murray *et al.*, 1997), individual items were dropped from the assessment if at least seven of the original ten language or country populations were shown not to have the same item parameters – *i.e.* if the response data for a particular item proved to have a poor fit to the item parameters common to the rest of the language or country populations. In addition, if there were items in which only one, two or three countries varied, these countries were allowed to have unique parameters for that item. This resulted in a total of 13 items being dropped from the assessment, with 31 items getting a unique parameter for one language or country population, 16 for two language or country populations, and 6 for three language or country populations. Another way to look at this is that there were a total of 1,010 constraints (114 items minus the 13 dropped times 10 language samples). Of these, unique item parameters were required or allowed in 81 instances, meaning that 92 per cent of the constraints support a common scale across the ten original language or country populations.

These discrepancies were due largely to differences in translations among countries, or to differences in interpretation of scoring rubrics for individual items. The different performance on some items also reflected the variation in language and culture, although no obvious or specific reason could be identified. The fact that not all items had identical item parameters resulted in two types of variation. First, differences could influence the distribution of proficiency scores for a particular language or country group, if only slightly. Analyses indicated that the consequence of using a partially different set of item parameters on the proficiency distribution for a particular population was minimal. For any population, when the proficiency distribution was estimated based either on a set of items which included those common across countries as well as those unique to a given country, or on a set of items which were optimal for a different population, the means and standard deviations of estimated proficiencies differed by less than half of a standard error. Typically, standard errors of estimation ranged between 1 and 3 points on the 500-point scales depending on a particular language or country population.

The second type of variation which results from having a small set of items with unique parameters occurs in the placement of particular tasks along the scales according to their response probability of 80 per cent (RP80). At the beginning of this annex, it was mentioned that a criterion of 80 per cent was used, meaning that tasks were placed along a scale based on the probability that someone with that level of proficiency would have an 80 per cent chance of getting that task and others like it correct. The fact that small subsets of tasks have unique parameters for particular country/language groups results in some tasks falling at different points along each scale.

To evaluate the variability of average probabilities of correct responses (RP80s) for each language or country population, the deviation of RP80s against the common RP80 was examined. It is important to note that no country received all common item parameters. That is, at least one item for each country received a unique set of parameters. However, at least seven of the original language or country populations received common parameters for each of the 101 items. In total, there are 24 language or country groups for which data are currently available to estimate this variation. Nine of the groups are from the first assessment reported in 1995, six are from the assessment cycle reported in 1997 and nine are from the final round of surveys. There were a total of 101 literacy tasks in the assessment so there could be as many as 1,515 deviations (101 times 15).

The mean deviation among the RP80s was 4.7, with a standard deviation of 15.3. This means that the average variation among the RP80s for the literacy tasks was 4.7 points on a 500-point scale, or less than 10 per cent of the 50 points making up a particular literacy level. In addition, a small number of items had large deviations, accounting for a significant percentage of this variation. Only 2 per cent of the deviations observed account for about 35 per cent of the average deviation. In other words, 98 per cent of the deviations have a mean of 3.0, or a 35 per cent reduction from the average of 4.7.

Table A.4 shows the average deviation of the RP80s for each of the 23 country or language groups; the average is seen to range from a low of 1.1 for the French-speaking Swiss to 10.3 for Hungary.

TABLE A.4

AVERAGE DEVIATION OF RP80 VALUES BY COUNTRY OR LANGUAGE GROUP

Australia	7.6	Germany	5.3	Poland	5.4
Belgium (Flanders)	5.8	Great Britain	5.2	Slovenia	5.3
Canada (English)	3.6	Hungary	10.3	Sweden	5.2
Canada (French)	3.2	Ireland	4.5	Switzerland (French)	1.1
Chile	3.5	Netherlands	3.4	Switzerland (German)	4.0
Czech Republic	3.7	New Zealand	7.2	Switzerland (Italian)	6.0
Denmark	3.2	Northern Ireland	6.9	United States	2.0
Finland	3.6	Norway (Bokmål)	2.7		

Conclusion

One of the goals of large-scale surveys is to provide information that can help policy makers during the decision-making process. Presenting that information in a way that will enhance understanding of what has been measured and the conclusions to be drawn from the data is important to reaching this goal. This annex has offered a framework for understanding the consistency of task responses demonstrated by adults from a number of countries. The framework identifies a set of variables that have been shown to underlie successful performance on a broad array of literacy tasks. Collectively, they provide a means for moving away from interpreting survey results in terms of discrete tasks or a single number, and towards identifying levels of performance sufficiently generalised to have validity across assessments and groups.

The concept of test design is evolving. Frameworks such as the one presented here can assist in that evolution. No longer should testing stop at assigning a numerical value; it should assign meaning to that number. And, as concern ceases to centre on discrete behaviours or isolated observations and focus is more on providing a *meaningful* score, a higher level of measurement is reached (Messick, 1989).

References

KIRSCH, I.S. and MOSENTHAL, P. (1993), "Interpreting the IEA reading literacy scales", in M. Binkley, K. Rust and M. Winglee (Eds.), *Methodological Issues in Comparative Educational Studies: The Case of the IEA Reading Literacy Study,* National Center for Education Statistics, United States Department of Education, Washington, DC.

KIRSCH, I.S., JUNGEBLUT, A., JENKINS, L., and KOLSTAD, A. (Eds.) (1993), *Adult Literacy in America: A First Look at the Results of the National Adult Literacy Survey,* National Center for Education Statistics, United States Department of Education, Washington, DC.

MESSICK, S. (1989), "Validity", in R. Linn (Ed.), *Educational Measurement*, 3rd edition, Macmillan, New York.

MONTIGNY, G., KELLY, K., and JONES, S. (1991), *Adult Literacy in Canada: Results of a National Study,* Statistics Canada, Catalogue No. 89-525-XPE, Minister of Industry, Science and Technology, Ottawa.

MURRAY, T.S., KIRSCH, I.S., and JENKINS, L. (Eds.) (1997), *Adult Literacy in OECD Countries: Technical Report on the First International Adult Literacy Survey,* National Center for Education Statistics, United States Department of Education, Washington, DC.

YAMAMOTO, K. (1997), "Scaling and scale linking", in T.S. Murray, I.S. Kirsch, and L. Jenkins (Eds.), *Adult Literacy in OECD Countries: Technical Report on the First International Adult Literacy Survey,* National Center for Education Statistics, United States Department of Education, Washington, DC.

ANNEX B

Survey Methodology and Data Quality

Introduction

The International Adult Literacy Survey (IALS) represents a first attempt at undertaking a large-scale household-based assessment of adult literacy skills at the international level. It incorporated an open-ended literacy test conducted in different languages and across different cultures. These features made sound survey methodology and continuous quality control a necessity. At the same time, the unique features of a household-based assessment meant that the international and national study teams were part of an on-going learning process in how to best carry out such surveys.

The methodology guidelines adopted for the IALS explicitly required that participating countries perform each of the survey steps in accordance with certain prescribed data quality procedures. These procedures were enhanced during the second cycle of the survey (SIALS) based on the experience gained from the first round. The enhanced procedures facilitated the effort to achieve a high level of data quality, allowing meaningful analysis and reliable international comparisons.

The IALS was conducted as a household survey of adults, aged 16 to 65 years of age, in each of the participating countries.[1] Each respondent completed a background questionnaire and then a literacy test, of approximately one-hour in length, during a personal interview. The background questionnaire contained a range of questions concerning, for example, the respondent's demographic characteristics, family background, labour force status, reading habits at work and at home, adult education and training, and self-reports on literacy proficiency. The literacy test was comprised of two parts: a core task booklet and a main task booklet. The former contained six easy test items designed to identify very low-literate individuals. Adults who were able to answer at least two of the six core questions correctly proceeded with the main literacy test.

This annex describes the main steps of the survey and explains the data quality procedures that were implemented. Because additional quality measures were taken during the second cycle, the results are presented separately for the countries participating in the first and second rounds.

---

1. Several countries extended their samples to also include persons below 16 and above 65 years of age.

Survey Instruments

During the development stage of the survey, countries were provided with a "master" English-language version of the background questionnaire and task booklets. With respect to the background questionnaire, the master copy clearly indicated which questions were optional or mandatory and whether and how countries could adapt response categories to country-specific needs.

For the task booklets extensive documentation was provided indicating what changes were allowed to the test items. For the SIALS cycle explanations were given of the theory and expected behaviour of each item. For example, one of the literacy tasks was the article about a marathon swimmer reproduced below.

Swimmer completes Manhattan marathon

The Associated Press

NEW YORK – University of Maryland senior Stacy Chanin on Wednesday became the first person to swim three 28-mile laps around Manhattan.

Chanin, 23, of Virginia, climbed out the East River at 96th Street at 9:30 p.m. She began the swim at noon on Tuesday.

A spokesman for the swimmer, Roy Brunett, said Chanin had kept up her strength with "banana and honey sandwiches, hot chocolate, lots of water and granola bars."

Chanin has twice circled Manhattan before and trained for the new feat by swimming about 28.4 miles a week.

The Yonkers native has competed as a swimmer since she was 15 and hoped to persuade Olympic authorities to add a long-distance swimming event.

The Leukemia Society of America solicited pledges for each mile she swam.

In July 1983, Julie Ridge became the first person to swim around Manhattan twice. With her three laps, Chanin came up just short of Diana Nyad's distance record, set on a Florida-to-Cuba swim.

Task: Underline the sentence that tells what Ms. Chanin ate during the swim.

The following changes or adaptations were allowed:

May delete "The Associated Press."

May change 28-mile to 45-km.

May change 9:30 p.m. to 21.30.

May change 28.4 miles to 45.7 km.

Comments: The article shall appear in the bottom right-hand corner of page 2 of the newspaper. The items eaten by Ms. Chanin must be written in a sentence that appears in the 3rd paragraph of the first column.

The description of what the task was trying to measure was provided by:

This is a locate task.

Directive specifies that a single sentence must be located in article in newspaper.

Article is relatively short making the locate task easier.

No exact match between question and text (for example, can't match on "ate").

Low-level inference required (banana, etc. = food = ate).

No other food mentioned in the article to act as a distractor.

Once such changes had been implemented the adapted and translated items and test booklets were reviewed at Statistics Canada. Any deviations from the guidelines were noted and given in writing to the country to either correct or to provide an explanation as to why the change could not be made.

Moreover, as a result of the pilot test, any items that failed the study's standards for psychometric equivalence were identified and countries requested to verify possible translation, adaptation or scoring problems. With this additional information in hand the countries were able to further improve the adaptations and translations of their instruments.

Target Population and Frame Coverage

Each country designed a sample that should be representative of their civilian, non-institutionalised population aged 16-65. Only a small number of exclusions were acceptable. Table B.1a and Table B.1b show the high rate of coverage achieved by each of the participating countries.

Countries were encouraged to field sample sizes large enough to yield 3,000 completed cases after non-response, so that secondary analysis and estimates of literacy profiles could be obtained reliably.

TABLE B.1a		
SURVEY COVERAGE AND EXCLUSIONS (FIRST CYCLE)		

Country	Coverage (per cent)	Exclusions
Australia	98	Members of the permanent armed forces, non-Australian diplomats, all persons in special dwellings, all persons in the aboriginal strata of Queensland and the Northern Territory
Belgium[1] (Flanders)	99	Residents of institutions
Canada	98	Residents of institutions, persons living on Indian reserves, members of the armed forces, residents of the Yukon and Northwest Territories
Ireland	100	None
Netherlands	99	Residents of institutions
New Zealand	99	Residents of institutions; offshore islands, onshore islands, waterways and inlets
Poland	99	Persons residing in the country for less than three months
Sweden	98	Persons living in institutions (including those doing their military service), persons living abroad during the survey period
Switzerland (French and German)	89	Persons in Italian and Rhaeto-Romanic regions, persons in institutions, persons without telephones
United Kingdom	97	Residents of institutions; the Scottish Highlands and islands north of the Caledonian Canal
United States	97	Members of the armed forces on active duty, those who reside outside the country, those without a fixed household address

1. The Belgium IALS-sample is representative of the "Flemish Region", excluding Brussels. Therefore, the label "Flanders" is used throughout this publication, rather than the more conventional "Flemish Community".

	TABLE B.1b	
	SURVEY COVERAGE AND EXCLUSIONS (SECOND CYCLE)	

Country	Coverage (per cent)	Exclusions
Chile	98	Residents of institutions; persons in remote areas
Czech Republic	98	Residents of institutions; members of the armed forces; citizens living abroad
Denmark	99	Residents of institutions
Finland	94	Residents of institutions; citizens living abroad; persons with Swedish as the mother tongue
Hungary	99	Residents of institutions; persons without a fixed address
Norway	99	Residents of institutions for more than six months
Portugal	91	Labour force survey exclusions; some remote areas with very small populations
Slovenia	98	Residents of institutions; refugees; foreigners
Switzerland (Italian)	99	Residents of institutions; persons without a telephone

The tests could be conducted in more than one language in a country. Canada, Norway and Switzerland chose to do so. In Canada respondents were given a choice of English or French. In Norway surveys were conducted in Bokmål and Nynorsk. In Switzerland, samples drawn from French, German or Italian-speaking cantons (mostly Ticino) were required to respond in those respective languages (Rhaeto-Romanic-speaking regions were excluded). For the Italian-speaking sample in Switzerland, the target sample size was fixed at 1,500 cases – the number necessary for producing reliable literacy profiles.

In all countries, when respondents could not speak the designated test language, attempts were made to collect information through the background questionnaire so as to allow for the imputation of missing literacy information and hence reduce the possibility of biased results.

Table B.2 shows the target populations and the test languages used in each country. Although the common target population was people aged 16-65, individual countries were free to sample younger or older adults. Canada, Sweden and Switzerland sampled persons at least 16 years of age but with no upper limit, while the Netherlands sampled persons aged 16 to 74, and Australia sampled those aged 15 to 74. Chile also took this opportunity, including young adults 15 years of age.

The total number of respondents in IALS over both of the two cycles is given in Table B.2c.

Sample Design

The IALS required all countries to employ a probability sample representative of the national population aged 16-65. No single sampling methodology was imposed due to differences in the data sources and resources available in each of the participating countries. A thorough review of the designs was conducted by Statistics Canada prior to the data collection operations to ensure that countries met the required sampling criteria. The second cycle required countries to supply more detailed sampling documentation. As such, a more comprehensive review was possible. The sample designs used by the participating countries are described below. Numbers of survey respondents refer to the full samples, see Tables B.6a and B.6b.

TABLE B.2a

TEST LANGUAGE, TARGET POPULATION SIZE AND NUMBER OF SURVEY RESPONDENTS (FIRST CYCLE)

Country	Test language	Population aged 16-65	Survey respondents aged 16-65
Australia	English	11,900,000	8,204
Belgium (Flanders)	Dutch	4,500,000	2,261
Canada	English French	13,700,000 4,800,000	3,130 1,370
France	French	36,432,474	2,996
Germany	German	53,800,000	2,062
Ireland	English	2,200,000	2,423
Netherlands	Dutch	10,500,000	2,837
New Zealand	English	2,100,000	4,223
Poland	Polish	24,500,000	3,000
Sweden	Swedish	5,400,000	2,645
Switzerland	French German	1,000,000 3,000,000	1,435 1,393
United Kingdom	English	37,000,000	6,718
United States	English	161,100,000	3,053

TABLE B.2b

TEST LANGUAGE, TARGET POPULATION SIZE AND NUMBER OF RESPONDENTS (SECOND CYCLE)

Country	Test language	Population aged 16-65	Survey respondents aged 16-65
Chile	Spanish	9,400,000	3,502
Czech Republic	Czech	7,100,000	3,132
Denmark	Danish	3,400,000	3,026
Finland	Finnish	3,200,000	2,928
Hungary	Hungarian	7,000,000	2,593
Norway	Bokmål	2,800,000	3,307
Portugal	Portuguese	6,700,000	1,239
Slovenia	Slovenian	1,400,000	2,972
Switzerland (Italian)	Italian	200,000	1,302

TABLE B.2c

TOTAL NUMBER OF RESPONDENTS (FIRST AND SECOND CYCLES)

Survey cycle	Survey respondents aged 16–65
First	44,754
Second	24,001
Total	**68,755**

Sample Designs—First Cycle

Australia: Sample selection in Australia was carried out using the same probability framework that is used for the Monthly Population Survey, an important large-scale household survey. This was a multi-stage area design where the first stage of sampling selects census collection districts, the second stage dwellings and the final stage one person per household. The total number of respondents was 9,302 persons.

Belgium (Flanders): The designated area of Flanders was divided into statistical sectors, from which 200 were selected with probability proportional to size. Then, 40 persons were chosen from a complete list of persons for each of these selected sectors. Finally, in order to get an equal distribution of persons by education level, the chosen persons were then selected into the final sample based on their level of education. Those people who were not sampled due to their education level were given a short questionnaire but these results were not included as part of the sample. This procedure explains, in part, the relatively low response rate achieved for the final sample. The total number of respondents was 2,261.

Canada: Two samples were combined. The main IALS sample was a sub-sample of the May 1994 Canadian Labour Force Survey (LFS) file using probability sampling at all stages. The sub-sample of 6,427 LFS respondents was stratified, with an over-sample of certain target groups of policy interest. The sample yielded 4,703 respondents. The other sample was a three-stage probability sample of Francophones from the province of Ontario selected from the 1991 census. This sample resulted in 1,044 respondents. The total number of respondents was 5,660.

Germany: The country used a master sample of sampling points, with the selection of addresses being made using the random route method. At each of the 525 sampling points, a single random route of addresses was followed, and along each route eight addresses were selected. In each household one person was selected for interview using the Kish method. The sample comprised 4,033 addresses, of which 997 did not belong to the target population. The total number of respondents was 2,062.

Ireland: Probability sampling was used at each of three stages of selection used. At the first stage of sampling, district electoral divisions were selected by stratum, where strata were defined in terms of population size and urban/rural type. Within each selected division, electoral registers were used to select a household. One adult per household was then selected randomly according to their date of birth. The total number of respondents was 2,423.

Netherlands: The Dutch approach was to use two-stage systematic sampling. In the first stage, postal codes were selected; in the second, one address was chosen from each selected postal code. The person to be interviewed in each sampled household was determined randomly according to their date of birth. The total number of respondents was 3,090.

New Zealand: The initial sampling frame was a list of geographical regions ("meshblocks"). The country was stratified by region and population size, and meshblocks were selected within strata with probability proportional to size. Households were then randomly selected within the meshblock. Finally, a Kish sampling grid was used to select one person per household. The total number of respondents was 4,223.

Poland: Poland used a stratified, multi-stage design employing probability sampling at the various stages. The sample was selected from the Polish National Register of Citizens, a register that covers all persons living permanently (longer than three months) in the country. The total number of respondents was 3,000.

Sweden: A stratified, self-weighting master sample was used. The sample was drawn from a national register of individuals. The total number of respondents was 3,038.

Switzerland (French and German): The target population was divided into two strata, corresponding to German- and French-speaking regions. Household telephone numbers were selected, and in each household the first member by alphabetical order of first name was selected. A complementary sample was selected in the canton of Geneva, using the same methods as the principal sample. The total number of respondents was 3,000.

United Kingdom: Two samples were selected – one for Great Britain and the other for Northern Ireland. In Great Britain, the Postal Code Address file was used to select the initial sample of addresses by postal code sectors. At each of the 35 addresses contained within each sector, the Kish method was used to select one adult. In Northern Ireland, a list of all private addresses was used to select an initial systematic sample of 7,000. At each of these addresses, one person was selected using the Kish method. The United Kingdom had a total sample of 6,718 respondents, 3,811 from Great Britain and 2,907 from Northern Ireland.

United States: The sample was selected from housing units undergoing their final Current Population Survey interviews during the period March-June 1994. A probability sample of 4,901 persons was selected using a disproportionate stratified design, with strata formed by race/ethnicity and education. This allocation was designed to provide an efficient linkage of the IALS survey to the earlier National Adult Literacy Survey (NALS). Students residing on college or university campus were excluded from the sample. The total number of respondents was 3,053.

All 12 first-cycle countries used probability sampling for most of the stages of their sample designs; in fact, ten used it in all stages. Two countries – Switzerland and Germany – used a non-probability sampling method in one stage of their multi-stage designs. Switzerland selected one household member using an alphabetic sort. This selection method is expected to yield unbiased results because of the unlikely correlation between first name and literacy skill level. Germany used the "random walk" method for selecting households for the sample. This non-probability method is often used with area frames because of practical constraints – namely the cost associated with enumerating every household within a geographic area, necessary for a probability sample. With non-probability sampling, there is no information about the properties of the resulting estimates, and so no definitive statement about their data quality can be made. This is not to say that the quality is better or worse than that of a probability sample; rather, the quality level is unknown. This issue is examined in greater detail in Murray *et al.* (1997).

Sample Designs – Second Cycle

Chile: A four-stage stratified sample design was used, with sampling units in a sequence extending from districts, census sectors, dwellings to individuals. Stratification of districts was performed according to region and type (urban/rural). Districts were selected with probability proportional to size in a systematic manner. In selected districts, census sectors were drawn again with probability proportional to size. A list of dwellings and individuals was drawn in those selected sectors during a preliminary visit. Dwellings were selected using the method of moving blocks and one individual in each selected dwelling was selected at random using a Kish table. Highly educated individuals were given a probability of selection twice as high as other individuals. The total number of respondents was 3,583.

Czech Republic: An area frame was used where primary sampling units were census units, defined as parts of cities, towns or villages with an average number of 80 households. Stratification of census units was done by size of locality and region. Selection of census units was carried out with probability proportional to the number of households, ensuring that there were at least two selections per stratum. The second stage of selection consisted in selecting an equal number of households in each unit, from an available list of households in those selected units. Finally, one individual was selected at random in each selected household, using a Kish table. The total number of respondents was 3,132.

Denmark: The sampling frame was the Population Register, which is kept up-to-date and includes all people living in Denmark. Individuals were directly selected from the frame at random. Stratification was done according to age and region. The total number of respondents was 3,026.

Finland: The sample of individuals was selected from the Central Population Register by systematic random sampling. The frame was sorted by a unique domicile code and by age. The sort order ensured implicit proportional stratification according to geographical population density. The total number of respondents was 2,928.

Hungary: The sampling frame was composed of two parts: a self-representing component (Budapest and the county seats) and the rest of the country. In the self-representing component, individuals were directly selected from the computerized database of the Central Office of Elections and Registration. In the rest of the country, stratification took place according to counties and size of settlements. The settlements themselves were the primary sampling units, selected with probability proportional to size. Individuals were then selected at random using the same database as for the self-representing component. The same number of individuals was selected in each settlement, which resulted in a self-weighting design. The total number of respondents was 2,593.

Norway: The sampling frame was composed of two parts: a self-representing component of municipalities with a population of 30,000 and over, and the rest of the country. In the self-representing component, individuals were directly selected from the Population Register in a systematic fashion. In the rest of the country, deep stratification took place first according to counties and second to a variety of characteristics. Primary sampling units were single municipalities or groups of municipalities, selected with probability proportional to size. At the second stage of selection (first in the self-representing component), individuals were further stratified according to their education, in order to over-sample individuals at both ends of the education spectrum. Individuals were selected using systematic sampling. The sample was supplemented by a special sample of job seekers, selected from a special register according to procedures similar to the main sample. The total number of respondents was 3,307.

Slovenia: The sample design was a two-stage cluster sample. The primary units were enumeration areas with an average size of 50 households. Stratification was performed implicitly as areas were sorted according first to regions and second to urban-rural type. Areas were selected with probability proportional to the number of eligible individuals. The Population Register maintained by the Ministry of Inner Affairs was used for the selection of individuals. Individuals in selected areas were sorted according to the street, house number, and family name and sampled in a systematic fashion. The total number of respondents was 2,972.

Switzerland (Italian): The sample covered only the Italian-speaking part of Switzerland, which includes the Canton of Ticino and the Italian-speaking regions of the Grison. A two-stage stratified sample of individuals was selected, where phone numbers represented the primary sampling units. Stratification of phone numbers took place according to statistical districts and territorial subdivisions. Individuals in contacted households were randomly selected according to pre-determined random numbers. The total number of respondents was 1,302.

The enhanced data quality procedures imposed during the second cycle of the survey led to the outcome that all countries implemented statistically sound sampling designs.

Portugal: The country conducted a literacy survey as part of an EU-sponsored research project undertaken independently of both IALS cycles but using a similar methodology and identical test instruments. For this reason the country was not subject to the data quality procedures and checks imposed on other participating countries. Based on information taken from ONS (2000), the following methodology was applied.

The Portuguese IALS sample was based on a follow-up to the Labour Force Survey where a two-stage sample was selected from the responding LFS sample. At the first stage, one sixth of the responding sample from the LFS was selected, and stratified according to their highest level of educational attainment. Individuals were randomly selected within each stratum from statistical sections (approximately 300 dwellings; some remote areas with very small populations were excluded). In order to ensure that sufficient items were completed for scaling, the sample was weighted towards more highly educated respondents; 10 per cent of the IALS sample were drawn from the group which had completed primary education, and 45 per cent each from those who had completed the first level of secondary education and the second level of secondary education or higher.

Because high levels of non-response were anticipated, one or two substitutes with the same characteristics were selected for each sampled individual. In total, 3,020 individuals were selected. Substitution was used when sampled individuals could not be located, when they refused to take part, were unable to respond or did not complete at least one third of the questions in the background questionnaire, the core booklet and the test booklet.

Data Collection and Processing

The IALS survey design combined educational testing techniques with those of household survey research to measure literacy and provide the information necessary to make these measures meaningful. The respondents were first asked a series of questions to obtain background and demographic information on educational attainment, literacy practices at work and at home, labour force information, adult education participation and literacy self-assessment.

Once the background questionnaire had been completed, the interviewer presented a booklet containing six simple tasks. Respondents who passed the screener test were given a much larger variety of tasks, drawn from a pool of 114 items, in a separate booklet. Each booklet contained about 45 items. These tests were not timed and respondents were urged to try each exercise in their booklet. Respondents were given maximum leeway to demonstrate their skill levels, even if their measured skills were minimal.

Data collection for the IALS project took place between 1994 and 1998, depending in which of the survey cycles a country participated. Table B.3 presents the collection periods.

To ensure high quality data, the IALS Survey Administration Guidelines[2] specified that each country should work with a reputable data collection agency or firm, preferably one with its own professional, experienced interviewers. The manner in which these interviewers were paid should encourage maximum response. The interviews were conducted in homes in a neutral, non-pressuring manner. Interviewer training and supervision was to be provided, emphasising the selection of one person per household (if applicable), the selection of one of the seven main task booklets (if applicable), the scoring of the core task booklet, and the assignment of status codes. Finally the interviewers' work was to have been supervised by using frequent quality checks at beginning of data collection, fewer quality checks throughout collection and having help available to interviewers during the data collection period.

---

2. For the IALS a large number of guidelines, technical specifications and other documents were written and made available to the national study teams in the participating countries. Examples are the IALS International Planning Report, the IALS Sampling Guidelines, the IALS Survey Administration Guidelines and the IALS Scoring Manual. These documents are available from the Special Surveys Division of Statistics Canada.

TABLE B.3a

SURVEY COLLECTION DATES (FIRST CYCLE)

Country	Collection date
Australia	May through July 1996
Belgium (Flanders)	1996
Canada	September through October 1994
Germany	September through November 1994
Ireland	1996
Netherlands	September through December 1994
New Zealand	1996
Poland	October 1994 through January 1995
Sweden	October 1994 through February 1995
Switzerland (French and German)	1994
United Kingdom	1996
United States	October through November 1994

TABLE B.3b

SURVEY COLLECTION DATES (SECOND CYCLE)

Country	Collection date
Chile	May through June 1998
Czech	December 1997 through March 1998
Denmark	April, May and August 1998
Finland	February until June 1998
Hungary	August through September 1998
Norway	November 1997 through May 1998
Portugal	1998
Slovenia	September through November 1998
Switzerland (Italian)	March through September 1998

The IALS took several precautions against non-response bias, as specified in the IALS Administration Guidelines. Interviewers were specifically instructed to return several times to non-responding households in order to obtain as many responses as possible. In addition, all countries were asked to trace respondents who had moved, where applicable according to the sample design.

During the SIALS cycle, data collection questionnaires were completed by study managers in order to demonstrate that the guidelines had been followed. Table B.4 presents information about interviewers derived from these questionnaires.

As a condition of their participation in the IALS, countries were required to capture and process their files using procedures that ensured logical consistency and acceptable levels of data capture error. Specifically, countries were advised to conduct complete verification of the captured scores (*i.e.* enter each record twice) in order to minimize error rates. Because the process of accurately capturing the test scores is essential to high data quality, 100 per cent keystroke validation was needed.

TABLE B.4

INTERVIEWER INFORMATION (SECOND CYCLE)

Country	Number of interviewers	Number of supervisors	Interviewer experience
Chile	230	12	About one-half of the interviewers were university students in the social sciences and the rest were professional survey interviewers with an average experience of two years
Czech Republic	No information provided		
Denmark	112	5	Professional interviewers with between five and ten years of experience
Finland	135	3	Professional interviewers with on average 13 years of service
Hungary	150	5	Professional interviewers
Norway	150	6	Professional interviewers with on average five years of survey experience
Slovenia	127	8	About 90 per cent were experienced in interviewing. The others had little or no survey experience
Switzerland (Italian)	56	2	Interviewers were trained especially for this survey

Each country was also responsible for coding industry, occupation, and education using standard coding schemes such as the International Standard Industrial Classification (ISIC), the International Standard Occupational Classification (ISCOC) and the International Standard Classification of Education (ISCED). Coding schemes were provided by Statistics Canada for all open-ended items, and countries were given specific instructions about the coding of such items.

In order to facilitate comparability in data analysis, each IALS country was required to map its national dataset into a highly structured, standardised record layout. In addition to specifying the position, format and length of each field, the international record layout included a description of each variable and indicated the categories and codes to be provided for that variable. Upon receiving a country's file, Statistics Canada performed a series of range checks to ensure compliance to the prescribed format. In the SIALS cycle, Statistics Canada additionally ran consistency and flow edits on the data files received. When anomalies were detected, countries were notified of the problems and were asked to submit cleaned files.

Scoring of the Literacy Tests

Persons charged with scoring in each IALS country received intense training in scoring responses to the open-ended items using the IALS Scoring Manual. To further ensure accuracy, countries were monitored as to the quality of their scoring in two ways.

First, within a country, at least 20 per cent of the tests had to be re-scored. The two sets of scores needed to match with at least 95 per cent accuracy before the next step of processing could begin. In fact, most of the intra-country scoring reliabilities were above 97 per cent. Where errors occurred, a country was required to go back to the questionnaires and booklets and re-score all the questions with problems and all the tests that belonged to a problem scorer.

Second, an international re-score was performed. Each country had 10 per cent of its sample re-scored by scorers in another country. For example, a sample of test booklets from the United States was re-scored by the persons who had scored Canadian English booklets, and vice versa. The main goal of the re-score was to verify that no country scored consistently differently from another. Inter-country score reliabilities were calculated by Statistics Canada and the results were evaluated by the Educational Testing Service based in Princeton. Again, strict accuracy was demanded: a 90 per cent correspondence was required before the scores were deemed acceptable. Any problems detected had to be re-scored. Table B.5 shows the high level of inter-country score agreement that was achieved.

Survey Response and Weighting

The IALS instrumentation consisted of three parts: (i) the background questionnaire, for demographic information about the respondent; (ii) the core tasks booklet, which identifies respondents with very low levels of literacy; and (iii) the main tasks booklet, used to calibrate the literacy levels.

TABLE B.5a

INTER-COUNTRY RE-SCORE RELIABILITY (FIRST CYCLE)

Original country	Number of booklets re-scored	Average agreement (per cent)	Re-scored by
Australia	300	96	New Zealand
Belgium (Flanders)	300	94	Netherlands
Canada (English)	158	97	United States
Canada (French)	142	97	France
Germany	270	94	Switzerland
Ireland	300	97	United States
Netherlands	300	96	Netherlands*
New Zealand	300	98	Australia
Poland	300	97	Canada
Sweden	300	97	Sweden*
Switzerland (French)	154	96	France
Switzerland (German)	153	96	Germany
United Kingdom / Great Britain	300	97	Northern Ireland
United Kingdom / Northern Ireland	300	98	Great Britain
United States	315	97	Canada

* The Netherlands and Sweden carried out both inter and intra re-scoring internally due to lack of available language experts in Dutch and Swedish; separate groups were established to perform the re-score.

TABLE B.5b

INTER-COUNTRY RE-SCORE RELIABILITY (SECOND CYCLE)

Original country	Number of booklets re-scored	Average agreement (per cent)	Re-scored by
Chile	349	92	Italy
Czech Republic	349	86	Canada
Denmark	350	88	Canada
Finland	354	95	Hungary
Hungary	346	91	Slovenia
Norway	346	90	Denmark
Portugal	n.a.	n.a.	n.a.
Slovenia	349	90	Canada
Switzerland (Italian)	327	80	Canada

Note: Inter-rater reliabilities for the SIALS countries are high but generally somewhat lower than those for the IALS countries. This result is thought to be due to greater language heterogeneity in the second round of data collection.

The definition of an IALS respondent is a person who has fully or partially completed the background questionnaire. With this information, as well as the reason why the tasks booklet was not completed, it was possible to impute a literacy profile (given a sufficient number of complete responses). Thus the IALS procedures stressed that at a minimum the background questionnaire should be completed by every person sampled. Table B.6 summarises the response rates achieved by the participating countries.

The variation in the number of out-of-scope cases appropriately reflects the fact that all countries used different sample designs.

At a meeting prior to the main data collection for the second survey, countries had been asked to provide their overall sample size, the one that would yield the requested number of respondents (1,500 or 3,000) after non-response. They had also been advised against selecting additional samples in order to reach their target. The idea was to avoid any use of quota samples. Nonetheless, two countries – the Czech Republic and Denmark – did select additional samples. Given the small size of these additional samples (especially for Denmark), and the fact that satisfactory response rates had been obtained for both countries, it was felt that any potential impact of the additional samples would be negligible.

TABLE B.6a

RESPONSE RATES BY COUNTRY (FIRST CYCLE)

Country	Age range	Number of respondents	Response rate (per cent)
Australia	15-74	9,302	96
Belgium (Flanders)[1]	16-65	2,261	36
Canada	16+	5,660	69
Germany	16-65	2,062	69
Ireland	16-65	2,423	60
Netherlands[1]	16-74	3,090	45
New Zealand	16-65	4,223	74
Poland[2]	16-65	3,000	75
Sweden	16+	3,038	60
Switzerland (French and German)	16+	3,000	55
United Kingdom	16-65	6,718	63
United States	16-65	3,053	60

1. Non-response follow-up surveys were conducted.

2. The response rate for Poland includes only the first wave of sampled persons, before interviewer follow-up.

TABLE B.6b

RESPONSE RATES[1] BY COUNTRY (SECOND CYCLE)

Country	Age range	Initial sample	Additional sample	Total sample	Out-of-scope cases	Number of respondents	Response rate[1] (per cent)
Chile	15-65	5,200		5,200	384	3,583	74.4
Czech Republic	16-65	5,000	643	5,643	554	3,132	61.5
Denmark	16-65	4,500	115	4,615	9	3,026	65.7
Finland	16-65	4,250		4,250	10	2,928	69.1
Hungary	16-65	5,000		5,000	9	2,593	52.0
Norway	16-65	5,500		5,500	68	3,307	60.9
Portugal	16-65	2,086		2,086	7	1,239	59.6
Slovenia	16-65	4,290		4,290	12	2,972	69.5
Switzerland (Italian)	16-65	4,000		4,000	1,229	1,302	47.0

1. Calculated as the number of respondents divided by the total sample minus out-of-scope cases.

The reason that low response rates are of concern in any survey is that bias might exist in the resulting estimates. Several precautions against non-response bias were taken. Interviewers were instructed to return several times to non-responding households in order to obtain as many responses as possible. In addition, all sample designs included some over-sampling. This refers to the inclusion in a sample of more randomly selected households than are necessary for the required number of completed interviews, to ensure a sufficient number of responses. Finally, the IALS sampling guidelines included an adjustment during the weighting procedure to help correct for non-response bias.

This correction, known as post-stratification, adjusts the population weights so that they match known population counts, *e.g.* by age group or education level. All countries post-stratified their data to such counts. The underlying assumption behind this compensation for non-response is that the respondents and non-respondents have the same literacy profile for the characteristic for which the adjustment is made. Table B.7 indicates the applied non-response adjustments.

TABLE B.7a

POST-STRATIFICATION VARIABLES BY COUNTRY (FIRST CYCLE)

Country	Benchmark variables
Australia	Age, sex, region
Belgium	Age, sex, education
Canada	Province, economic region, census metropolitan area, age, sex, in-school youth, out-of-school youth, unemployment insurance recipients, social assistance recipients
Germany	Number of household members aged 16-65, age, sex, citizenship
Ireland	Area, sex, age
Netherlands	Region, age, sex, education
New Zealand	Sex, age, household size, urban/rural
Poland	Region, urban/rural, age
Sweden	Region, education, age, sex
Switzerland (French and German)	Number of household members aged 16-65, total number of persons in the household, level of education, size of community, age, sex
United Kingdom	Education, employment, region, age, sex
United States	Education

TABLE B.7b

POST-STRATIFICATION VARIABLES BY COUNTRY (SECOND CYCLE)

Country	Benchmark variables (number of categories)
Chile	Urban/rural (2), age (5), sex (2)
Czech Republic	Education (4), age (3), sex (2), then region (8)
Denmark	Region (4), education (3), age (5), sex (2)
Finland	Province (6), education (5), age (5), sex (2), population density (3)
Hungary	Region (4), age (5), sex (2)
Norway	Age (5), sex (2), then education (3)
Portugal	Age (2), sex (2), education (3)
Slovenia	Age (10), sex (2)
Switzerland (Italian)	Education (3), age (3), sex (2)

In the Czech Republic and Norway post-stratification was done in two stages. As a result, final estimates would not coincide perfectly with the benchmark totals obtained for the first group of variables.

Overall Assessment of Data Quality

In-depth analysis of data quality issues was implemented in the second cycle for each country. Through these analyses a few problems were identified with certain methodologies that could potentially have an effect on international comparability. These problems are described below.

Hungary: Two problems occurred in Hungary. First, the response rate in Budapest was extremely low, at 26 per cent compared with 55 per cent or higher for other regions of the country. Second, the data suggest that quota sampling was used in rural areas. This gives rise to a concern about the probabilistic nature of the sample. As a consequence, the presence of bias with a non-negligible impact on the literacy estimates for the country cannot be ruled out.

Norway: It appears that the replicate weights produced for the calculation of the precision of the estimates do not appropriately reflect the sample design used in the country. The complication is not related to the fact that the country fielded surveys of both national languages, one of Bokmål and the other of Nynorsk. As a consequence, variances, coefficients of variation and confidence intervals will be slightly underestimated. Estimates of literacy levels are not affected.

Switzerland (Italian): Switzerland has a rather low response rate (47 per cent). A non-response follow-up study indicated that the problem was due mainly to the selection of the sample of individuals. Analysis of the results revealed an over-representation of women, which called into question the random nature of the selection. An independent investigation carried out by the Swiss Federal Statistical Office confirmed that a sizeable proportion of interviewers had not properly followed the procedures for random selection. The Swiss Italian-speaking sample is considered to be somewhat biased in favour of people most likely to be at home during the day.

Conclusion

The primary goal of the International Adult Literacy Survey was to generate valid, reliable and comparable profiles of adult literacy skills both within and between countries, a challenge never before attempted. The findings presented in this report leave little question that the study has produced a wealth of data of importance to public policy, a fact that has whetted the appetite of policy makers for more.

The IALS study also set a number of scientific goals, many of which were related to containing measurement error to acceptable levels in a previously untried combination of educational assessment and household survey research. The data presented in this annex suggest that the study achieved many of these goals, often to a remarkable degree.

References

MURRAY, T.S., KIRSCH, I.S., and JENKINS, L.B. (Eds.) (1998), *Adult Literacy in OECD Countries: Technical Report on the First International Adult Literacy Survey,* National Center for Education Statistics, US Department of Education, Washington DC.

ONS (2000), *Measuring Adult Literacy: The International Adult Literacy Survey in the European Context*, Office for National Statistics, London.

ANNEX C

Note on International Comparability of IALS Data

Introduction

After the completion of data collection and analysis for the first group of countries participating in the International Adult Literacy Survey (IALS), and before publication of the findings (OECD and Statistics Canada, 1995), France withdrew its results from the study. The European Commission (EC) then commissioned a review of the IALS, undertaken by the United Kingdom Office of National Statistics (ONS).[1] Before that review commenced, data for a further four countries or regions had been collected. These were published in 1997, together with those already reported in the 1995 publication (OECD and Human Resources Development Canada, 1997). While the ONS review was underway, data were being gathered by the nine additional countries or regions included in the current report. The ONS review was published (ONS, 2000) as the current report was being prepared. This note provides a considered response to some of the criticisms of IALS raised in the review.

The IALS brought together, in a novel way, the procedures of educational measurement and those of household surveys. Data from the three rounds of IALS, provided in this volume, attest to the fact that the skills that have been measured differ across countries in interesting ways and seem to play a key role in the labour market outcomes of individuals and societies.

With the novelty has come some controversy. The French withdrawal, which came despite French participation in the design, development and testing of the study, was motivated by concerns about the comparability of the IALS results about to be published, especially that they tended to underestimate the true literacy skills of the adult population of France relative to the populations of other countries participating in the survey. Three specific objections raised were said to have resulted in an underestimation of French literacy levels. One was that the test items were biased in favour of "Anglo-Saxon" cultures, at the expense of Latin cultures, due to the origins of the survey in North America. A second was that the translation and adaptation of some items into French had increased their difficulty level. The third was that French respondents had been less motivated than respondents in other countries.

A review of the IALS methods, conducted by three independent international experts prior to the first publication, recommended that the results be published but

---

1. The review was in part also motivated by a desire on the part of the Commission to explore the feasibility of eventually undertaking a European Adult Literacy Survey.

identified several ways in which survey methods could be improved (Kalton *et al.*, 1995). Potential weaknesses in the IALS methods were further documented in the technical report produced following the first round of IALS data collection (NCES, 1998). The ONS review (ONS, 2000) offers a range of evidence and opinion on the IALS methodology and on the validity, reliability and comparability of the IALS data, specifically in the European context. It is focused exclusively on the methods employed in the first round of IALS data collection so it does not reflect the enhancements that were incorporated into the second and third waves of data collection, a point that ONS acknowledges (p. 239).

The IALS Programme of Work

By the mid-1980s, some policy makers had become dissatisfied with the use of educational attainment as a proxy for what workers and students knew and could do (Niece and Adset, 1992). This dissatisfaction manifested itself in a desire to measure such skills more directly, through the administration of actual proficiency tests. Jones (1998a) characterises three different approaches to direct assessment:

- Item models, which make no attempt to generalise beyond the actual test items themselves;

- Competency models, which assume that general performance is perfectly correlated with performance on the items selected for inclusion in the test; and

- Skill models, which rely on explicit theories of item difficulty to support generalisation beyond the items selected for inclusion in the test.

The IALS opted for the latter approach. In particular, it was built upon the theoretical and methodological insights offered by four large-scale North American surveys that embodied skill models:

- the Functional Reading Study conducted in the United States by the Educational Testing Service in the early 1970s;

- the Young Adult Literacy Study conducted in the United States by the Educational Testing Service in 1985;

- the Survey of Literacy Skills Used in Daily Activities conducted in Canada by Statistics Canada in 1989; and

- the National Adult Literacy Survey conducted in the United States by the Educational Testing Service in 1990.

International interest in the results of these studies was sufficiently great for a consortium consisting of Statistics Canada, the United States National Center for Education Statistics and the Educational Testing Service to decide to develop and subsequently field the IALS in collaboration with the OECD, EUROSTAT and the UNESCO Institute for Education. Interested countries, including France, participated in the design of the IALS instrumentation and methods and nine, including France, fielded the pilot survey designed to validate the instrumentation and data collection methods. All countries reviewed the empirical results of the pilot survey and agreed to implement the study as specified. Of the texts used for test items in the final assessment, 48 per cent were drawn from the United States and Canada, a fact dictated in large measure by the decision by the participating countries to link IALS to the scales originating from the NALS study. The rest of the test items were drawn largely from European countries,[2] as shown in Table C.1.

---

2. Mexico and Taiwan participated in the early development of the project, but were unable to collect data. The Dutch study team co-operated very actively in the design of the study and submitted a large number of prototype texts for consideration by the teams from other countries. Table C.1 indicates that quite a few texts of Dutch origin made it into the final assessment. Poland and Sweden joined the survey at a late stage and hence were unable to contribute prototype texts.

TABLE C.1

SOURCES OF TEXTS FOR LITERACY ITEMS USED IN THE FIRST ROUND OF IALS

Country of origin	Number of texts	Per cent of texts
United States	17	44
Canada	2	5
Mexico	2	5
North America subtotal	**21**	**54**
France	2	5
Germany	4	10
Ireland	1	2
Netherlands	9	24
Europe subtotal	**16**	**42**
Taiwan	2	5
Asia subtotal	**2**	**5**
Total	**39**	**100**

Participating countries were required to translate and adapt the model English-language assessment instruments into their national languages. A quality assurance protocol was put in place to minimise the impact of the process of translation and adaptation on the psychometric equivalence of the instruments. This procedure involved a re-translation and review of the adapted assessment with a view to identifying problematic adaptations and negotiating appropriate modifications. A second review of problematic items was conducted on the basis of the results from the pilot survey, which had identified a small number of poorly performing items. In these cases the problems were either fixed or the item was dropped from the assessment. Several items with problems were identified in the course of the review of the instruments from various countries but national study teams were not in all cases willing to implement the suggested alterations. This points to a weakness in the collegial approach employed in the IALS study – achieved quality depended ultimately on the ability of participants to adhere to agreed specifications and procedures. To the extent that participants are unwilling, or lack sufficient resources or technical expertise to comply with procedures, the comparability and quality of the resultant estimates will be diminished.

In the first stage of the data analysis carried out for IALS a statistical procedure was used to determine empirically whether some test items performed differently in some countries, most often due to difficulties in translation and adaptation. The difficulty indices calculated for each item and country indicate not only whether differences in the relative difficulty level of items may have occurred but also the extent of the deviation. In the IALS analyses, such deviating items were permitted to have unique difficulty parameters for the country concerned rather than the international difficulty parameters. This strategy minimised any bias in the estimation of overall literacy levels of the country that would have been due to shifts in relative difficulty of the test items. Since the adjustment depends on shifts in relative difficulty of individual items, the procedure could not detect whether an effect on difficulty might have occurred across all the items for a country. Overall, 92 per cent of the items satisfied the criterion of consistent relative difficulty across all countries and were assigned international difficulty parameters in all cases.[3] The numbers of items for which unique national parameters were required to accommodate arbitrary shifts in relative difficulty are shown in Table C.2.

---

3. See Table 10.8 in NCES (1998), p. 171.

TABLE C.2

Uɴɪǫᴜᴇ ɪᴛᴇᴍ ᴅɪꜰꜰɪᴄᴜʟᴛʏ ᴘᴀʀᴀᴍᴇᴛᴇʀꜱ ꜰᴏʀ ᴄᴏᴜɴᴛʀɪᴇꜱ ɪɴ ꜰɪʀꜱᴛ ʀᴏᴜɴᴅ ᴏꜰ **IALS**

Country	Number of unique items
Canada (English)	12
Canada (French)	8
France	6
Germany	12
Netherlands	11
Poland	1
Sweden	14
Switzerland (French)	2
Switzerland (German)	3
United States	4

The information in Table C.2 shows that, for France, six items were detected as having their relative difficulty levels shifted by the translation and adaptation processes. This suggests that 23 out of 27 items identified in the INED (Institut National d'Etudes Démographiques) analysis performed as designed.

Conclusions Concerning the ONS Review

The ONS research study was divided into several distinct strands, each designed to explore a different aspect of the IALS methodology. The ONS report is divided into two parts: Part A provides expert opinion on the approach taken to measurement and scaling whereas Part B presents empirical evidence based upon secondary analysis of IALS data and upon additional data collected in several countries. Of these two, the latter information is particularly useful as it is based on new empirical evidence.

For the purposes of this annex, it is useful to re-group the ONS material into the following three categories: conclusions with respect to survey practice in Europe, conclusions with respect to the psychometric models used to summarize the IALS proficiency results, and conclusions with respect to the translation and adaptation of instruments and the issue of differential motivation.

Sᴜʀᴠᴇʏ ᴘʀᴀᴄᴛɪᴄᴇ ɪɴ Eᴜʀᴏᴘᴇ

The review of survey practice centred on three aspects:

- Sample design and sampling procedures;
- Survey experience; and
- Field work organisations and survey processing.

The results of the ONS review are somewhat mixed. With respect to IALS methods, as applied in the first round of data collection, it identifies several cases where an unnecessary amount of inter-country variation in execution was permitted, variation that may or may not have had a deleterious impact on the comparability of survey results. Given the differences in technical expertise and institutional infrastructure that exist between countries, some variability is unavoidable in this type of study. What is clear, however, is that the reduction of such variation depends on the presence of clear and realistic standards, consortia of skilled and experienced institutions, sufficient budgets to fulfil the complex technical and operational demands imposed in such a study, well developed quality assurance procedures to minimise deviation from specification and to identify problems at a stage where they can be dealt with and, finally, and perhaps most importantly, a willingness on the part of participating countries to adhere to agreed standards and guidelines. In many respects, this goal has been achieved over the course of the second and third round of IALS data collection, where more stringent specifications and quality assurance procedures helped to reduce unnecessary inter-country variation in survey practice.

In an effort to assess the impact that variation in administration might have had on the comparability of national mean proficiency, ONS selected representative sub-samples of IALS respondents in Great Britain, France, Portugal[4] and Sweden and re-tested them using "best practice" survey methods (ONS, 2000, p. 9). The results for the "best practice" and IALS control groups are published in ONS (*op. cit.*, pp. 172-177).[5] Only in Great Britain did the use of "best practice" collection procedures yield small but statistically significant improvement in assessed proficiency levels – in other countries the results obtained were, for all intents and purposes, the same as in the original IALS (*op. cit.*, p. 177).

PSYCHOMETRIC MODELS USED TO SUMMARISE *IALS* PROFICIENCY RESULTS

The ONS report presents conflicting views among experts on the advisability of the reliance in IALS on Item Response Theory[6] (IRT) to provide summary measures of proficiency for population subgroups. On the one hand, Albert Beaton of Boston College and Director of a number of international and US national surveys of student performance asserts that use of an IRT is the best method for handling large-scale assessment data (ONS, 2000, pp. 26-33). He cites its successful use in all of the recent international comparative assessments and in virtually all large-scale assessment programmes at national and sub-national level.

In contrast, Harvey Goldstein of the Institute of Education in London argues that IRT does not provide a satisfactory basis for test development, psychometric calibration or, as a consequence, country comparisons (*op. cit.*, pp. 34-40). Goldstein reaches this conclusion solely on theoretical grounds. Despite the fact that the IALS database has been available to interested researchers since 1996, the alternative models he commends have not been tested empirically. His conclusions also seem somewhat counter-intuitive in the face of evidence from extensive analyses of the IALS data sets conducted by researchers in participating countries, analyses that reveal a high degree of both internal and external coherence in the data set.

Goldstein makes a further point that reflects a clear division of opinion about how the science and art of measurement in education is best approached. The strategy that Goldstein prefers is first to gather data with a wide variety of tasks and then to explore the dimensionality that may be present in the data. An alternative strategy is to start with a clear theory of the phenomenon to be measured, grounded in prior empirical research, and to have it guide the test development process. Dimensionality is then not something to be discovered but something imposed on the design but then verified using actual data. As mentioned in Annex A, the IALS test development team used the work of Kirsch and Mosenthal as the theoretical view of literacy with which to construct its instruments. The IRT used provided the means to test the conformity of the data to the theoretical model. The efficacy of the theory was confirmed with analyses showing that a large proportion of the observed variability in item difficulties could be predicted from the theory.[7]

---

4. In Portugal the IALS assessment was administered to a sample based on the national labour force survey.
5. IALS estimates of mean levels and distributions of literacy skills in France are given on pages 181-185 of the ONS publication.
6. Referred to also as Item Response Models in the scholarly literature.
7. The proportions of variance accounted for were 80 per cent for the prose scale, 88 per cent for the document scale and 78 per cent for the quantitative scale, see Table 7.8 in NCES (1998, p. 127).

Patrick Heady of ONS shares Goldstein's preference for empirical "discovery" of dimensionality rather than *a priori* specification of it (ONS, 2000, pp. 99-117). Unlike Goldstein who suggests that more dimensions could have been established if a different item set had been used, Heady concludes that fewer dimensions are needed to account for the IALS data than the three imposed by the applied theory, namely prose, document and quantitative literacy. While this might be statistically true, it would transform the IALS assessment from a skill model to a competency or even an item model. Such simplification would, by focusing more on discrete behaviours and isolated observations, reduce the meaningfulness and interpretability of the resultant scale and result in a serious downgrading of the quality of measurement (Messick, 1989). Assessments such as the IALS attempt to incorporate representative samples of both individuals and the domains of interest. A reductionist approach, such as the one Heady proposes, would compromise the latter objective and, thereby, seriously reduce both the scientific and face validity of the measures in the eyes of the end users of the data.

TRANSLATION AND ADAPTATION OF INSTRUMENTS AND DIFFERENTIAL MOTIVATION

Alain Blum and France Guérin-Pace of the Institut National d'Etudes Démographiques (INED) in Paris identify items in the French version of the IALS instruments that they believe to have translation and adaptation problems, but fail to establish whether these errors had any significant impact on the French results in IALS. Of the 27 problematic items identified by Blum and Guérin-Pace in their INED analysis, four had been assigned unique French difficulty parameters rather than the international difficulty parameters used for the IALS analysis.[8] Furthermore, individual respondents answered only some of the total set of items used in the survey. To determine whether the problems of translation and adaptation of the IALS instruments in France affected the French results, it is not enough to know only how many items were affected. One has to know also what was the impact on the actual results for the population subgroups answering particular blocks of items. An analysis that draws information value from the entire response pattern for all of the population subgroups and that accounts for the underlying proficiency distribution using major covariates of literacy skills such as educational attainment, conducted by the Educational Testing Service, concludes that the anomalies identified by Blum and Guérin-Pace are spurious and have no impact on the ability of the IALS test to discriminate and reflect relative item difficulty and proficiency.

While Blum and Guérin-Pace provide no conclusive evidence on the key question of whether the national estimates for France were significantly affected by the problems of translation they identify, there is evidence elsewhere in the ONS report in the results of a sub-sample of original French IALS respondents re-tested with "corrected" assessment instruments[9] and the "best practice" data collection procedures. The estimates of mean proficiency obtained from this exercise are within the standard error of the original estimates, suggesting that the net impact of translation and adaptation errors on the comparability of French results with those of other countries was insignificant.

At a broader level, claims of cultural bias in favour of respondents of "Anglo-Saxon" origin[10] are not supported by similar re-test data for Portugal. In 1996, literacy estimates for Portugal were obtained using tests based upon the IALS theoretical framework and applying the IALS collection methods but employing only authentic

---

8. The 27 poorly fitting items were identified using proportion correct scores, and not on the basis of the plausible values generated by the two-parameter model that was applied. Proportion correct scores can offer a basis for deriving crude estimates but should not be used for ranking the countries.

9. Among other measures, the Swiss-French instrument was used.

10. The heterogeneity of the 28 populations in the countries that participated in the IALS extends far beyond primarily English-speaking populations.

Portuguese texts and tasks, as well as a much simpler scaling method to derive the proficiency estimates for the adult population (Benevente *et al.*, 1996). Re-testing of a representative sub-sample of these respondents, as part of the ONS review, with IALS instruments duly adapted into Portuguese and results scaled using the IALS item response model, provides estimates of mean literacy proficiency that are not statistically different from the original estimates. Were serious cultural bias a factor this simply would not be the case.

Suggesting that potential cultural bias in the initial test materials and problems of translation and adaptation had no substantial impact on the French IALS results is not to say that these issues are unimportant. In order to guard further against the possibility of linguistic, cultural or geographic biases in the forthcoming Adult Literacy and Lifeskills (ALL) survey, for example, item development has been undertaken by an extensive international network. As a result, the pilot instruments proposed for the ALL survey have been drawn from 15 languages and more than 25 countries.

Finally, several small-scale experiments with the payment of financial incentives (ONS, 2000, p. 9), in-depth follow-up interviews conducted with sub-samples of respondents in several European countries (*op. cit.*, Chapters 9 and 12) and analysis of test interview duration, item omission and item-not-reached rates published in the IALS Technical Report (Jones, 1998b) suggest that differential motivation is not a factor in explaining differences in national proficiency levels.

Conclusion

As with any new measurement technology, much room remains for improvement. In each successive round of collection, quality assurance procedures have been enhanced and extended in response to identified problems. The initial design assumption in IALS was that instrument adaptation, particularly of the assessment instruments, was the design element that carried the most inherent risk. Thus, most quality assurance procedures deployed in the first round of collection were devoted to the psychometric aspects of the study.

Post-collection evaluation of achieved quality suggests, however, that most quality concerns identified were associated with the more pedestrian aspects of household survey research, such as selection of a representative sample of the adult population, administration of the survey instruments in keeping with a prescribed set of collection procedures and processing of data (NCES, 1998). Quality assurance procedures related to these aspects of the study were, therefore, enhanced in the subsequent rounds of data collection for IALS.

One must not lose sight of the fact that the measurement technology deployed in IALS is new, combining two previously distinct measurement traditions – educational assessment and social survey. The IALS Technical Report (NCES, 1998), the annexes included in the international IALS publications and the ONS study each identify areas for improvement. Many of these improvements were, in fact, incorporated into subsequent rounds of data collection in IALS. Thinking prospectively, more improvements will be incorporated in the design and implementation of the planned ALL survey. Further development will depend largely on continued international co-operation and on the emergence of an associated empirical research literature, the basis for most scientific advance.

References

BENEVENTE, A., ROSA, A., DA COSTA, F., and AVILA, P. (1996), *A Literacia em Portugal: Resultados de uma pesquisa extensiva e monographica,* Fundacao Calouste Gulbenkian and Conselho Nacional de Educacao, Lisbon.

JONES, S. (1998a), "Measuring adult basic skills: A literature review", in A.C. Tuijnman, I.S. Kirsch and D.A. Wagner (Eds.), *Adult Basic Skills: Innovations in Measurement and Policy Analysis*, Hampton Press, Creskil, NJ.

JONES, S. (1998b), "Incentives and the motivation to do well", *Adult Literacy in OECD Countries: Technical Report on the First International Adult Literacy Survey*, National Center for Education Statistics, United States Department for Education, Washington, DC.

KALTON, G., LYBERG, L., and REMPP, J.M. (1995), "Review of methodology, Statistics Canada, Ottawa", Reprinted in NCES (1998), *Adult Literacy in OECD Countries: Technical Report on the First International Adult Literacy Survey*, National Center for Education Statistics, United States Department for Education, Washington, DC.

MESSICK, S. (1989), "Validity", in R. Linn (Ed.), *Educational Measurement,* 3rd edition, McMillan, New York.

NCES (1998), *Adult Literacy in OECD Countries: Technical Report on the First International Adult Literacy Survey*, National Center for Education Statistics, United States Department for Education, Washington, DC.

NIECE, D., and ADSET, M. (1992), "Direct versus proxy measures of adult functional literacy: A preliminary re-examination", *Adult Illiteracy and Economic Performance*, OECD, Paris.

MURRAY, T.S. (Forthcoming), "The assessment of adult literacy: History and prospects", Background Papers for the 2000 INES General Assembly, OECD, Paris

OECD and STATISTICS CANADA (1995), *Literacy, Economy and Society: Results of the First International Adult Literacy Survey,* Paris and Ottawa.

ONS (2000), *Measuring Adult Literacy: The International Adult Literacy Survey in the European Context*, Office for National Statistics, London.

STATISTICS CANADA (1990), "An international assessment of adult literacy: A proposal", Unpublished mimeo, Ottawa.

ANNEX D

Data Values for the Figures

This annex presents data tables showing the numeric values used for the production of the graphs featured in the text. For clarity, the countries are ordered alphabetically into three groups according to the period in which most of the main data collection occurred. The fact that some countries collected data a few years earlier or later than others is thought not to affect the international comparability of the survey data because the literacy population profiles are quite stable and are normally expected to change only slowly with the passing of time.

The values in parentheses are the standard errors of the estimates. Standard jack-knife procedures have been used for the calculation of these errors, which should be seen as indicators of the probable range of error, given that other methods might produce slightly different results. For information about the reliability and comparability of data values not derived from IALS the reader is referred to the original sources.

All IALS estimates based on less than 30 cases are flagged with an asterisk (*). In all such cases the estimates are considered to be unreliable, even though the standard errors might be small. In certain cases, countries did not include all of the common questions in their background questionnaire, or asked them in ways that differed from the standard format. Such cases are noted by a dash (—).

TABLE 1.1

OECD[1] MANUFACTURING TRADE[2] BY TECHNOLOGY INTENSITY (INDEX 1985 = 100)

	High technology	Medium-high technology	Medium-low technology	Low technology	Total manufacturing
1985	100	100	100	100	100
1986	121	124	107	123	119
1987	145	147	125	150	143
1988	177	166	142	168	162
1989	194	177	157	177	174
1990	226	205	178	206	202
1991	243	207	175	210	205
1992	258	222	179	226	218
1993	262	212	171	214	210
1994	298	240	186	236	235
1995	361	286	222	275	279
1996	379	294	223	276	285

1. Total OECD excludes Czech Republic, Hungary, Korea, Mexico and Poland.
2. Average value of exports and imports.

Source: OECD (1999), *Science, Technology and Industry Scoreboard 1999.*

TABLE 1.2

KNOWLEDGE-BASED INDUSTRIES AND SERVICES

	Medium-high technology manufactures	High technology manufactures	Communication services	Finance, insurance and other business services	Community, social and personal services	Total
Australia	3.16	0.93	2.93	26.13	14.86	48.01
Austria	9.64 [1]	x	2.91	25.24	5.97	43.76
Belgium	8.68 [1]	x	2.20	35.37 [2]	x	46.25
Canada	6.05	2.19	3.29	24.09	15.39	51.01
Denmark (1995)	6.86	1.77	2.48	23.93	7.04	42.07
Finland	8.17	2.99	2.99	24.48	3.44	42.08
France	7.02	2.97	2.87	29.10	8.00	49.95
Germany	11.07	2.86	2.57	42.08 [2]	x	58.57
Greece (1995)	2.01	0.89	2.39	33.58 [2]	x	38.88
Iceland (1995)	0.68	0.00	2.34	21.76	6.65	31.42
Italy	6.39	1.45	2.13	31.37	x	41.33
Japan	8.61	3.75	2.98	37.67 [2]	x	52.99
Korea	8.39	5.35	2.37	19.51	4.68	40.31
Mexico	6.42	1.78	1.59	17.82	13.98	41.59
Netherlands (1995)	5.01	2.72	2.51	27.51	12.46	50.22
New Zealand (1995)	3.85	0.52	3.59	26.41	5.51	39.88
Norway	4.12	0.87	2.55	21.09	6.63	35.26
Portugal (1993)	3.95	1.45	2.80	16.42	9.25	33.87
Spain (1994)	7.18	1.58	2.48	20.41	6.27	37.93
Sweden (1994)	9.13	2.65	3.00	30.29	5.65	50.72
United Kingdom (1995)	7.22	3.26	3.31	28.33	9.38	51.51
United States	6.12	3.03	2.95	30.79	12.36	55.25
EU (1994)	7.69	2.54	2.72	35.46 [2]	x	48.42
OECD (1994)	6.95	2.92	2.84	38.19 [2]	x	50.89

x Included in the preceding category.
1. Includes high-technology manufactures.
2. Includes community, social and personal services.

Source: OECD (1999), *Science, Technology and Industry Scoreboard 1999.*

TABLE 1.2 (concluded)

KNOWLEDGE-BASED INDUSTRIES AND SERVICES

	Knowledge-based industry	Total business sector		Knowledge-based industry	Total business sector
Australia	4.3	3.4	Mexico (1988-96)	3.8	2.9
Austria	3.7	2.9	Netherlands (1986-95)	2.9	2.7
Belgium	3.0	2.4	Norway	1.7	3.2
Canada	3.2	2.3	Portugal (1986-93)	6.9	4.6
Denmark (1985-95)	1.4	2.0	Spain (1986-94)	2.9	2.5
Finland	4.0	2.0	Sweden (1985-94)	2.4	1.7
France	2.8	2.0	United Kingdom	4.1	2.9
Germany	3.7	2.5	United States	3.1	3.0
Greece (1985-95)	2.9	1.8			
Italy	2.8	2.2	EU (1986-94)	3.1	2.4
Japan	4.0	3.3			
Korea	12.5	9.1	OECD (1986-94)	3.4	2.9

Source: OECD (1999), *Science, Technology and Industry Scoreboard 1999.*

TABLE 1.3   See text, page 5

TABLE 1.4

EMPLOYMENT GROWTH RATES BY INDUSTRY AND BY TECHNOLOGY INTENSITY, TOTAL OECD (INDEX 1980=100)

	By industry[1]					Total manufacturing	By technology intensity			
	Whole-sale and retail trade, hotels and restaurants	Transport, storage and communi-cations	Finance, insurance, real estate and business services	Com-munity, social and personal services	Total services		High-tech-nology	Medium-high-tech-nology	Medium-low-tech-nology	Low-tech-nology
1980	100.00	100.00	100.00	100.00	100.00	100.00	100.00	100.00	100.00	100.00
1981	101.18	100.14	103.60	102.85	101.87	98.29	102.19	97.99	97.19	98.38
1982	101.28	99.99	106.27	106.19	103.21	94.59	100.92	93.37	92.95	95.18
1983	102.47	99.36	110.42	110.04	105.35	92.77	102.73	90.39	89.88	94.24
1984	105.85	99.97	116.53	114.49	109.08	93.76	109.68	91.56	90.77	93.80
1985	108.01	100.86	122.15	118.83	112.20	93.76	111.77	92.41	89.72	93.39
1986	109.90	102.03	127.87	122.26	115.02	93.58	113.42	92.11	88.79	93.42
1987	112.63	102.98	135.27	127.12	118.82	93.82	111.43	92.63	88.81	94.09
1988	115.11	104.40	141.10	131.95	122.32	95.16	113.48	94.32	90.21	95.01
1989	117.53	106.68	146.97	137.16	126.01	96.21	114.78	96.13	91.74	95.12
1990	118.53	107.46	151.57	143.26	128.92	96.39	114.44	96.99	92.35	94.62
1991	118.13	107.32	151.83	148.47	130.16	95.11	112.72	96.05	91.02	93.21
1992	117.89	107.41	152.29	153.08	131.37	93.43	109.33	94.69	89.16	91.82
1993	118.39	108.27	155.50	156.27	133.06	91.55	104.84	92.14	87.76	90.68
1994	118.02	107.22	159.03	160.76	134.52	91.09	102.33	91.40	87.92	90.45
1995	118.41	107.38	162.54	165.03	136.41	90.62	103.29	91.81	87.49	89.14

1. Aggregated International Standard Industry Classification (ISIC) categories.
Source: OECD (1998), *Technology, Productivity and Job Creation.*

TABLE 1.5   See text, page 7

TABLE 1.6

PER CENT CONTRIBUTIONS OF OCCUPATIONAL CATEGORIES TO AVERAGE ANNUAL EMPLOYMENT GROWTH
BETWEEN INDICATED YEARS

		White-collar high-skilled workers	All other occupational categories
Australia	(1986-91)	1.09	0.71
Canada	(1981-91)	0.87	0.45
Finland	(1980-90)	0.86	-0.47
France	(1982-95)	0.55	-0.51
Germany	(1980-90)	0.55	-0.12
Ireland	(1987-95)	0.80	0.92
Italy	(1981-95)	0.28	-0.58
Japan	(1980-90)	0.56	0.32
New Zealand	(1981-95)	1.25	0.74
United Kingdom	(1981-95)	0.91	-0.53
United States	(1983-93)	0.68	1.18

Source: OECD (1998), *Technology, Productivity and Job Creation.*

TABLE 1.7

PER CENT CONTRIBUTIONS OF OCCUPATIONAL CATEGORIES TO AVERAGE ANNUAL EMPLOYMENT GROWTH
IN MANUFACTURING AND SERVICES BETWEEN INDICATED YEARS

		Manufacturing				Services			
		White-collar high-skilled workers	White-collar low-skilled workers	Blue-collar high-skilled workers	Blue-collar low-skilled workers	White-collar high-skilled workers	White-collar low-skilled workers	Blue-collar high-skilled workers	Blue-collar low-skilled workers
Australia	(1986-91)	0.61	0.11	0.03	-0.50	1.55	0.83	0.01	0.34
Canada	(1981-91)	0.42	0.08	-0.20	-0.75	1.06	0.83	0.01	0.12
Finland	(1980-90)	0.37	-0.15	-1.03	-0.87	1.28	0.54	0.01	0.10
France	(1982-90)	0.34	-0.21	-0.22	-1.43	1.07	0.45	0.02	0.19
Germany	(1980-90)	0.34	0.02	-0.01	-0.53	0.84	0.62	0.13	-0.15
Italy	(1981-91)	0.21	-0.05	-0.99	-0.48	0.56	0.72	0.09	0.25
Japan	(1980-90)	0.33	0.52	-0.15	0.22	0.74	0.97	-0.11	0.13
New Zealand	(1981-91)	0.06	-0.23	-1.73	-0.74	2.68	0.49	-0.10	0.19
United Kingdom	(1981-91)	0.29	-0.56	-0.88	-0.94	1.40	0.48	-0.04	-0.02
United States	(1983-93)	0.14	-0.09	-0.08	-0.10	0.85	1.39	0.07	0.22

Source: OECD (1998), *Technology, Productivity and Job Creation.*

TABLE 2.1

MEAN SCORES, STANDARD DEVIATIONS, AND SCORES AT THE 5TH, 25TH, 75TH AND 95TH PERCENTILES ON A SCALE WITH
RANGE 0-500 POINTS, PROSE, DOCUMENT, AND QUANTITATIVE LITERACY SCALES, POPULATION AGED 16-65, 1994-1998

	5th percentile	25th percentile	Mean		Standard deviation	75th percentile	95th percentile
A. Prose							
Canada	144.5	242.6	278.8	(3.2)	10.0	321.7	363.4
Germany	199.6	245.0	275.9	(1.0)	11.2	308.0	350.2
Ireland	159.6	230.6	265.7	(3.3)	19.8	307.4	352.3
Netherlands	202.8	257.7	282.7	(0.8)	30.0	312.7	349.0
Poland	115.3	194.4	229.5	(1.1)	15.3	272.3	318.1
Sweden	214.0	271.1	301.3	(0.8)	11.9	335.1	381.1
Switzerland (French)	150.8	240.6	264.8	(1.7)	12.3	302.6	336.9
Switzerland (German)	150.3	238.2	263.3	(1.4)	10.5	299.2	341.0
United States	136.7	236.7	273.7	(1.6)	10.4	320.0	368.1
Australia	145.1	245.8	274.2	(1.0)	25.5	315.7	359.0
Belgium (Flanders)	161.0	240.3	271.8	(3.9)	30.0	308.8	353.6
New Zealand	164.8	240.7	275.2	(1.3)	19.1	315.3	362.9
United Kingdom	151.2	233.0	266.7	(1.8)	29.2	311.0	353.2
Chile	123.4	186.5	220.8	(2.1)	21.0	259.1	301.4
Czech Republic	195.1	244.1	269.4	(0.8)	28.5	299.2	334.0
Denmark	209.5	253.6	275.0	(0.7)	14.9	301.0	329.6
Finland	198.8	259.0	288.6	(0.7)	27.9	322.2	360.9
Hungary	162.1	214.3	242.4	(1.1)	18.1	274.2	313.3
Norway	208.8	264.1	288.5	(1.0)	16.9	317.5	351.7
Portugal	93.3	172.6	222.6	(3.7)	18.7	272.7	324.6
Slovenia	117.9	192.6	229.7	(1.5)	25.9	272.8	316.9
Switzerland (Italian)	162.8	235.3	264.3	(2.2)	21.3	301.9	337.0
B. Document							
Canada	133.9	243.3	279.3	(3.0)	11.7	326.1	377.4
Germany	207.2	256.1	285.1	(1.0)	17.8	317.8	361.1
Ireland	146.7	225.3	259.3	(3.2)	14.0	300.6	345.3
Netherlands	202.4	260.1	286.9	(0.9)	29.3	319.0	355.6
Poland	85.2	181.1	223.9	(1.8)	11.2	274.3	330.2
Sweden	218.6	276.0	305.6	(0.9)	11.6	341.4	386.8
Switzerland (French)	153.8	246.9	274.1	(1.7)	10.6	313.5	353.6
Switzerland (German)	117.1	241.2	269.7	(2.0)	7.8	313.2	360.1
United States	125.4	230.1	267.9	(1.7)	15.8	315.8	368.0
Australia	143.7	246.0	273.3	(1.0)	26.6	314.1	358.0
Belgium (Flanders)	170.4	251.2	278.2	(3.2)	30.0	314.2	353.6
New Zealand	153.8	233.8	269.1	(1.3)	15.7	312.0	360.5
United Kingdom	143.3	230.2	267.5	(1.9)	30.0	314.4	363.6
Chile	120.4	187.7	218.9	(2.2)	20.0	256.7	299.0
Czech Republic	190.6	249.9	282.9	(0.9)	18.0	318.8	365.8
Denmark	211.5	265.3	293.8	(0.8)	19.5	326.6	363.7
Finland	189.9	257.8	289.2	(0.9)	19.7	326.4	372.2
Hungary	146.4	212.5	249.0	(1.2)	19.2	287.4	341.2
Norway	202.5	268.4	296.9	(1.2)	15.1	331.3	369.5
Portugal	92.7	180.6	220.4	(3.7)	23.5	268.6	314.1
Slovenia	102.1	190.8	231.9	(1.7)	21.5	279.5	327.4
Switzerland (Italian)	167.6	243.8	271.0	(2.2)	25.6	307.6	346.2

TABLE 2.1 (concluded)

MEAN SCORES, STANDARD DEVIATIONS, AND SCORES AT THE 5TH, 25TH, 75TH AND 95TH PERCENTILES ON A SCALE WITH RANGE 0-500 POINTS, PROSE, DOCUMENT, AND QUANTITATIVE LITERACY SCALES, POPULATION AGED 16-65, 1994-1998

	5th percentile	25th percentile	Mean		Standard deviation	75th percentile	95th percentile
C. Quantitative							
Canada	155.1	246.8	281.0	(3.8)	7.8	323.0	375.6
Germany	217.8	265.0	293.3	(1.1)	9.0	323.7	366.5
Ireland	146.2	226.4	264.6	(3.2)	20.5	308.8	360.7
Netherlands	200.9	260.8	287.7	(1.0)	30.0	319.5	359.4
Poland	97.6	192.9	234.9	(1.7)	12.8	286.2	334.9
Sweden	215.9	275.6	305.9	(1.0)	8.9	342.0	390.7
Switzerland (French)	145.7	257.7	280.1	(1.7)	15.8	319.6	356.7
Switzerland (German)	146.1	252.1	278.9	(1.8)	9.9	318.4	357.2
United States	138.3	236.9	275.2	(1.7)	17.2	322.5	376.3
Australia	149.5	246.0	275.9	(1.0)	28.7	316.6	359.9
Belgium (Flanders)	158.4	249.9	282.0	(3.8)	30.0	322.6	369.3
New Zealand	154.1	236.6	270.7	(1.3)	22.3	312.7	360.0
United Kingdom	141.5	230.5	267.2	(1.9)	30.0	314.1	362.0
Chile	83.7	166.5	208.9	(2.8)	18.3	257.9	312.5
Czech Republic	198.1	265.9	298.1	(1.0)	21.4	334.1	381.5
Denmark	219.0	272.1	298.4	(0.7)	19.3	329.5	366.5
Finland	197.1	258.5	286.1	(1.0)	21.7	318.4	356.9
Hungary	162.9	235.2	269.9	(1.4)	14.1	310.4	357.7
Norway	208.9	269.1	296.8	(1.0)	17.4	328.8	367.0
Portugal	103.0	185.3	231.4	(3.8)	22.5	280.0	326.2
Slovenia	106.2	200.7	242.8	(1.9)	21.0	292.0	340.1
Switzerland (Italian)	159.5	241.4	274.4	(2.3)	30.0	314.0	354.7

Source: International Adult Literacy Survey, 1994-1998.

TABLE 2.2

PER CENT OF POPULATION AGED 16-65 AT EACH PROSE, DOCUMENT AND QUANTITATIVE LITERACY LEVEL, 1994-1998

	Level 1		Level 2		Level 3		Level 4/5	
A. Prose								
Canada	16.6	(1.6)	25.6	(1.8)	35.1	(2.4)	22.7	(2.3)
Germany	14.4	(0.9)	34.2	(1.0)	38.0	(1.3)	13.4	(1.0)
Ireland	22.6	(1.4)	29.8	(1.6)	34.1	(1.2)	13.5	(1.4)
Netherlands	10.5	(0.6)	30.1	(0.9)	44.1	(1.0)	15.3	(0.6)
Poland	42.6	(0.9)	34.5	(0.9)	19.8	(0.7)	3.1	(0.3)
Sweden	7.5	(0.5)	20.3	(0.6)	39.7	(0.9)	32.4	(0.5)
Switzerland (French)	17.6	(1.3)	33.7	(1.6)	38.6	(1.8)	10.0	(0.7)
Switzerland (German)	19.3	(1.0)	35.7	(1.6)	36.1	(1.3)	8.9	(1.0)
United States	20.7	(0.8)	25.9	(1.1)	32.4	(1.2)	21.1	(1.2)
Australia	17.0	(0.5)	27.1	(0.6)	36.9	(0.5)	18.9	(0.5)
Belgium (Flanders)	18.4	(1.5)	28.2	(2.1)	39.0	(2.4)	14.3	(1.2)
New Zealand	18.4	(0.9)	27.3	(1.0)	35.0	(0.8)	19.2	(0.7)
United Kingdom	21.8	(1.0)	30.3	(1.2)	31.3	(1.1)	16.6	(0.7)
Chile	50.1	(1.7)	35.0	(1.2)	13.3	(1.2)	1.6	(0.4)
Czech Republic	15.7	(0.5)	38.1	(1.0)	37.8	(0.9)	8.4	(0.4)
Denmark	9.6	(0.6)	36.4	(0.9)	47.5	(1.0)	6.5	(0.4)
Finland	10.4	(0.4)	26.3	(0.7)	40.9	(0.7)	22.4	(0.6)
Hungary	33.8	(1.0)	42.7	(1.4)	20.8	(0.9)	2.6	(0.4)
Norway	8.5	(0.5)	24.7	(1.0)	49.2	(0.9)	17.6	(0.9)
Portugal	48.0	(2.0)	29.0	(2.3)	18.5	(1.2)	4.4	(0.5)
Slovenia	42.2	(1.1)	34.5	(1.0)	20.1	(0.9)	3.2	(0.3)
Switzerland (Italian)	19.6	(1.3)	34.7	(1.5)	37.5	(1.8)	8.3	(0.9)

TABLE 2.2 (concluded)

PER CENT OF POPULATION AGED **16-65** AT EACH PROSE, DOCUMENT AND QUANTITATIVE LITERACY LEVEL, **1994-1998**

	Level 1		Level 2		Level 3		Level 4/5	
B. Document								
Canada	18.2	(1.9)	24.7	(1.5)	32.1	(1.8)	25.1	(1.3)
Germany	9.0	(0.7)	32.7	(1.2)	39.5	(1.0)	18.9	(1.0)
Ireland	25.3	(1.7)	31.7	(1.2)	31.5	(1.3)	11.5	(1.2)
Netherlands	10.1	(0.7)	25.7	(0.8)	44.2	(0.9)	20.0	(0.8)
Poland	45.4	(1.3)	30.7	(1.0)	18.0	(0.7)	5.8	(0.3)
Sweden	6.2	(0.4)	18.9	(0.7)	39.4	(0.8)	35.5	(0.6)
Switzerland (French)	16.2	(1.3)	28.8	(1.4)	38.9	(1.3)	16.0	(1.1)
Switzerland (German)	18.1	(1.0)	29.1	(1.5)	36.6	(0.8)	16.1	(1.0)
United States	23.7	(0.8)	25.9	(1.1)	31.4	(0.9)	19.0	(1.0)
Australia	17.0	(0.5)	27.8	(0.7)	37.7	(0.7)	17.4	(0.6)
Belgium (Flanders)	15.3	(1.7)	24.2	(2.8)	43.2	(4.1)	17.2	(0.9)
New Zealand	21.4	(0.9)	29.2	(1.1)	31.9	(0.8)	17.6	(0.7)
United Kingdom	23.3	(1.0)	27.1	(1.0)	30.5	(1.0)	19.1	(1.0)
Chile	51.5	(1.8)	35.4	(1.0)	11.7	(0.9)	1.5	(0.5)
Czech Republic	14.3	(0.7)	28.0	(1.0)	38.1	(0.9)	19.6	(0.7)
Denmark	7.8	(0.5)	24.2	(0.8)	42.6	(0.9)	25.4	(0.7)
Finland	12.6	(0.5)	24.1	(0.8)	38.1	(0.8)	25.1	(0.6)
Hungary	32.9	(0.9)	34.2	(1.0)	25.0	(0.9)	8.0	(0.7)
Norway	8.6	(0.5)	21.0	(1.0)	40.9	(1.0)	29.4	(1.2)
Portugal	49.1	(2.5)	31.0	(2.4)	16.6	(0.9)	3.2	(0.4)
Slovenia	40.9	(1.1)	31.8	(0.9)	22.0	(0.9)	5.3	(0.5)
Switzerland (Italian)	17.5	(1.3)	30.7	(1.6)	38.3	(1.4)	13.6	(1.1)
C. Quantitative								
Canada	16.9	(1.8)	26.1	(2.5)	34.8	(2.1)	22.2	(1.8)
Germany	6.7	(0.4)	26.6	(1.2)	43.2	(0.8)	23.5	(0.9)
Ireland	24.8	(1.5)	28.3	(0.8)	30.7	(1.0)	16.2	(1.6)
Netherlands	10.3	(0.7)	25.5	(0.9)	44.3	(1.0)	19.9	(0.8)
Poland	39.1	(1.1)	30.1	(1.2)	23.9	(0.6)	6.8	(0.5)
Sweden	6.6	(0.4)	18.6	(0.6)	39.0	(0.9)	35.8	(0.7)
Switzerland (French)	12.9	(0.9)	24.5	(1.4)	42.2	(1.6)	20.4	(1.0)
Switzerland (German)	14.2	(1.0)	26.2	(1.3)	40.7	(1.5)	19.0	(1.3)
United States	21.0	(0.7)	25.3	(1.1)	31.3	(0.8)	22.5	(1.0)
Australia	16.8	(0.5)	26.5	(0.6)	37.7	(0.7)	19.1	(0.6)
Belgium (Flanders)	16.7	(1.8)	23.0	(1.7)	37.8	(2.0)	22.6	(1.3)
New Zealand	20.4	(1.0)	28.9	(1.1)	33.4	(0.8)	17.2	(0.8)
United Kingdom	23.2	(0.9)	27.8	(1.0)	30.4	(0.9)	18.6	(1.0)
Chile	56.4	(1.8)	26.6	(1.1)	14.3	(1.6)	2.6	(0.5)
Czech Republic	8.9	(0.5)	22.3	(0.9)	37.0	(0.9)	31.9	(1.0)
Denmark	6.2	(0.4)	21.5	(0.8)	43.9	(1.2)	28.4	(0.9)
Finland	11.0	(0.4)	27.2	(0.8)	42.1	(0.8)	19.7	(0.6)
Hungary	20.5	(1.0)	31.6	(1.0)	31.7	(1.0)	16.1	(0.8)
Norway	7.7	(0.5)	22.0	(1.0)	42.9	(1.3)	27.4	(1.2)
Portugal	41.6	(2.0)	30.2	(1.8)	23.0	(1.3)	5.2	(0.6)
Slovenia	35.0	(1.2)	30.4	(1.0)	26.0	(1.0)	8.6	(0.6)
Switzerland (Italian)	17.0	(1.4)	28.1	(1.7)	37.9	(1.6)	17.0	(1.9)

Source: International Adult Literacy Survey, 1994-1998.

TABLE 2.3   For data values of Figure 2.3 see Table 2.1, page 135

TABLE 2.4

MEAN PROSE, DOCUMENT AND QUANTITATIVE SCORES ON A SCALE WITH RANGE 0-500 POINTS,
BY LEVEL OF EDUCATIONAL ATTAINMENT, POPULATION AGED 16-65, 1994-1998

	With less than upper secondary education		Completed upper secondary education		Completed tertiary education	
A. Prose						
Canada	233.4	(4.6)	283.8	(3.8)	314.8	(5.3)
Germany	265.6	(1.4)	283.8	(2.2)	310.1	(2.6)
Ireland	238.8	(2.8)	288.2	(2.7)	308.3	(2.6)
Netherlands	257.5	(1.2)	297.0	(1.3)	312.1	(1.4)
Poland	210.5	(1.2)	252.7	(1.6)	277.3	(2.3)
Sweden	275.4	(2.1)	302.3	(1.2)	329.1	(1.7)
Switzerland (French)	228.1	(4.3)	274.1	(2.0)	298.3	(2.7)
Switzerland (German)	227.3	(5.0)	273.4	(1.8)	288.9	(2.4)
United States	207.1	(3.5)	270.7	(2.8)	308.4	(2.5)
Australia	250.6	(1.6)	280.0	(1.3)	310.4	(1.4)
Belgium (Flanders)	242.5	(6.9)	281.0	(2.1)	312.3	(1.7)
New Zealand	252.1	(2.3)	290.6	(1.9)	307.3	(1.5)
United Kingdom	247.9	(2.2)	281.9	(2.7)	309.5	(1.8)
Chile	196.8	(1.7)	243.5	(2.6)	271.4	(2.8)
Czech Republic	254.9	(0.8)	285.5	(1.5)	302.4	(1.9)
Denmark	252.8	(1.1)	278.1	(0.8)	298.5	(1.0)
Finland	261.6	(1.6)	295.9	(1.3)	316.9	(1.4)
Hungary	213.2	(2.1)	249.6	(1.1)	271.2	(2.5)
Norway	254.5	(2.8)	284.4	(1.2)	315.1	(1.0)
Portugal	206.6	(4.5)	291.5	(2.7)	304.8	(2.7)
Slovenia	191.8	(2.4)	243.2	(1.7)	279.2	(2.5)
Switzerland (Italian)	239.7	(4.8)	273.3	(1.7)	302.7	(2.7)
B. Document						
Canada	227.1	(5.7)	288.0	(5.3)	318.4	(4.9)
Germany	276.1	(1.1)	295.4	(2.2)	314.5	(1.6)
Ireland	231.5	(2.6)	280.5	(2.9)	303.5	(3.3)
Netherlands	262.6	(1.5)	302.3	(1.4)	311.2	(1.6)
Poland	201.5	(1.7)	251.5	(2.0)	275.6	(3.9)
Sweden	280.6	(2.4)	308.3	(1.0)	331.2	(2.0)
Switzerland (French)	235.0	(4.1)	283.4	(2.2)	312.5	(2.7)
Switzerland (German)	230.6	(6.2)	283.2	(2.1)	300.4	(2.7)
United States	199.9	(4.6)	266.1	(2.3)	302.5	(2.4)
Australia	248.5	(1.5)	281.9	(1.3)	308.0	(1.2)
Belgium (Flanders)	250.9	(5.3)	288.6	(2.1)	313.3	(1.5)
New Zealand	244.5	(2.3)	287.3	(2.0)	302.1	(1.5)
United Kingdom	247.4	(2.4)	285.5	(3.1)	311.8	(1.9)
Chile	196.5	(2.1)	239.0	(2.9)	266.2	(2.9)
Czech Republic	266.3	(1.0)	301.0	(1.6)	320.1	(2.3)
Denmark	266.9	(1.5)	298.2	(1.0)	319.3	(1.5)
Finland	257.3	(1.7)	297.4	(1.2)	322.3	(1.7)
Hungary	214.1	(2.6)	258.1	(1.5)	280.9	(3.5)
Norway	257.0	(3.8)	293.1	(1.7)	326.7	(1.2)
Portugal	206.7	(4.6)	282.9	(2.3)	289.9	(3.0)
Slovenia	189.5	(2.7)	246.6	(1.8)	285.4	(2.7)
Switzerland (Italian)	248.2	(4.6)	279.6	(1.8)	306.3	(2.9)

TABLE 2.4 (concluded)

MEAN PROSE, DOCUMENT AND QUANTITATIVE SCORES ON A SCALE WITH RANGE 0-500 POINTS, BY LEVEL OF EDUCATIONAL ATTAINMENT, POPULATION AGED 16-65, 1994-1998

	With less than upper secondary education		Completed upper secondary education		Completed tertiary education	
C. Quantitative						
Canada	233.7	(4.5)	285.6	(5.6)	320.5	(6.0)
Germany	285.2	(1.6)	300.2	(2.4)	321.0	(2.4)
Ireland	236.8	(2.6)	285.6	(3.1)	310.5	(3.2)
Netherlands	263.7	(1.6)	300.2	(1.5)	316.2	(2.0)
Poland	213.2	(1.7)	263.2	(1.8)	285.8	(3.2)
Sweden	282.3	(2.1)	307.4	(1.1)	331.7	(2.0)
Switzerland (French)	243.8	(3.8)	293.0	(1.9)	311.7	(3.1)
Switzerland (German)	245.4	(6.4)	289.7	(1.7)	305.3	(2.4)
United States	208.4	(4.8)	270.1	(2.3)	311.8	(2.5)
Australia	250.0	(1.5)	284.7	(1.2)	311.9	(1.3)
Belgium (Flanders)	251.7	(7.0)	291.3	(2.3)	324.2	(2.0)
New Zealand	246.9	(2.3)	287.8	(2.0)	302.9	(1.6)
United Kingdom	246.4	(2.4)	285.0	(2.8)	314.6	(1.8)
Chile	179.2	(2.7)	236.1	(3.6)	272.8	(3.3)
Czech Republic	280.7	(1.2)	317.2	(1.9)	336.7	(2.1)
Denmark	272.3	(1.4)	303.6	(1.1)	321.3	(1.4)
Finland	259.9	(1.6)	291.6	(1.3)	316.2	(1.6)
Hungary	231.5	(2.6)	278.6	(1.5)	308.5	(3.2)
Norway	262.2	(3.5)	291.6	(1.4)	326.6	(1.0)
Portugal	218.0	(4.7)	289.4	(2.4)	304.3	(3.1)
Slovenia	198.2	(2.9)	258.0	(2.0)	300.3	(3.2)
Switzerland (Italian)	246.0	(4.7)	286.3	(2.0)	313.9	(3.6)

Source: International Adult Literacy Survey, 1994-1998.

TABLE 2.5

PER CENT OF POPULATION AGED 16-65 WHO HAVE NOT COMPLETED UPPER SECONDARY EDUCATION, BUT WHO SCORE AT LEVELS 3 AND 4/5 ON THE DOCUMENT SCALE, 1994-1998

	Per cent at Levels 3 and 4/5	
Canada	27.3	(2.7)
Germany	50.6	(1.1)
Ireland	23.0	(1.7)
Netherlands	42.3	(1.2)
Poland	14.0	(0.7)
Sweden	59.3	(2.3)
Switzerland (French)	20.6	(2.8)
Switzerland (German)	24.6	(3.7)
United States	17.1	(1.9)
Australia	37.6	(0.8)
Belgium (Flanders)	40.2	(8.3)
New Zealand	30.3	(1.3)
United Kingdom	36.7	(1.2)
Chile	4.0	(0.6)
Czech Republic	46.2	(1.3)
Denmark	45.0	(1.5)
Finland	39.6	(1.7)
Hungary	11.6	(1.2)
Norway	42.9	(3.9)
Portugal	12.2	(1.1)
Slovenia	11.2	(1.1)
Switzerland (Italian)	34.5	(3.0)

Source: International Adult Literacy Survey, 1994-1998.

TABLE 3.1

MEAN PROSE, DOCUMENT AND QUANTITATIVE SCORES ON A SCALE WITH RANGE 0-500 POINTS,
BY LEVEL OF EDUCATIONAL ATTAINMENT, POPULATION AGED 20-25, 1992-1998

	With less than upper secondary education		Completed upper secondary education		Completed tertiary education	
A. Prose						
Canada	231.3	(36.1)	293.5	(11.9)	309.9	(6.4)
Germany	269.5	(7.7)	298.8	(6.5)	328.9*	(12.9)
Ireland	236.1	(6.8)	287.1	(3.7)	306.2	(5.6)
Netherlands	266.1	(5.3)	305.5	(3.6)	321.8	(6.3)
Poland	227.1	(4.9)	270.0	(4.2)	291.5	(5.7)
Sweden	282.9	(15.2)	311.3	(2.6)	341.0	(5.7)
Switzerland[1]	263.3*	(8.0)	288.6	(3.4)	300.0	(6.1)
United States[2]	227.7	(4.0)	270.2	(2.0)	313.4	(2.3)
Australia	262.3	(3.3)	291.3	(2.2)	312.6	(4.9)
Belgium (Flanders)	259.9*	(13.4)	295.8	(5.9)	319.3	(5.0)
New Zealand	242.2	(10.4)	289.7	(4.2)	313.1	(5.6)
United Kingdom	261.0	(5.5)	290.6	(6.5)	304.7	(7.6)
Chile	206.4	(5.3)	248.6	(3.5)	276.8	(4.0)
Czech Republic	267.5	(4.3)	294.2	(2.3)	325.2	(6.7)
Denmark	257.5	(4.4)	295.5	(1.8)	303.9	(4.3)
Finland	280.2	(9.6)	321.6	(3.1)	336.0*	(5.1)
Hungary	216.4	(6.5)	265.6	(3.1)	287.0	(9.0)
Norway	265.7	(8.7)	298.1	(3.9)	326.9	(3.5)
Portugal	237.9	(4.6)	302.0	(3.0)	315.0	(6.3)
Slovenia	202.9	(7.8)	272.9	(3.9)	300.2	(7.4)
B. Document						
Canada	217.8	(37.0)	301.9	(13.7)	322.6	(9.1)
Germany	277.3	(5.2)	311.3	(6.9)	344.6*	(10.1)
Ireland	230.0	(7.3)	281.1	(3.2)	300.5	(6.9)
Netherlands	273.0	(6.5)	311.7	(3.2)	320.9	(5.9)
Poland	217.4	(6.7)	272.6	(4.2)	292.1	(6.3)
Sweden	292.7	(10.9)	314.4	(2.8)	339.1	(5.5)
Switzerland[1]	265.4*	(16.1)	300.9	(4.5)	316.1	(7.3)
United States[2]	228.0	(4.3)	271.5	(2.1)	312.2	(1.9)
Australia	263.0	(2.9)	293.9	(2.3)	312.4	(4.0)
Belgium (Flanders)	276.2*	(12.9)	303.7	(5.1)	323.3	(4.4)
New Zealand	238.3	(12.1)	291.1	(3.6)	311.0	(5.3)
United Kingdom	261.3	(6.6)	294.6	(7.3)	304.4	(6.6)
Chile	207.1	(5.5)	241.0	(4.5)	272.6	(4.0)
Czech Republic	275.8	(6.4)	311.6	(4.2)	348.0	(8.9)
Denmark	277.4	(5.6)	321.8	(2.0)	327.2	(6.3)
Finland	280.0	(9.7)	325.2	(3.4)	341.0*	(6.6)
Hungary	212.0	(8.9)	276.5	(4.2)	300.7	(9.6)
Norway	265.8	(12.4)	307.6	(5.0)	341.4	(4.1)
Portugal	237.7	(7.5)	288.7	(3.3)	294.7	(7.0)
Slovenia	210.6	(8.9)	277.2	(3.8)	310.0	(6.6)

TABLE 3.1 (concluded)

MEAN PROSE, DOCUMENT AND QUANTITATIVE SCORES ON A SCALE WITH RANGE 0-500 POINTS,
BY LEVEL OF EDUCATIONAL ATTAINMENT, POPULATION AGED 20-25, 1992-1998

	With less than upper secondary education		Completed upper secondary education		Completed tertiary education	
C. Quantitative						
Canada	226.6	(35.7)	286.3	(14.9)	310.9	(7.8)
Germany	282.4	(4.7)	313.2	(6.3)	344.3*	(15.0)
Ireland	233.0	(6.2)	283.6	(4.1)	302.8	(6.8)
Netherlands	266.9	(5.8)	306.4	(3.9)	322.0	(5.6)
Poland	224.0	(5.6)	276.4	(4.4)	289.5	(6.6)
Sweden	288.8	(11.8)	309.3	(2.9)	332.6	(6.0)
Switzerland[1]	274.4*	(8.7)	300.2	(3.4)	307.5	(6.7)
United States[2]	221.9	(4.1)	270.1	(2.2)	310.0	(2.4)
Australia	259.1	(3.2)	291.4	(2.4)	308.5	(4.3)
Belgium (Flanders)	277.1*	(15.1)	304.4	(6.3)	331.5	(5.7)
New Zealand	236.2	(11.4)	286.8	(3.6)	302.5	(5.3)
United Kingdom	251.4	(6.3)	285.8	(6.8)	300.7	(7.0)
Chile	189.9	(8.0)	235.1	(6.9)	275.9	(4.6)
Czech Republic	289.2	(6.1)	320.2	(3.5)	354.0	(9.3)
Denmark	272.5	(5.5)	317.3	(2.5)	321.4	(6.5)
Finland	272.9	(9.3)	308.4	(3.1)	323.0*	(7.6)
Hungary	222.0	(8.6)	291.3	(3.5)	324.7	(10.9)
Norway	264.7	(9.0)	298.7	(4.5)	331.3	(5.5)
Portugal	244.2	(6.4)	294.5	(2.9)	305.3	(6.6)
Slovenia	217.8	(9.4)	286.0	(3.6)	324.0	(8.5)

* Unreliable estimate.

1. Combined estimate for whole country population, 1994 and 1998.

2. Values for the United States youth population are derived from the US National Adult Literacy Survey (1992) because a sampling anomaly involving college students limits the comparability of the IALS data for this cohort.

Note: Belgium (Flanders), Finland, Germany and Switzerland are excluded from Figure 3.1a-c because the data are unreliable.

Sources: International Adult Literacy Survey, 1994-1998; US National Adult Literacy Survey, 1992.

TABLE 3.2

RELATIONSHIP BETWEEN RESPONDENT'S DOCUMENT LITERACY SCORES AND PARENTS' EDUCATION IN YEARS,
POPULATION AGED 16-25, 1992-1998

		Unstandardised Coefficients		Standardised Coefficients	Mean	
		B		β		
Canada	Constant	-1.49	(0.15)			
	Parents' education	0.16	(0.01)	0.34	11.47	(0.07)
Germany	Constant	-1.40	(0.34)			
	Parents' education	0.16	(0.03)	0.27	10.74	(0.07)
Ireland	Constant	-1.52	(0.18)			
	Parents' education	0.15	(0.02)	0.32	9.61	(0.08)
Netherlands	Constant	-0.92	(0.21)			
	Parents' education	0.13	(0.02)	0.32	10.59	(0.09)
Poland	Constant	-2.45	(0.23)			
	Parents' education	0.19	(0.02)	0.31	10.13	(0.07)
Sweden	Constant	-0.22	(0.16)			
	Parents' education	0.08	(0.01)	0.23	10.95	(0.10)
Switzerland[1]	Constant	-1.04	(0.20)			
	Parents' education	0.12	(0.02)	0.30	11.91	(0.09)
United States[2]	Constant	-1.76	(0.05)			
	Parents' education	0.14	(0.00)	0.48	12.41	(0.05)
Australia	Constant	-1.00	(0.12)			
	Parents' education	0.10	(0.01)	0.25	11.26	(0.06)
Belgium (Flanders)	Constant	-0.87	(0.11)			
	Parents' education	0.11	(0.01)	0.39	10.99	(0.10)
New Zealand	Constant	-1.66	(0.26)			
	Parents' education	0.15	(0.02)	0.27	11.47	(0.08)
United Kingdom	Constant	-1.28	(0.23)			
	Parents' education	0.12	(0.02)	0.18	10.78	(0.05)
Chile	Constant	-1.61	(0.07)			
	Parents' education	0.10	(0.01)	0.42	9.10	(0.12)
Czech Republic	Constant	-0.84	(0.20)			
	Parents' education	0.10	(0.02)	0.25	11.27	(0.10)
Denmark	Constant	-1.13	(0.23)			
	Parents' education	0.13	(0.02)	0.29	12.26	(0.07)
Finland	Constant	-0.26*	(0.21)			
	Parents' education	0.08	(0.02)	0.18	11.84	(0.08)
Hungary	Constant	-3.04	(0.26)			
	Parents' education	0.25	(0.02)	0.43	11.58	(0.07)
Norway	Constant	-0.75	(0.21)			
	Parents' education	0.11	(0.02)	0.24	12.35	(0.07)
Portugal	Constant	-1.42	(0.15)			
	Parents' education	0.13	(0.02)	0.32	8.17	(0.10)
Slovenia	Constant	-2.55	(0.20)			
	Parents' education	0.20	(0.02)	0.41	11.40	(0.07)

* Unreliable estimate.

1. Combined estimate for whole country population, 1994 and 1998.

2. Values for the United States youth population are derived from the US National Adult Literacy Survey (1992) because a sampling anomaly involving college students limits the comparability of the IALS data for this cohort.

Note: The values differ slightly from those published previously in *Literacy Skills for the Knowledge Society: Further Results from the International Adult Literacy Survey* (OECD and HRDC, 1997) because the international mean and standard deviation for all 20 countries are used to standardise the estimates.

Sources: International Adult Literacy Survey, 1994-1998; US National Adult Literacy Survey, 1992.

TABLE 3.3

RELATIONSHIP BETWEEN RESPONDENT'S DOCUMENT LITERACY SCORES AND PARENTS' EDUCATION IN YEARS,
POPULATION AGED 26-65, 1994-1998

		Unstandardised Coefficients		Standardised Coefficients		
		B		β	Mean	
Canada	Constant	-1.22	(0.05)			
	Parents' education	0.15	(0.01)	0.47	9.42	(0.06)
Germany	Constant	-0.92	(0.18)			
	Parents' education	0.12	(0.02)	0.17	10.33	(0.03)
Ireland	Constant	-1.64	(0.09)			
	Parents' education	0.18	(0.01)	0.39	8.71	(0.05)
Netherlands	Constant	-1.01	(0.07)			
	Parents' education	0.14	(0.01)	0.35	9.49	(0.04)
Poland	Constant	-2.01	(0.07)			
	Parents' education	0.17	(0.01)	0.40	8.03	(0.05)
Sweden	Constant	-0.56	(0.06)			
	Parents' education	0.13	(0.01)	0.39	9.03	(0.05)
Switzerland[1]	Constant	-1.41	(0.06)			
	Parents' education	0.14	(0.01)	0.41	10.73	(0.04)
United States	Constant	-1.86	(0.10)			
	Parents' education	0.18	(0.01)	0.40	11.21	(0.05)
Australia	Constant	-1.10	(0.04)			
	Parents' education	0.13	(0.00)	0.38	9.86	(0.04)
Belgium (Flanders)	Constant	-0.63	(0.06)			
	Parents' education	0.09	(0.01)	0.33	8.75	(0.08)
New Zealand	Constant	-0.99	(0.07)			
	Parents' education	0.11	(0.01)	0.33	10.22	(0.05)
United Kingdom	Constant	-1.76	(0.10)			
	Parents' education	0.19	(0.01)	0.28	10.06	(0.02)
Chile	Constant	-1.35	(0.03)			
	Parents' education	0.10	(0.00)	0.47	6.59	(0.08)
Czech Republic	Constant	-0.84	(0.08)			
	Parents' education	0.11	(0.01)	0.28	9.89	(0.04)
Denmark	Constant	-1.02	(0.09)			
	Parents' education	0.13	(0.01)	0.31	10.98	(0.03)
Finland	Constant	-0.97	(0.06)			
	Parents' education	0.14	(0.01)	0.40	9.10	(0.05)
Hungary	Constant	-1.57	(0.09)			
	Parents' education	0.13	(0.01)	0.32	9.71	(0.13)
Norway	Constant	-1.16	(0.09)			
	Parents' education	0.15	(0.01)	0.34	10.97	(0.04)
Portugal	Constant	-1.38	(0.05)			
	Parents' education	0.13	(0.01)	0.48	4.33	(0.08)
Slovenia	Constant	-2.17	(0.07)			
	Parents' education	0.17	(0.01)	0.44	9.57	(0.06)

1. Combined estimate for whole country population, 1994 and 1998.

Note: The values differ slightly from those published previously in *Literacy Skills for the Knowledge Society: Further Results from the International Adult Literacy Survey* (OECD and HRDC, 1997) because the international mean and standard deviation for all 20 countries are used to standardise the estimates.

Source: International Adult Literacy Survey, 1994-1998.

TABLE 3.4

MEAN SCORES AND SCORES AT THE 5TH, 25TH, 75TH AND 95TH PERCENTILES ON A SCALE WITH RANGE 0-500 POINTS, PROSE, DOCUMENT, AND QUANTITATIVE LITERACY SCALES, POPULATION AGED 26-35 AND 56-65, 1994-1998

	Age	5th percentile	25th percentile	Mean		75th percentile	95th percentile
A. Prose							
Canada	26-35	179.8	255.2	287.3	(5.0)	326.2	365.6
	56-65	105.3	174.8	234.1	(11.9)	290.3	328.2
Germany	26-35	205.6	255.2	284.3	(3.3)	315.5	353.9
	56-65	178.9	234.9	256.8	(2.0)	283.3	326.0
Ireland	26-35	184.0	246.8	272.3	(3.5)	305.0	344.1
	56-65	127.6	199.4	237.3	(9.3)	283.1	330.8
Netherlands	26-35	219.7	276.0	295.0	(2.0)	322.1	351.6
	56-65	184.6	234.3	255.7	(2.6)	284.2	314.5
Poland	26-35	139.9	212.0	241.8	(2.6)	276.3	322.1
	56-65	84.9	132.2	186.1	(3.7)	233.0	285.9
Sweden	26-35	232.1	291.7	313.5	(2.7)	344.6	381.3
	56-65	179.6	244.7	275.5	(3.6)	309.9	354.7
Switzerland[1]	26-35	157.3	251.5	273.1	(3.7)	307.0	338.4
	56-65	131.2	218.6	243.9	(3.9)	276.1	318.3
United States	26-35	124.8	241.3	275.4	(3.3)	322.4	364.5
	56-65	136.8	238.2	265.6	(3.2)	306.2	356.6
Australia	26-35	186.5	258.5	284.1	(1.1)	321.4	356.7
	56-65	86.8	211.8	241.4	(2.5)	289.1	335.3
Belgium (Flanders)	26-35	179.5	260.0	284.8	(3.4)	320.4	353.2
	56-65	128.3	194.5	234.1	(4.0)	275.0	321.9
New Zealand	26-35	179.4	250.5	277.4	(2.2)	313.6	350.9
	56-65	175.4	228.0	261.2	(3.8)	298.2	342.6
United Kingdom	26-35	173.7	247.1	275.2	(2.4)	316.7	352.1
	56-65	125.3	207.8	235.9	(2.9)	275.4	324.7
Chile	26-35	135.1	193.7	226.7	(2.4)	260.3	306.5
	56-65	109.3	149.3	190.4	(6.2)	229.0	270.2
Czech Republic	26-35	216.6	256.6	279.7	(2.3)	307.0	334.3
	56-65	178.7	226.8	248.6	(3.1)	277.0	309.0
Denmark	26-35	225.1	268.4	283.9	(1.2)	304.9	328.4
	56-65	190.5	229.2	253.2	(1.7)	281.6	306.3
Finland	26-35	238.5	284.8	306.9	(1.9)	333.4	365.1
	56-65	173.8	217.9	248.9	(1.8)	282.1	317.3
Hungary	26-35	176.3	225.9	250.6	(2.6)	277.2	315.3
	56-65	141.0	190.6	214.7	(2.5)	241.2	284.5
Norway	26-35	218.7	280.6	296.7	(2.1)	321.5	351.0
	56-65	184.8	228.9	258.3	(3.0)	286.4	322.4
Portugal	26-35	122.7	184.2	231.6	(7.0)	284.9	325.1
	56-65	92.8	121.3	184.4	(11.2)	239.7	287.8
Slovenia	26-35	139.4	219.3	245.6	(2.0)	282.1	320.0
	56-65	102.7	142.3	183.6	(3.9)	226.4	267.5

TABLE 3.4 (continued)

MEAN SCORES AND SCORES AT THE 5TH, 25TH, 75TH AND 95TH PERCENTILES ON A SCALE WITH RANGE 0-500 POINTS, PROSE, DOCUMENT, AND QUANTITATIVE LITERACY SCALES, POPULATION AGED 26-35 AND 56-65, 1994-1998

	Age	5th percentile	25th percentile	Mean		75th percentile	95th percentile
B. Document							
Canada	26-35	163.6	260.6	292.3	(5.6)	336.7	396.5
	56-65	66.7	159.3	221.0	(16.4)	282.1	330.3
Germany	26-35	223.6	267.4	293.6	(2.3)	325.1	363.0
	56-65	193.0	238.6	266.2	(3.0)	293.8	336.2
Ireland	26-35	164.2	236.0	266.5	(3.9)	301.5	344.7
	56-65	118.0	190.1	228.6	(9.1)	276.0	325.0
Netherlands	26-35	221.3	278.5	299.2	(1.8)	328.2	357.7
	56-65	178.1	233.1	258.0	(2.9)	284.9	321.1
Poland	26-35	101.7	199.7	237.2	(3.7)	280.0	333.1
	56-65	63.6	105.3	176.2	(3.9)	238.3	288.9
Sweden	26-35	242.2	294.2	319.2	(3.1)	352.9	385.7
	56-65	189.0	248.6	279.3	(3.7)	316.9	360.6
Switzerland[1]	26-35	128.9	259.6	281.3	(4.5)	322.8	356.4
	56-65	116.8	228.4	252.8	(4.1)	291.0	328.3
United States	26-35	125.4	239.1	271.8	(2.9)	323.5	358.5
	56-65	112.0	218.8	254.1	(3.2)	299.5	339.8
Australia	26-35	185.8	257.8	283.8	(1.4)	319.5	356.4
	56-65	82.7	207.7	238.7	(2.5)	285.9	331.5
Belgium (Flanders)	26-35	203.8	269.6	292.3	(3.2)	325.9	351.9
	56-65	134.3	204.4	241.0	(3.8)	284.6	326.2
New Zealand	26-35	154.8	248.3	274.3	(2.2)	310.3	353.7
	56-65	148.8	203.8	244.9	(4.6)	281.6	329.3
United Kingdom	26-35	170.0	242.3	277.8	(2.6)	323.9	366.7
	56-65	109.0	198.8	232.6	(3.6)	279.1	324.4
Chile	26-35	137.0	195.6	225.6	(2.5)	257.0	302.0
	56-65	103.8	141.5	187.4	(5.7)	227.5	260.1
Czech Republic	26-35	217.6	264.9	295.3	(2.2)	326.6	370.9
	56-65	172.9	234.6	262.4	(3.3)	297.0	333.2
Denmark	26-35	237.6	288.6	308.0	(1.5)	332.9	364.6
	56-65	184.2	236.4	265.3	(2.3)	299.5	335.9
Finland	26-35	229.7	285.0	309.9	(2.4)	339.3	376.8
	56-65	152.6	214.4	244.8	(2.5)	281.6	323.3
Hungary	26-35	162.8	228.2	258.9	(3.4)	291.7	336.3
	56-65	121.8	187.5	216.6	(3.2)	249.2	295.1
Norway	26-35	224.3	287.9	307.9	(2.4)	339.4	368.0
	56-65	163.7	229.2	259.5	(3.6)	293.8	337.4
Portugal	26-35	114.2	194.4	228.6	(7.5)	274.1	316.1
	56-65	84.1	138.3	183.2	(11.4)	226.0	287.7
Slovenia	26-35	130.8	222.2	250.6	(2.6)	290.8	329.2
	56-65	84.5	129.7	179.1	(4.7)	229.0	280.6

TABLE 3.4 (concluded)

MEAN SCORES AND SCORES AT THE 5TH, 25TH, 75TH AND 95TH PERCENTILES ON A SCALE WITH RANGE 0-500 POINTS, PROSE, DOCUMENT, AND QUANTITATIVE LITERACY SCALES, POPULATION AGED 26-35 AND 56-65, 1994-1998

	Age	5th percentile	25th percentile	Mean		75th percentile	95th percentile
C. Quantitative							
Canada	26-35	168.3	258.5	291.5	(5.5)	329.9	382.2
	56-65	122.3	192.2	237.6	(11.5)	292.4	332.9
Germany	26-35	229.5	275.3	299.8	(2.5)	329.9	366.9
	56-65	206.8	252.0	277.6	(2.5)	300.3	345.0
Ireland	26-35	160.1	239.4	270.7	(4.2)	311.2	360.7
	56-65	117.0	196.3	238.0	(9.5)	285.5	341.7
Netherlands	26-35	213.3	275.3	298.2	(1.6)	329.0	360.3
	56-65	182.5	241.2	267.3	(3.1)	298.7	333.3
Poland	26-35	114.5	212.3	246.4	(3.5)	291.2	336.1
	56-65	82.6	126.7	197.0	(3.8)	258.8	309.1
Sweden	26-35	235.0	288.6	316.5	(3.3)	350.7	389.9
	56-65	188.3	250.3	285.1	(3.9)	322.5	367.0
Switzerland[1]	26-35	142.4	268.0	287.3	(3.8)	325.0	355.4
	56-65	144.9	241.8	266.7	(3.5)	300.8	340.0
United States	26-35	132.4	243.3	278.2	(3.2)	326.5	370.5
	56-65	142.5	234.5	267.6	(3.5)	310.3	353.6
Australia	26-35	183.8	256.8	285.1	(1.3)	320.9	360.7
	56-65	104.1	214.0	247.5	(2.7)	295.2	340.8
Belgium (Flanders)	26-35	198.4	269.5	297.7	(3.9)	333.4	369.2
	56-65	115.6	202.6	242.3	(4.3)	293.5	353.4
New Zealand	26-35	161.5	247.8	274.1	(2.2)	309.8	350.9
	56-65	153.5	220.8	253.3	(4.5)	291.3	338.6
United Kingdom	26-35	175.7	239.9	276.5	(2.6)	323.1	365.0
	56-65	122.8	204.5	240.6	(3.4)	284.8	333.6
Chile	26-35	99.3	176.9	216.4	(3.3)	259.6	313.5
	56-65	66.7	117.0	175.7	(7.5)	229.6	276.6
Czech Republic	26-35	223.2	280.1	309.0	(2.3)	343.3	381.6
	56-65	178.8	255.7	282.2	(3.6)	317.8	356.0
Denmark	26-35	234.1	288.0	307.0	(1.3)	332.3	364.7
	56-65	195.8	252.7	280.4	(2.2)	313.4	349.5
Finland	26-35	228.3	277.5	299.8	(2.0)	326.8	357.8
	56-65	167.0	225.4	255.7	(2.5)	289.4	327.7
Hungary	26-35	176.2	244.3	276.3	(3.3)	314.1	356.6
	56-65	145.9	211.4	244.5	(2.7)	281.1	330.6
Norway	26-35	216.6	283.6	304.1	(2.2)	333.8	364.5
	56-65	181.6	244.9	271.9	(3.2)	304.9	344.7
Portugal	26-35	111.9	192.2	237.8	(7.0)	287.4	334.6
	56-65	99.9	140.4	198.9	(10.6)	248.1	297.7
Slovenia	26-35	127.2	228.8	259.5	(2.6)	302.5	346.8
	56-65	93.1	138.8	194.8	(5.0)	252.2	301.0

1. Combined estimate for whole country population, 1994 and 1998.
Source: International Adult Literacy Survey, 1994-1998.

TABLE 3.5

MEAN LITERACY SCORES ON THE PROSE, DOCUMENT AND QUANTITATIVE SCALES FOR PERSONS
IN DIFFERENT AGE GROUPS WITH COMPLETED SECONDARY EDUCATION, 1992-1998

	16-25		26-35		36-45		46-65	
A. Prose								
Canada	295.1	(8.0)	283.3	(7.0)	291.8	(8.6)	273.9	(8.5)
Germany	297.7	(5.6)	292.2	(4.9)	275.6	(7.0)	270.3	(3.7)
Ireland	287.8	(3.1)	290.1	(4.7)	286.4	(4.5)	285.3	(6.2)
Netherlands	306.3	(3.2)	303.7	(2.5)	296.5	(3.0)	278.8	(2.9)
Poland	270.4	(3.7)	261.2	(2.5)	252.5	(3.7)	234.0	(3.8)
Sweden	311.1	(2.4)	310.2	(2.5)	299.6	(2.9)	285.3	(4.3)
Switzerland[1]	286.7	(2.8)	282.5	(2.2)	268.0	(3.9)	260.9	(3.2)
United States[2]	273.3	(1.9)	272.4	(4.5)	276.6	(7.1)	273.8	(3.7)
Australia	294.0	(2.3)	286.3	(2.1)	278.7	(3.4)	258.6	(2.5)
Belgium (Flanders)	297.6	(4.9)	279.0	(4.9)	279.6	(3.8)	265.0	(5.2)
New Zealand	288.4	(4.3)	291.8	(5.0)	288.6	(3.9)	288.3	(5.8)
United Kingdom	284.0	(5.7)	286.4	(4.9)	278.2	(5.2)	273.7	(6.0)
Chile	252.1	(3.6)	242.3	(4.0)	237.4	(5.3)	243.2	(6.7)
Czech Republic	292.3	(2.3)	291.1	(3.4)	287.6	(3.4)	276.0	(2.4)
Denmark	294.5	(2.0)	282.9	(1.7)	280.2	(2.1)	263.4	(1.4)
Finland	321.4	(2.8)	306.2	(2.3)	289.4	(2.6)	274.1	(2.1)
Hungary	264.8	(3.0)	253.4	(2.4)	243.2	(2.2)	233.7	(2.1)
Norway	298.6	(2.6)	290.5	(2.7)	285.9	(2.3)	270.9	(2.5)
Portugal	301.7	(3.3)	288.3	(5.5)	271.2	(6.3)	276.7	(8.1)
Slovenia	271.1	(3.3)	249.4	(2.5)	239.9	(4.0)	216.5	(3.1)
B. Document								
Canada	305.3	(9.5)	289.0	(3.8)	295.1	(11.1)	269.6	(8.0)
Germany	309.7	(5.3)	301.9	(4.7)	287.2	(8.4)	281.3	(3.5)
Ireland	281.8	(2.7)	283.8	(5.7)	279.9	(4.2)	274.6	(6.0)
Netherlands	312.4	(3.1)	309.0	(2.1)	300.8	(3.0)	284.0	(3.3)
Poland	270.8	(3.0)	259.8	(3.2)	255.3	(5.0)	228.1	(4.6)
Sweden	314.1	(2.2)	316.3	(2.4)	305.9	(2.9)	292.5	(3.5)
Switzerland[1]	299.4	(3.9)	292.6	(3.1)	276.3	(3.8)	270.3	(3.7)
United States[2]	274.2	(1.9)	270.0	(4.8)	269.9	(6.6)	265.7	(2.6)
Australia	296.0	(2.1)	288.2	(2.3)	279.8	(3.5)	259.4	(2.6)
Belgium (Flanders)	304.8	(4.3)	290.3	(5.0)	284.0	(3.9)	271.9	(5.3)
New Zealand	288.1	(3.2)	290.4	(5.5)	283.2	(4.2)	280.4	(5.8)
United Kingdom	288.2	(6.1)	290.2	(5.6)	284.6	(6.0)	275.4	(6.2)
Chile	245.7	(4.4)	238.6	(3.1)	233.4	(6.5)	237.6	(6.3)
Czech Republic	307.5	(3.7)	307.1	(3.4)	303.0	(4.1)	291.7	(2.8)
Denmark	320.4	(2.3)	307.4	(1.9)	301.4	(2.9)	276.9	(1.6)
Finland	324.6	(3.1)	310.0	(2.6)	290.1	(2.3)	274.5	(2.3)
Hungary	275.4	(4.1)	260.6	(3.3)	253.3	(3.0)	241.0	(2.9)
Norway	307.2	(3.2)	301.2	(3.2)	295.4	(3.2)	278.1	(3.0)
Portugal	289.2	(3.3)	281.0	(4.0)	267.2	(7.2)	267.0	(6.7)
Slovenia	274.1	(3.4)	254.9	(3.4)	246.9	(4.5)	218.0	(3.6)

TABLE 3.5 (concluded)

MEAN LITERACY SCORES ON THE PROSE, DOCUMENT AND QUANTITATIVE SCALES FOR PERSONS
IN DIFFERENT AGE GROUPS WITH COMPLETED SECONDARY EDUCATION, 1992-1998

	16-25		26-35		36-45		46-65	
C. Quantitative								
Canada	288.7	(10.3)	291.4	(4.4)	292.7	(9.2)	273.0	(8.5)
Germany	310.3	(5.4)	306.9	(4.6)	290.6	(8.0)	290.0	(4.3)
Ireland	284.4	(3.0)	289.1	(6.4)	285.1	(4.4)	284.9	(7.1)
Netherlands	306.5	(3.6)	305.6	(2.3)	299.7	(2.8)	289.0	(3.5)
Poland	273.2	(3.2)	270.1	(2.8)	268.2	(4.2)	246.7	(5.1)
Sweden	308.8	(2.2)	312.0	(2.6)	308.4	(2.7)	297.1	(3.6)
Switzerland[1]	298.6	(2.9)	297.7	(2.7)	288.7	(3.3)	281.0	(3.0)
United States[2]	271.8	(2.1)	272.7	(4.9)	275.8	(6.9)	275.3	(3.0)
Australia	292.2	(2.2)	290.4	(2.1)	286.1	(3.0)	267.7	(2.7)
Belgium (Flanders)	305.5	(5.2)	290.7	(5.8)	288.9	(4.6)	278.0	(6.1)
New Zealand	284.6	(3.6)	290.2	(5.3)	286.3	(3.9)	288.6	(5.3)
United Kingdom	278.7	(5.9)	289.9	(5.0)	288.4	(5.9)	283.9	(8.0)
Chile	239.5	(6.2)	233.1	(3.9)	234.0	(7.2)	242.6	(7.8)
Czech Republic	317.3	(3.3)	321.8	(4.1)	319.7	(4.7)	311.2	(3.0)
Denmark	315.9	(2.6)	307.5	(2.0)	306.7	(3.0)	290.9	(1.5)
Finland	307.2	(3.0)	299.6	(2.5)	287.6	(2.5)	278.7	(2.4)
Hungary	290.1	(3.5)	280.6	(4.0)	277.3	(4.0)	265.2	(3.0)
Norway	296.7	(2.7)	295.7	(3.0)	293.7	(3.0)	284.8	(3.2)
Portugal	294.2	(3.1)	285.6	(4.6)	279.0	(6.9)	285.2	(8.1)
Slovenia	282.5	(3.4)	264.3	(3.7)	257.6	(4.5)	234.1	(3.7)

1. Combined estimate for whole country population, 1994 and 1998.
2. Values for the United States youth population are derived from the US National Adult Literacy Survey (1992) because a sampling anomaly involving college students limits the comparability of the IALS data for the cohort aged 16-25.
Sources: International Adult Literacy Survey, 1994-1998; US National Adult Literacy Survey, 1992.

TABLE 3.6

RATES OF LABOUR FORCE PARTICIPATION BY LOW (LEVELS 1 AND 2) AND MEDIUM TO HIGH (LEVELS 3 AND 4/5)
LITERACY PROFICIENCY FOR PROSE, DOCUMENT AND QUANTITATIVE SCALES, POPULATION AGED 25-65, 1994-1998

		In the labour force		Not in the labour force	
A. Prose					
Canada	Levels 1 and 2	67.1	(4.2)	32.9	(4.2)
	Levels 3 and 4/5	81.7	(4.6)	18.3	(4.6)
Germany	Levels 1 and 2	60.9	(3.1)	39.1	(3.1)
	Levels 3 and 4/5	72.0	(1.3)	28.0	(1.3)
Ireland	Levels 1 and 2	55.5	(1.7)	44.5	(1.7)
	Levels 3 and 4/5	72.9	(1.3)	27.1	(1.3)
Netherlands	Levels 1 and 2	55.8	(1.6)	44.2	(1.6)
	Levels 3 and 4/5	77.0	(1.3)	23.0	(1.3)
Poland	Levels 1 and 2	66.8	(0.7)	33.2	(0.7)
	Levels 3 and 4/5	81.9	(2.2)	18.1	(2.2)
Sweden	Levels 1 and 2	71.0	(1.7)	29.0	(1.7)
	Levels 3 and 4/5	87.0	(1.1)	13.0	(1.1)
Switzerland[1]	Levels 1 and 2	75.8	(2.8)	24.2	(2.8)
	Levels 3 and 4/5	83.8	(2.0)	16.2	(2.0)
United States	Levels 1 and 2	73.8	(1.7)	26.2	(1.7)
	Levels 3 and 4/5	83.7	(1.3)	16.3	(1.3)
Australia	Levels 1 and 2	67.0	(1.1)	33.0	(1.1)
	Levels 3 and 4/5	84.0	(0.6)	16.0	(0.6)
Belgium (Flanders)	Levels 1 and 2	63.1	(1.7)	36.9	(1.7)
	Levels 3 and 4/5	83.4	(1.3)	16.6	(1.3)

TABLE 3.6 (continued)

RATES OF LABOUR FORCE PARTICIPATION BY LOW (LEVELS 1 AND 2) AND MEDIUM TO HIGH (LEVELS 3 AND 4/5)
LITERACY PROFICIENCY FOR PROSE, DOCUMENT AND QUANTITATIVE SCALES, POPULATION AGED 25-65, 1994-1998

		In the labour force		Not in the labour force	
New Zealand	Levels 1 and 2	70.0	(1.9)	30.0	(1.9)
	Levels 3 and 4/5	81.4	(1.1)	18.6	(1.1)
United Kingdom	Levels 1 and 2	67.9	(1.3)	32.1	(1.3)
	Levels 3 and 4/5	87.0	(0.9)	13.0	(0.9)
Chile	Levels 1 and 2	65.2	(1.4)	34.8	(1.4)
	Levels 3 and 4/5	80.8	(2.3)	19.2	(2.3)
Czech Republic	Levels 1 and 2	71.0	(1.4)	29.0	(1.4)
	Levels 3 and 4/5	84.5	(1.4)	15.5	(1.4)
Denmark	Levels 1 and 2	74.6	(0.9)	25.4	(0.9)
	Levels 3 and 4/5	85.6	(1.3)	14.4	(1.3)
Finland	Levels 1 and 2	68.7	(1.5)	31.3	(1.5)
	Levels 3 and 4/5	86.0	(0.8)	14.0	(0.8)
Hungary	Levels 1 and 2	63.0	(1.1)	37.0	(1.1)
	Levels 3 and 4/5	84.6	(2.2)	15.4	(2.2)
Norway	Levels 1 and 2	72.7	(1.5)	27.3	(1.5)
	Levels 3 and 4/5	88.8	(0.8)	11.2	(0.8)
Portugal	Levels 1 and 2	71.1	(2.9)	28.9	(2.9)
	Levels 3 and 4/5	89.8	(3.6)	10.2 *	(3.6)
Slovenia	Levels 1 and 2	71.8	(0.7)	28.2	(0.7)
	Levels 3 and 4/5	92.0	(1.3)	8.0	(1.3)
B. Document					
Canada	Levels 1 and 2	66.3	(3.2)	33.7	(3.2)
	Levels 3 and 4/5	82.7	(4.9)	17.3	(4.9)
Germany	Levels 1 and 2	59.1	(3.2)	40.9	(3.2)
	Levels 3 and 4/5	71.9	(1.1)	28.1	(1.1)
Ireland	Levels 1 and 2	55.7	(1.3)	44.3	(1.3)
	Levels 3 and 4/5	74.6	(1.4)	25.4	(1.4)
Netherlands	Levels 1 and 2	51.6	(1.6)	48.4	(1.6)
	Levels 3 and 4/5	78.2	(1.2)	21.8	(1.2)
Poland	Levels 1 and 2	65.2	(0.7)	34.8	(0.7)
	Levels 3 and 4/5	86.9	(1.5)	13.1	(1.5)
Sweden	Levels 1 and 2	70.6	(2.5)	29.4	(2.5)
	Levels 3 and 4/5	86.4	(0.9)	13.6	(0.9)
Switzerland[1]	Levels 1 and 2	76.1	(3.0)	23.9	(3.0)
	Levels 3 and 4/5	82.4	(1.9)	17.6	(1.9)
United States	Levels 1 and 2	72.0	(1.6)	28.0	(1.6)
	Levels 3 and 4/5	86.1	(1.2)	13.9	(1.2)
Australia	Levels 1 and 2	65.0	(1.2)	35.0	(1.2)
	Levels 3 and 4/5	86.1	(0.7)	13.9	(0.7)
Belgium (Flanders)	Levels 1 and 2	60.1	(1.8)	39.9	(1.8)
	Levels 3 and 4/5	83.2	(1.5)	16.8	(1.5)
New Zealand	Levels 1 and 2	67.1	(1.8)	32.9	(1.8)
	Levels 3 and 4/5	85.8	(0.9)	14.2	(0.9)
United Kingdom	Levels 1 and 2	67.2	(1.1)	32.8	(1.1)
	Levels 3 and 4/5	87.2	(0.9)	12.8	(0.9)
Chile	Levels 1 and 2	65.2	(1.3)	34.8	(1.3)
	Levels 3 and 4/5	82.4	(2.2)	17.6	(2.2)
Czech Republic	Levels 1 and 2	70.8	(1.6)	29.2	(1.6)
	Levels 3 and 4/5	81.9	(1.4)	18.1	(1.4)
Denmark	Levels 1 and 2	69.6	(1.2)	30.4	(1.2)
	Levels 3 and 4/5	85.9	(0.9)	14.1	(0.9)
Finland	Levels 1 and 2	68.1	(1.3)	31.9	(1.3)

TABLE 3.6 (concluded)

RATES OF LABOUR FORCE PARTICIPATION BY LOW (LEVELS 1 AND 2) AND MEDIUM TO HIGH (LEVELS 3 AND 4/5) LITERACY PROFICIENCY FOR PROSE, DOCUMENT AND QUANTITATIVE SCALES, POPULATION AGED 25-65, 1994-1998

		In the labour force		Not in the labour force	
	Levels 3 and 4/5	86.5	(0.9)	13.5	(0.9)
Hungary	Levels 1 and 2	60.9	(1.2)	39.1	(1.2)
	Levels 3 and 4/5	81.9	(1.7)	18.1	(1.7)
Norway	Levels 1 and 2	69.7	(1.9)	30.3	(1.9)
	Levels 3 and 4/5	89.2	(0.8)	10.8	(0.8)
Portugal	Levels 1 and 2	72.2	(2.8)	27.8	(2.8)
	Levels 3 and 4/5	87.4	(3.0)	12.6 *	(3.0)
Slovenia	Levels 1 and 2	70.5	(0.9)	29.5	(0.9)
	Levels 3 and 4/5	92.9	(1.0)	7.1	(1.0)
C. Quantitative					
Canada	Levels 1 and 2	67.2	(2.9)	32.8	(2.9)
	Levels 3 and 4/5	81.6	(4.8)	18.4	(4.8)
Germany	Levels 1 and 2	56.7	(3.0)	43.3	(3.0)
	Levels 3 and 4/5	71.3	(1.6)	28.7	(1.6)
Ireland	Levels 1 and 2	53.6	(1.4)	46.4	(1.4)
	Levels 3 and 4/5	75.3	(1.6)	24.7	(1.6)
Netherlands	Levels 1 and 2	51.7	(1.7)	48.3	(1.7)
	Levels 3 and 4/5	77.5	(1.0)	22.5	(1.0)
Poland	Levels 1 and 2	64.9	(0.8)	35.1	(0.8)
	Levels 3 and 4/5	81.5	(1.0)	18.5	(1.0)
Sweden	Levels 1 and 2	72.2	(2.1)	27.8	(2.1)
	Levels 3 and 4/5	85.7	(1.1)	14.3	(1.1)
Switzerland[1]	Levels 1 and 2	75.5	(3.7)	24.5	(3.7)
	Levels 3 and 4/5	82.0	(1.7)	18.0	(1.7)
United States	Levels 1 and 2	72.8	(1.6)	27.2	(1.6)
	Levels 3 and 4/5	84.3	(1.2)	15.7	(1.2)
Australia	Levels 1 and 2	64.0	(1.2)	36.0	(1.2)
	Levels 3 and 4/5	85.7	(0.7)	14.3	(0.7)
Belgium (Flanders)	Levels 1 and 2	60.1	(1.8)	39.9	(1.8)
	Levels 3 and 4/5	82.8	(1.4)	17.2	(1.4)
New Zealand	Levels 1 and 2	68.7	(1.9)	31.3	(1.9)
	Levels 3 and 4/5	83.5	(1.0)	16.5	(1.0)
United Kingdom	Levels 1 and 2	67.7	(1.1)	32.3	(1.1)
	Levels 3 and 4/5	86.5	(1.0)	13.5	(1.0)
Chile	Levels 1 and 2	64.0	(1.3)	36.0	(1.3)
	Levels 3 and 4/5	84.1	(2.3)	15.9	(2.3)
Czech Republic	Levels 1 and 2	70.5	(1.3)	29.5	(1.3)
	Levels 3 and 4/5	80.0	(1.3)	20.0	(1.3)
Denmark	Levels 1 and 2	69.5	(1.3)	30.5	(1.3)
	Levels 3 and 4/5	84.6	(0.9)	15.4	(0.9)
Finland	Levels 1 and 2	69.3	(1.6)	30.7	(1.6)
	Levels 3 and 4/5	85.4	(1.0)	14.6	(1.0)
Hungary	Levels 1 and 2	58.2	(1.3)	41.8	(1.3)
	Levels 3 and 4/5	78.0	(1.5)	22.0	(1.5)
Norway	Levels 1 and 2	72.3	(1.9)	27.7	(1.9)
	Levels 3 and 4/5	87.7	(0.9)	12.3	(0.9)
Portugal	Levels 1 and 2	70.9	(2.9)	29.1	(2.9)
	Levels 3 and 4/5	85.9	(3.3)	14.1	(3.3)
Slovenia	Levels 1 and 2	69.4	(1.0)	30.6	(1.0)
	Levels 3 and 4/5	89.6	(1.2)	10.4	(1.2)

* Unreliable estimate.

1. Combined estimate for whole country population, 1994 and 1998.

Source: International Adult Literacy Survey, 1994-1998.

TABLE 3.7

UNEMPLOYMENT RATE BY LEVEL OF LITERACY PROFICIENCY FOR THE LABOUR FORCE AGED 16-65,
PROSE, DOCUMENT AND QUANTITATIVE SCALES, 1994-1998

	Prose				Document				Quantitative			
	Levels 1 and 2		Levels 3 and 4/5		Levels 1 and 2		Levels 3 and 4/5		Levels 1 and 2		Levels 3 and 4/5	
Canada	16.0	(3.9)	7.8	(1.1)	17.0	(2.6)	7.2	(1.5)	17.7	(2.5)	6.6	(1.9)
Germany	14.2	(1.7)	7.8	(1.4)	16.5	(1.9)	7.2	(1.3)	16.1	(1.8)	8.6	(1.3)
Ireland	23.1	(2.9)	11.3	(1.9)	23.4	(2.9)	9.9	(1.6)	24.4	(3.0)	10.2	(1.4)
Netherlands	9.3	(1.2)	5.1	(0.7)	9.8	(1.4)	5.2	(0.7)	10.3	(1.3)	5.1	(0.6)
Poland	16.9	(1.1)	11.1	(1.9)	17.0	(1.1)	11.5	(1.6)	17.3	(1.0)	12.1	(1.7)
Sweden	11.1	(1.2)	7.4	(0.6)	12.8	(1.5)	7.0	(0.6)	11.2	(1.6)	7.5	(0.7)
Switzerland[1]	4.5	(0.9)	3.4	(0.8)	4.1	(0.9)	3.8	(0.8)	5.4	(1.0)	3.1	(0.7)
United States	6.9	(1.2)	3.6	(0.8)	7.1	(1.0)	3.4	(0.9)	7.4	(1.1)	3.3	(0.8)
Australia	10.5	(0.8)	5.1	(0.5)	11.3	(0.8)	4.6	(0.5)	11.3	(0.9)	4.8	(0.5)
Belgium (Flanders)	17.4	(2.7)	6.8	(1.0)	17.7	(3.0)	8.0	(1.0)	20.3	(3.2)	6.6	(1.0)
New Zealand	16.1	(1.7)	3.8	(0.7)	15.2	(1.6)	3.8	(0.6)	15.0	(1.4)	4.1	(0.7)
United Kingdom	15.5	(1.2)	9.1	(0.9)	17.5	(1.4)	7.7	(0.8)	17.0	(1.4)	8.0	(0.8)
Chile	14.0	(1.0)	8.2*	(1.8)	13.7	(1.1)	9.0*	(2.3)	14.5	(1.1)	7.2*	(1.7)
Czech Republic	7.6	(0.9)	4.3	(0.7)	7.7	(0.9)	4.9	(0.6)	8.3	(1.1)	5.1	(0.7)
Denmark	9.0	(1.1)	5.3	(0.7)	10.7	(1.5)	5.3	(0.6)	11.5	(1.8)	5.4	(0.6)
Finland	20.6	(1.7)	9.3	(0.7)	21.7	(1.7)	8.8	(0.6)	19.1	(1.4)	10.0	(0.7)
Hungary	15.0	(1.2)	13.4	(2.2)	17.2	(1.5)	10.2	(1.7)	18.2	(1.7)	11.4	(1.5)
Norway	5.6	(0.8)	3.0	(0.4)	6.2	(0.8)	2.9	(0.4)	5.8	(0.8)	3.0	(0.3)
Portugal	15.4	(2.3)	9.0	(1.3)	14.4	(2.2)	12.0*	(3.1)	16.0	(2.4)	8.8	(2.1)
Slovenia	13.6	(1.0)	7.5	(1.5)	14.6	(1.1)	5.9	(1.0)	14.6	(1.2)	7.8	(1.2)

* Unreliable estimate.
1. Combined estimate for whole country population, 1994 and 1998.
Note: Chile is excluded from Figure 3.7 because the data are unreliable.
Source: International Adult Literacy Survey, 1994-1998.

TABLE 3.8

MEAN NUMBER OF WEEKS WORKED BY PERSONS WHO WERE EMPLOYED DURING THE YEAR PRECEDING THE INTERVIEW,
BY LITERACY LEVEL, QUANTITATIVE SCALE, POPULATION AGED 25-65, 1994-1998

	Level 1		Level 2 and above		All levels	
Canada	38.9	(2.2)	45.8	(0.8)	44.9	(0.7)
Germany	48.5	(1.4)	50.2	(0.4)	50.1	(0.3)
Ireland	46.3	(0.7)	48.5	(0.4)	48.1	(0.4)
Netherlands	46.8	(1.3)	49.0	(0.3)	48.9	(0.3)
Poland	47.9	(0.3)	49.2	(0.2)	48.7	(0.2)
Sweden	48.0	(1.6)	47.3	(0.2)	47.4	(0.3)
Switzerland[1]	47.6	(1.1)	48.9	(0.2)	48.7	(0.2)
United States	46.4	(0.9)	48.4	(0.4)	48.1	(0.3)
Australia	44.5	(0.7)	47.8	(0.2)	47.4	(0.2)
Belgium (Flanders)	49.4	(1.4)	49.9	(0.3)	49.8	(0.3)
New Zealand	43.5	(1.3)	46.5	(0.3)	46.1	(0.4)
United Kingdom	47.6	(0.9)	48.3	(0.3)	48.2	(0.3)
Chile	45.7	(0.8)	48.5	(0.4)	46.9	(0.4)
Czech Republic	50.5	(0.7)	50.3	(0.1)	50.3	(0.2)
Denmark	49.4	(0.8)	48.9	(0.2)	49.0	(0.2)
Finland	42.6	(1.4)	46.2	(0.2)	45.9	(0.2)
Hungary	46.9	(1.1)	48.9	(0.4)	48.6	(0.4)
Norway	44.3	(1.8)	48.3	(0.3)	48.1	(0.3)
Slovenia	49.8	(0.5)	50.8	(0.2)	50.5	(0.2)

1. Combined estimate for whole country population, 1994 and 1998.
Note: Portugal is excluded because the survey did not ask about number of weeks worked.
Source: International Adult Literacy Survey, 1994-1998.

TABLE 3.9

TABLE 3.9

INDEX SCORES FOR ENGAGEMENT IN READING AT WORK BY LITERACY LEVEL, DOCUMENT SCALE,
POPULATION AGED **16-65, 1994-1998**

	Level 1		Level 2		Level 3		Level 4/5	
Canada	1.4	(0.4)	2.6	(0.1)	3.0	(0.2)	3.6	(0.1)
Germany	2.4	(0.1)	3.4	(0.1)	3.7	(0.2)	3.8	(0.1)
Ireland	1.3	(0.2)	2.3	(0.1)	2.6	(0.1)	3.3	(0.2)
Netherlands	1.4	(0.2)	2.6	(0.1)	3.0	(0.1)	3.3	(0.1)
Poland	1.1	(0.0)	1.7	(0.1)	2.3	(0.1)	2.8	(0.2)
Sweden[1]	—		—		—		—	
Switzerland[2]	1.9	(0.1)	3.0	(0.1)	3.5	(0.1)	3.7	(0.1)
United States	1.9	(0.1)	2.9	(0.1)	3.5	(0.1)	3.8	(0.1)
Australia	1.9	(0.1)	2.8	(0.1)	3.5	(0.1)	3.9	(0.0)
Belgium (Flanders)	1.2	(0.2)	2.1	(0.2)	2.7	(0.2)	3.3	(0.2)
New Zealand	2.2	(0.2)	3.0	(0.1)	3.6	(0.1)	3.8	(0.1)
United Kingdom	2.2	(0.1)	2.7	(0.1)	3.2	(0.1)	3.6	(0.1)
Chile	1.2	(0.1)	2.1	(0.1)	2.9	(0.2)	3.7	(0.4)
Czech Republic	1.6	(0.1)	2.3	(0.1)	2.6	(0.1)	3.0	(0.1)
Denmark	1.8	(0.2)	2.7	(0.1)	3.3	(0.1)	3.7	(0.1)
Finland	2.1	(0.1)	2.6	(0.1)	3.1	(0.1)	3.6	(0.1)
Hungary	1.8	(0.1)	2.3	(0.1)	2.7	(0.1)	3.3	(0.1)
Norway	1.7	(0.1)	2.4	(0.1)	2.8	(0.1)	3.2	(0.1)
Portugal	1.2	(0.1)	2.3	(0.2)	3.2	(0.2)	3.7	(0.3)
Slovenia	1.3	(0.1)	2.3	(0.1)	3.0	(0.1)	3.3	(0.2)

1. The Swedish survey did not ask about reading practices at work in a comparable way.
2. Combined estimate for whole country population, 1994 and 1998.
Source: International Adult Literacy Survey, 1994-1998.

TABLE 3.10

INDEX SCORES FOR ENGAGEMENT IN WRITING AT WORK BY LITERACY LEVEL, PROSE SCALE,
POPULATION AGED **16-65, 1994-1998**

	Level 1		Level 2		Level 3		Level 4/5	
Canada	0.9	(0.2)	1.5	(0.1)	1.9	(0.1)	1.9	(0.1)
Germany	1.4	(0.1)	2.0	(0.1)	2.2	(0.1)	2.3	(0.2)
Ireland	0.8	(0.1)	1.4	(0.1)	1.7	(0.1)	2.0	(0.1)
Netherlands	0.8	(0.1)	1.4	(0.1)	1.5	(0.0)	1.7	(0.1)
Poland	0.5	(0.0)	0.9	(0.1)	1.2	(0.1)	1.6	(0.2)
Sweden[1]	1.0	(0.1)	1.2	(0.0)	1.5	(0.0)	1.6	(0.1)
Switzerland[2]	1.1	(0.1)	1.9	(0.1)	2.2	(0.1)	2.4	(0.1)
United States	1.0	(0.1)	1.7	(0.1)	2.1	(0.1)	2.2	(0.1)
Australia	0.8	(0.0)	1.2	(0.0)	1.4	(0.0)	1.7	(0.0)
Belgium (Flanders)	0.7	(0.1)	1.1	(0.1)	1.5	(0.1)	1.7	(0.1)
New Zealand	0.9	(0.1)	1.5	(0.1)	1.8	(0.1)	2.0	(0.1)
United Kingdom	1.1	(0.1)	1.4	(0.1)	1.9	(0.0)	1.9	(0.1)
Chile	0.8	(0.1)	1.5	(0.1)	2.0	(0.1)	2.5	(0.3)
Czech Republic	1.0	(0.1)	1.5	(0.1)	1.7	(0.1)	1.9	(0.1)
Denmark	0.9	(0.1)	1.3	(0.1)	1.8	(0.0)	1.8	(0.1)
Finland	0.9	(0.1)	1.3	(0.1)	1.6	(0.0)	1.8	(0.0)
Hungary	0.9	(0.1)	1.2	(0.1)	1.5	(0.1)	1.3	(0.1)
Norway	0.7	(0.1)	1.0	(0.1)	1.2	(0.0)	1.3	(0.0)
Portugal	0.6	(0.1)	1.3	(0.1)	1.8	(0.1)	2.5	(0.2)
Slovenia	0.8	(0.0)	1.5	(0.1)	1.8	(0.1)	1.7	(0.2)

1. The Swedish survey did not ask about writing practices at work in a comparable way.
2. Combined estimate for whole country population, 1994 and 1998.
Source: International Adult Literacy Survey, 1994-1998.

TABLE 3.11

PARTICIPATION IN ADULT EDUCATION AND TRAINING AND AVERAGE NUMBER OF HOURS
OF PARTICIPATION IN THE PREVIOUS YEAR, BY TYPE OF TRAINING, POPULATION AGED 16-65, 1994-1998

	All continuing education and training			Job-related education and training		
	Total participation rate[1]	Mean number of hours per participant	Mean number of hours per adult[2]	Participation rate[1]	Mean number of hours per participant	Mean number of hours per adult[2]
Canada	37.7 (1.0)	305.07 (54.3)	115.1	31.8 (1.3)	309.69 (69.4)	98.3
Ireland	24.3 (2.3)	331.72 (19.4)	80.7	18.6 (1.8)	323.08 (21.6)	60.0
Netherlands	37.4 (1.2)	242.38 (14.1)	90.6	25.4 (1.1)	274.09 (23.1)	69.5
Poland	13.9 (0.9)	149.22 (18.3)	20.8	10.5 (0.7)	119.95 (11.4)	12.6
Sweden[3]	52.5 (1.1)	— —	—	— —	— —	—
Switzerland[4]	41.8 (1.1)	140.14 (7.9)	58.6	27.2 (0.8)	145.50 (12.9)	39.6
United States	39.7 (1.4)	169.62 (14.6)	67.4	38.0 (1.6)	162.97 (16.1)	61.9
Australia	38.8 (0.7)	263.66 (8.2)	102.2	33.0 (0.7)	205.78 (8.7)	67.8
Belgium (Flanders)	21.2 (1.1)	129.11 (15.4)	27.4	13.8 (1.0)	101.63 (15.0)	14.0
New Zealand	47.5 (1.2)	284.27 (14.8)	135.0	40.8 (1.3)	276.78 (16.8)	112.9
United Kingdom	43.9 (0.9)	213.85 (11.6)	93.9	40.9 (1.0)	188.71 (13.4)	77.2
Chile	18.9 (1.1)	259.82 (22.4)	49.2	11.1 (0.7)	163.19 (22.8)	18.2
Czech Republic	25.5 (0.9)	167.56 (20.3)	42.7	21.1 (1.0)	117.96 (12.1)	24.9
Denmark	55.7 (0.7)	219.62 (9.8)	122.2	48.3 (0.8)	212.95 (10.8)	102.9
Finland	56.8 (0.9)	213.47 (9.2)	121.2	39.9 (0.8)	213.62 (11.3)	85.2
Hungary	19.3 (0.7)	187.62 (16.6)	36.1	13.4 (0.7)	147.85 (15.7)	19.8
Norway	47.9 (1.5)	239.69 (13.9)	114.9	44.7 (1.3)	212.76 (13.4)	95.0
Portugal[3]	14.2 (1.0)	— —	—	— —	— —	—
Slovenia	31.9 (1.1)	210.92 (12.7)	67.3	25.4 (1.0)	185.54 (12.2)	47.1
Average	**35.0 (0.6)**	**195.98 (8.0)**	**68.7**	**30.3 (0.8)**	**178.25 (9.8)**	**54.0**

1. Full-time students aged 16-24 and people who obtained less than 6 hours of training are excluded.
2. Mean number of hours per adult = Mean number of hours per participant * Participation rate/100.
3. Sweden and Portugal did not ask about job-related training in a comparable way, nor did they ask about training duration.
4. Combined estimate for whole country population, 1994 and 1998.
Note: Germany is excluded because the survey did not ask about adult education and training in a comparable way.
Source: International Adult Literacy Survey, 1994-1998.

TABLE 3.12

PER CENT OF POPULATION AGED 16-65[1] PARTICIPATING IN ADULT EDUCATION AND TRAINING DURING THE YEAR PRECEDING
THE INTERVIEW AT EACH LITERACY LEVEL AND IN TOTAL, DOCUMENT SCALE, 1994-1998

	Total participation rate	Level 1	Level 2	Level 3	Level 4/5
Canada	37.7 (1.0)	16.6 (6.2)	29.4 (2.4)	39.6 (2.9)	60.4 (2.2)
Ireland	24.3 (2.3)	10.1 (2.0)	19.6 (2.3)	34.2 (2.8)	47.3 (4.2)
Netherlands	37.4 (1.2)	16.8 (2.3)	27.0 (1.6)	41.6 (1.8)	53.4 (3.1)
Poland	13.9 (0.9)	8.4 (1.0)	14.8 (1.8)	22.8 (2.4)	31.9 (6.2)
Sweden	52.5 (1.1)	29.3 (5.2)	40.1 (2.2)	54.5 (1.8)	61.6 (1.3)
Switzerland[2]	41.8 (1.1)	20.2 (2.7)	34.0 (2.2)	48.2 (1.4)	63.5 (3.4)
United States	39.7 (1.4)	17.3 (2.1)	32.3 (1.8)	49.0 (1.8)	59.1 (3.0)
Australia	38.8 (0.7)	13.6 (1.2)	29.3 (1.2)	46.5 (1.2)	62.4 (1.5)
Belgium (Flanders)	21.2 (1.1)	4.4* (1.3)	15.1 (2.4)	25.6 (1.6)	37.2 (3.2)
New Zealand	47.5 (1.2)	28.7 (2.3)	40.8 (2.3)	55.2 (2.0)	68.3 (1.9)
United Kingdom	43.9 (0.9)	21.8 (1.7)	33.6 (1.8)	53.9 (1.8)	70.7 (2.0)

TABLE 3.12 (concluded)

PER CENT OF POPULATION AGED 16-65[1] PARTICIPATING IN ADULT EDUCATION AND TRAINING DURING THE YEAR PRECEDING THE INTERVIEW AT EACH LITERACY LEVEL AND IN TOTAL, DOCUMENT SCALE, 1994-1998

	Total participation rate		Level 1		Level 2		Level 3		Level 4/5	
Chile	18.9	(1.1)	11.2	(1.1)	24.2	(2.1)	39.0	(3.7)	51.2*	(11.1)
Czech Republic	25.5	(0.9)	10.9	(1.9)	23.1	(1.2)	28.7	(1.9)	35.0	(2.0)
Denmark	55.7	(0.7)	25.0	(3.3)	44.1	(1.8)	60.2	(1.4)	70.1	(1.5)
Finland	56.8	(0.9)	19.3	(1.8)	44.0	(2.5)	66.2	(1.6)	78.1	(1.7)
Hungary	19.3	(0.7)	8.4	(1.1)	16.7	(1.7)	31.0	(1.7)	44.4	(4.7)
Norway	47.9	(1.5)	18.0	(2.3)	35.8	(2.8)	50.7	(1.6)	62.7	(2.0)
Portugal	14.2	(1.0)	5.0	(1.4)	18.7	(2.6)	33.1	(3.4)	52.5	(7.0)
Slovenia	31.9	(1.1)	13.6	(1.3)	37.2	(1.7)	59.1	(2.1)	61.4	(5.2)
Average	**35.0**	**(0.6)**	**14.2**	**(0.9)**	**28.7**	**(0.9)**	**45.7**	**(0.9)**	**59.2**	**(1.4)**

* Unreliable estimate.

1. Full-time students aged 16-24 and people who obtained less than 6 hours of training are excluded.

2. Combined estimate for whole country population, 1994 and 1998.

Note: Germany is excluded because the survey did not ask about adult education and training in a comparable way.

Source: International Adult Literacy Survey, 1994-1998.

TABLE 3.13

ODDS RATIOS AND ADJUSTED ODDS VALUES[1,2] OF PARTICIPATING IN EMPLOYER-SPONSORED ADULT EDUCATION AND TRAINING, BY OCCUPATIONAL CATEGORY, POPULATION AGED 16-65[3], 1994-1998

	Blue-collar worker[4]	Clerk		Services worker		Manager		Technician		Professional	
Canada											
Odds	1.00	2.06	(0.15)	1.47	(0.16)	2.52	(0.17)	3.24	(0.15)	4.80	(0.13)
Adjusted odds	1.00	1.74	(0.19)	2.44	(0.22)	1.98	(0.21)	3.03	(0.22)	2.45	(0.19)
Ireland											
Odds	1.00	3.22	(0.23)	1.46*	(0.29)	2.05	(0.33)	3.42	(0.26)	3.01	(0.23)
Adjusted odds	1.00	1.98	(0.34)	1.37*	(0.40)	1.88*	(0.42)	1.90*	(0.35)	1.53*	(0.36)
Netherlands											
Odds	1.00	1.41*	(0.19)	0.73*	(0.22)	1.09*	(0.20)	1.86	(0.15)	2.45	(0.16)
Adjusted odds	1.00	0.98*	(0.22)	0.86*	(0.26)	0.64	(0.23)	0.81*	(0.19)	0.84*	(0.21)
Poland											
Odds	1.00	3.43	(0.26)	0.63*	(0.37)	2.92	(0.31)	2.80	(0.20)	4.79	(0.22)
Adjusted odds	1.00	1.62*	(0.32)	0.74*	(0.45)	1.32*	(0.36)	1.31*	(0.26)	1.73*	(0.30)
Sweden											
Odds	1.00	1.76	(0.22)	1.53	(0.17)	2.46	(0.24)	3.32	(0.14)	3.45	(0.13)
Adjusted odds	1.00	1.15*	(0.25)	1.44*	(0.21)	1.44*	(0.27)	2.18	(0.18)	2.09	(0.17)
Switzerland[5]											
Odds	1.00	1.45	(0.17)	1.39	(0.17)	2.78	(0.17)	2.64	(0.13)	2.63	(0.15)
Adjusted odds	1.00	1.03*	(0.20)	1.21*	(0.22)	1.66	(0.20)	1.71	(0.16)	1.42*	(0.19)
United States											
Odds	1.00	3.11	(0.16)	1.11*	(0.16)	3.44	(0.16)	4.54	(0.25)	4.79	(0.16)
Adjusted odds	1.00	1.88	(0.20)	1.24*	(0.21)	1.83	(0.20)	2.15	(0.30)	2.07	(0.21)

TABLE 3.13 (concluded)

ODDS RATIOS AND ADJUSTED ODDS VALUES[1,2] OF PARTICIPATING IN EMPLOYER-SPONSORED ADULT EDUCATION AND TRAINING, BY OCCUPATIONAL CATEGORY, POPULATION AGED 16-65[3], 1994-1998

	Blue-collar worker[4]	Clerk		Services worker		Manager		Technician		Professional	
Australia											
Odds	1.00	1.97	(0.09)	0.88*	(0.11)	2.62	(0.11)	2.49	(0.11)	3.31	(0.09)
Adjusted odds	1.00	1.39	(0.11)	0.92*	(0.14)	1.48	(0.14)	1.21*	(0.13)	1.37	(0.12)
New Zealand											
Odds	1.00	2.20	(0.14)	0.97*	(0.15)	2.44	(0.14)	3.07	(0.15)	3.59	(0.15)
Adjusted odds	1.00	1.14*	(0.18)	0.81*	(0.20)	1.25*	(0.19)	1.18*	(0.20)	1.44*	(0.21)
United Kingdom											
Odds	1.00	2.02	(0.09)	1.51	(0.09)	2.29	(0.10)	2.90	(0.13)	4.37	(0.10)
Adjusted odds	1.00	1.20*	(0.12)	1.71	(0.15)	1.62	(0.14)	1.77	(0.17)	1.93	(0.14)
Chile											
Odds	1.00	6.44	(0.22)	1.64	(0.26)	2.73	(0.39)	7.29	(0.26)	7.60	(0.26)
Adjusted odds	1.00	2.07	(0.28)	1.39*	(0.34)	1.71*	(0.46)	2.06	(0.33)	2.45	(0.36)
Czech Republic											
Odds	1.00	1.92	(0.22)	0.41	(0.26)	1.44	(0.18)	2.05	(0.13)	2.40	(0.17)
Adjusted odds	1.00	1.48*	(0.25)	0.60*	(0.31)	1.18*	(0.22)	1.42	(0.17)	1.46*	(0.22)
Denmark											
Odds	1.00	2.72	(0.17)	2.16	(0.15)	3.60	(0.16)	5.21	(0.14)	3.53	(0.20)
Adjusted odds	1.00	1.79	(0.20)	1.72	(0.18)	2.14	(0.19)	2.80	(0.17)	1.46*	(0.24)
Finland											
Odds	1.00	3.31	(0.18)	1.89	(0.17)	3.08	(0.18)	3.43	(0.15)	4.66	(0.15)
Adjusted odds	1.00	1.85	(0.23)	1.81	(0.24)	2.86	(0.24)	2.07	(0.20)	2.25	(0.21)
Hungary											
Odds	1.00	3.43	(0.32)	1.20*	(0.27)	4.76	(0.36)	3.34	(0.20)	5.74	(0.23)
Adjusted odds	1.00	1.53*	(0.42)	1.39*	(0.36)	4.52	(0.45)	1.78	(0.26)	3.25	(0.30)
Norway											
Odds	1.00	1.96	(0.16)	1.16*	(0.13)	2.72	(0.14)	3.00	(0.13)	3.15	(0.15)
Adjusted odds	1.00	1.07*	(0.19)	0.87*	(0.17)	1.52	(0.17)	1.27*	(0.16)	1.17*	(0.19)
Slovenia											
Odds	1.00	3.94	(0.18)	2.33	(0.18)	7.36	(0.21)	6.06	(0.17)	8.99	(0.19)
Adjusted odds	1.00	1.57	(0.21)	1.44*	(0.24)	3.37	(0.25)	2.33	(0.20)	2.69	(0.25)

See Box 3C in text for further information on odds ratios.

* Unreliable estimate.

1. Odds are adjusted for literacy engagement at work, industry classification, firm size, and full- or part-time work.
2. Standard errors are of the logarithm of the odds ratios and adjusted odds values.
3. Full-time students aged 16-24 and people who obtained less than 6 hours of training are excluded.
4. Blue-collar workers include skilled agricultural and fishery workers, craft and related trades workers, plant and machine operators and assemblers, and elementary occupations.
5. Combined estimate for whole country population, 1994 and 1998.

Note: Germany is excluded because the survey did not ask about adult education and training in a comparable way. Belgium (Flanders) is excluded because the survey did not ask about occupation in a comparable way. Portugal did not ask about firm size and full- or part-time work. Czech Republic, Ireland, Netherlands, New Zealand, Norway, Poland, Switzerland and Sweden are excluded from Figure 3.13 because the data are unreliable.

Source: International Adult Literacy Survey, 1994-1998.

TABLE 3.14

Pᴇʀ ᴄᴇɴᴛ ᴏꜰ ᴘᴀʀᴛɪᴄɪᴘᴀɴᴛꜱ ɪɴ ᴀᴅᴜʟᴛ ᴇᴅᴜᴄᴀᴛɪᴏɴ ᴀɴᴅ ᴛʀᴀɪɴɪɴɢ ᴡʜᴏ ʀᴇᴄᴇɪᴠᴇ ꜰɪɴᴀɴᴄɪᴀʟ ꜱᴜᴘᴘᴏʀᴛ[1] ꜰʀᴏᴍ ᴠᴀʀɪᴏᴜꜱ ꜱᴏᴜʀᴄᴇꜱ,
ʙʏ ɢᴇɴᴅᴇʀ, ɢᴇɴᴇʀᴀʟ ᴘᴏᴘᴜʟᴀᴛɪᴏɴ ᴀɴᴅ ᴇᴍᴘʟᴏʏᴇᴅ ᴘᴏᴘᴜʟᴀᴛɪᴏɴ ᴀɢᴇᴅ 16-65[2], 1994-1998

		General population		Employed population	
		Men	Women	Men	Women
Canada	Self or family	22.9	27.7	25.7	23.9
	Employers	26.0	19.8	31.9	24.2
	Government	9.8	13.9	8.2	10.3
	Other	5.9	5.2	5.9	5.3
Ireland	Self or family	13.7	27.4	13.9	21.1
	Employers	21.4	16.3	29.3	21.0
	Government	9.5	7.6	8.0*	6.0*
	Other	4.7*	5.2	5.1*	3.1*
Netherlands	Self or family	17.4	29.6	18.2	20.6
	Employers	34.0	16.5	43.6	20.6
	Government	6.5	5.3	6.0	4.0
	Other	3.5	2.9	3.1*	1.6*
Poland	Self or family	16.1	19.3	12.9	18.1
	Employers	34.0	23.8	39.2	26.7
	Government	3.3*	3.8*	2.2*	2.6*
	Other	7.5*	5.7*	7.7*	5.6*
Sweden	Self or family	—	—	—	—
	Employers	48.5	51.5	48.7	51.3
	Government	—	—	—	—
	Other	—	—	—	—
Switzerland[3]	Self or family	25.6	33.0	27.5	27.3
	Employers	28.3	19.2	32.8	21.1
	Government	8.5	8.2	8.0	7.5
	Other	3.4	4.7	3.5	4.3
United States	Self or family	16.1	21.1	17.1	17.8
	Employers	32.4	30.1	35.4	31.3
	Government	4.8	6.5	5.1	5.9
	Other	3.2	5.0	3.1	4.5
Australia	Self or family	22.6	29.5	22.7	27.7
	Employers	28.4	18.0	32.3	20.3
	Government	8.3	7.3	6.6	5.7
	Other	3.7	3.8	3.7	3.5
Belgium (Flanders)	Self or family	21.0	27.0	23.6	18.5
	Employers	33.1	17.3	40.1	20.0
	Government	7.3*	5.9*	8.2*	4.3*
	Other	4.1*	6.0*	4.6*	3.6*
New Zealand	Self or family	18.8	27.2	20.6	23.4
	Employers	27.6	24.5	32.9	28.6
	Government	11.3	13.3	9.7	11.4
	Other	5.6	7.8	6.0	6.1
United Kingdom	Self or family	9.6	14.4	9.2	11.7
	Employers	37.7	29.2	42.3	32.9
	Government	9.6	10.6	7.8	8.2
	Other	5.2	3.7	5.1	3.2

TABLE 3.14 (concluded)

PER CENT OF PARTICIPANTS IN ADULT EDUCATION AND TRAINING WHO RECEIVE FINANCIAL SUPPORT[1] FROM VARIOUS SOURCES, BY GENDER, GENERAL POPULATION AND EMPLOYED POPULATION AGED 16-65[2], 1994-1998

		General population		Employed population	
		Men	Women	Men	Women
Chile	Self or family	15.8	21.6	17.1	19.0
	Employers	21.5	15.8	27.5	19.8
	Government	8.9	13.2	10.7	9.4
	Other	6.8*	8.1	5.0*	5.8*
Czech Replublic	Self or family	14.1	14.9	14.3	12.2
	Employers	46.2	28.0	48.5	29.4
	Government	6.0	4.5	5.8	4.2
	Other	5.0*	5.0	5.3*	4.6
Denmark	Self or family	10.7	15.5	9.9	13.9
	Employers	33.3	28.3	39.6	33.0
	Government	12.6	17.1	10.6	13.5
	Other	10.5	12.9	10.7	10.8
Finland	Self or family	11.9	21.1	10.6	17.1
	Employers	30.4	31.5	36.0	37.0
	Government	9.3	10.5	6.8	8.1
	Other	7.9	6.8	7.6	6.1
Hungary	Self or family	19.2	23.0	16.3	22.1
	Employers	27.4	31.3	29.3	34.2
	Government	6.4*	8.8	7.0*	9.1
	Other	7.4*	7.9	6.4*	7.9
Norway	Self or family	14.3	15.9	13.4	15.1
	Employers	38.4	34.6	41.9	38.0
	Government	17.1	18.2	14.5	16.0
	Other	11.3	8.1	11.6	8.5
Slovenia	Self or family	18.2	15.9	17.0	12.8
	Employers	32.3	30.3	36.7	34.2
	Government	12.5	10.2	11.8	8.6
	Other	7.3	6.4	6.5	4.9
Average	**Self or family**	**16.1**	**20.9**	**16.3**	**17.6**
	Employers	**32.2**	**26.9**	**36.4**	**29.3**
	Government	**7.1**	**8.4**	**6.5**	**7.0**
	Other	**4.3**	**5.0**	**4.2**	**4.4**

* Unreliable estimate.

1. Respondents could indicate more than one source of financial support so totals may exceed 100 per cent for a country.

2. Full-time students aged 16-24 and people who obtained less than 6 hours of training are excluded.

3. Combined estimate for whole country population, 1994 and 1998.

Note: Germany is excluded because the survey did not ask about adult education and training in a comparable way. Portugal did not ask about source of financial support. The Swedish survey only asked about employer-sponsored training.

Source: International Adult Literacy Survey, 1994-1998.

TABLE 3.15

ODDS RATIOS AND ADJUSTED ODDS VALUES[1,2] OF RECEIVING EMPLOYER-SPONSORED ADULT EDUCATION AND TRAINING
BY LEVEL OF LITERACY ENGAGEMENT[3] AT WORK, EMPLOYED POPULATION AGED 16-65[4], 1994-1998

		1st quartile		2nd quartile		3rd quartile		4th quartile	
Canada	Odds	1.00		3.90	(0.21)	8.08	(0.20)	11.40	(0.19)
	Adjusted odds	1.00		2.82	(0.22)	5.17	(0.21)	6.33	(0.22)
Ireland	Odds	1.00		2.46	(0.27)	3.87	(0.26)	6.61	(0.25)
	Adjusted odds	1.00		2.38	(0.34)	2.70	(0.35)	5.39	(0.34)
Netherlands[5]	Odds	1.00		3.17	(0.23)	7.35	(0.22)	11.55	(0.22)
	Adjusted odds	1.00		3.13	(0.24)	6.61	(0.24)	8.80	(0.24)
Poland	Odds	1.00		3.00	(0.21)	6.88	(0.21)	6.94	(0.24)
	Adjusted odds	1.00		2.14	(0.23)	3.86	(0.25)	3.30	(0.30)
Sweden[5]	Odds	1.00		2.49	(0.19)	5.12	(0.19)	7.27	(0.18)
	Adjusted odds	1.00		2.03	(0.20)	3.60	(0.20)	4.58	(0.20)
Switzerland[6]	Odds	1.00		2.00	(0.23)	5.89	(0.21)	8.00	(0.21)
	Adjusted odds	1.00		1.79	(0.26)	5.07	(0.24)	5.33	(0.25)
United States	Odds	1.00		2.31	(0.20)	6.30	(0.18)	11.42	(0.18)
	Adjusted odds	1.00		1.58	(0.21)	3.78	(0.20)	5.76	(0.20)
Australia	Odds	1.00		2.77	(0.13)	6.63	(0.12)	11.20	(0.12)
	Adjusted odds	1.00		2.07	(0.14)	3.70	(0.14)	5.31	(0.14)
New Zealand	Odds	1.00		2.29	(0.18)	4.86	(0.17)	8.25	(0.16)
	Adjusted odds	1.00		2.21	(0.20)	3.77	(0.19)	4.73	(0.19)
United Kingdom	Odds	1.00		2.52	(0.11)	6.22	(0.11)	10.65	(0.11)
	Adjusted odds	1.00		2.27	(0.13)	4.42	(0.13)	5.90	(0.14)
Chile	Odds	1.00		5.70	(0.29)	15.56	(0.28)	20.20	(0.27)
	Adjusted odds	1.00		3.97	(0.33)	9.59	(0.33)	7.99	(0.35)
Czech Republic	Odds	1.00		1.80	(0.15)	3.16	(0.15)	5.45	(0.16)
	Adjusted odds	1.00		1.60	(0.17)	2.39	(0.18)	3.68	(0.20)
Denmark	Odds	1.00		2.58	(0.19)	5.58	(0.18)	9.03	(0.18)
	Adjusted odds	1.00		2.05	(0.20)	3.42	(0.20)	4.49	(0.20)
Finland	Odds	1.00		2.66	(0.18)	6.47	(0.18)	9.34	(0.19)
	Adjusted odds	1.00		2.12	(0.21)	3.86	(0.21)	4.66	(0.23)
Hungary	Odds	1.00		4.30	(0.24)	6.67	(0.25)	9.37	(0.28)
	Adjusted odds	1.00		3.24	(0.28)	3.75	(0.30)	3.93	(0.35)
Norway	Odds	1.00		2.36	(0.16)	4.62	(0.15)	7.83	(0.15)
	Adjusted odds	1.00		2.07	(0.17)	3.34	(0.17)	4.58	(0.18)
Slovenia	Odds	1.00		3.11	(0.15)	7.46	(0.16)	8.16	(0.17)
	Adjusted odds	1.00		2.25	(0.17)	4.11	(0.19)	3.54	(0.21)

See Box 3C in text for further information on odds ratios.

1. Odds are adjusted for ocupational status, industry classification, firm size, and full- or part-time work.
2. Standard errors are of the logarithm of the odds ratios and adjusted odds values.
3. The literacy engagement at work index is constructed using frequencies of nine literacy tasks – reading magazines or journals; manuals or reference books; diagrams or schematics; reports or articles; reading or writing letters or memos; bills, invoices or budgets; writing reports or articles; estimates or technical specifications; and calculating prices, costs or budgets. The 1st quartile represents workers who use workplace literacy skills the least; the 4th quartile represents workers who use workplace literacy skills the most.
4. Full-time students aged 16-24 and people who obtained less than 6 hours of training are excluded.
5. Odds are not adjusted for firm size because the country omitted this question.
6. Combined estimate for whole country population, 1994 and 1998.
Note: Germany is excluded because the survey did not ask about adult education and training in a comparable way. Belgium (Flanders) is excluded because the survey did not ask about occupation in a comparable way. Portugal did not ask about firm size and full- or part-time work.
Source: International Adult Literacy Survey, 1994-1998.

TABLE 3.16

PER CENT OF POPULATION AGED 16-65 WHO REPORTED READING BOOKS AND WATCHING TELEVISION, 1994-1998

	(a) Reading books				(b) Watching television			
	At least once a month		Less than once a month		More than 2 hours a day		2 hours or fewer a day	
Canada	65.4	(3.1)	34.6	(3.1)	39.2	(2.2)	60.8	(2.2)
Germany	70.5	(0.9)	29.5	(0.9)	50.2	(1.6)	49.8	(1.6)
Ireland	70.6	(2.6)	29.4	(2.6)	46.2	(1.4)	53.8	(1.4)
Netherlands	59.2	(0.8)	40.8	(0.8)	44.9	(1.2)	55.1	(1.2)
Poland	58.9	(1.0)	41.1	(1.0)	37.8	(0.8)	62.2	(0.8)
Sweden[1]	69.5	(0.7)	30.5	(0.7)	0.0	(0.0)	0.0	(0.0)
Switzerland[2]	68.9	(1.1)	31.1	(1.1)	21.5	(1.9)	78.5	(1.9)
United States	64.7	(1.6)	35.3	(1.6)	40.0	(1.4)	60.0	(1.4)
Australia[1]	70.3	(0.6)	29.7	(0.6)	0.0	(0.0)	0.0	(0.0)
Belgium (Flanders)	44.2	(2.7)	55.8	(2.7)	37.0	(2.9)	63.0	(2.9)
New Zealand	73.8	(1.2)	26.2	(1.2)	54.1	(1.3)	45.9	(1.3)
United Kingdom	60.3	(1.1)	39.7	(1.1)	59.9	(1.0)	40.1	(1.0)
Chile	48.1	(1.4)	51.9	(1.4)	40.4	(1.0)	59.6	(1.0)
Czech Republic	72.7	(1.3)	27.3	(1.3)	48.5	(1.1)	51.5	(1.1)
Denmark	62.9	(0.9)	37.1	(0.9)	41.1	(0.9)	58.9	(0.9)
Finland	60.5	(0.9)	39.5	(0.9)	42.8	(0.9)	57.2	(0.9)
Hungary	65.3	(1.3)	34.7	(1.3)	46.0	(1.2)	54.0	(1.2)
Norway	54.9	(1.1)	45.1	(1.1)	40.7	(1.3)	59.3	(1.3)
Portugal	23.4	(2.1)	76.6	(2.1)	41.1	(1.9)	58.9	(1.9)
Slovenia	56.4	(1.2)	43.6	(1.2)	30.1	(1.1)	69.9	(1.1)
Average	**62.5**	**(0.7)**	**37.5**	**(0.7)**	**44.6**	**(0.6)**	**55.4**	**(0.6)**

1. Sweden and Australia did not ask about watching television.
2. Combined estimate for whole country population, 1994 and 1998.

Source: International Adult Literacy Survey, 1994-1998.

TABLE 3.17

PER CENT OF POPULATION AGED 16-65 WHO REPORTED ENGAGING IN COMMUNITY ACTIVITIES, 1994-1998

	Participation in community activities			
	At least once a month		Less than once a month	
Canada	23.4	(1.8)	76.6	(1.8)
Germany	25.6	(0.8)	74.4	(0.8)
Ireland	28.9	(1.6)	71.1	(1.6)
Netherlands	31.5	(0.9)	68.5	(0.9)
Poland	8.9	(0.5)	91.1	(0.5)
Sweden	47.2	(0.9)	52.8	(0.9)
Switzerland[1]	22.3	(1.0)	77.7	(1.0)
United States	33.5	(1.7)	66.5	(1.7)
Australia	25.8	(0.8)	74.2	(0.8)
Belgium (Flanders)	24.1	(1.0)	75.9	(1.0)
New Zealand	32.9	(1.2)	67.1	(1.2)
United Kingdom	19.2	(0.9)	80.8	(0.9)
Chile	20.9	(1.2)	79.1	(1.2)
Czech Republic	14.3	(1.0)	85.7	(1.0)
Denmark	29.5	(0.9)	70.5	(0.9)
Finland	22.3	(0.8)	77.7	(0.8)
Hungary	11.3	(0.7)	88.7	(0.7)
Norway	32.1	(0.9)	67.9	(0.9)
Portugal	10.1	(1.0)	89.9	(1.0)
Slovenia	17.2	(1.0)	82.8	(1.0)
Average	**25.3**	**(0.6)**	**74.7**	**(0.6)**

1. Combined estimate for whole country population, 1994 and 1998.

Source: International Adult Literacy Survey, 1994-1998.

TABLE 3.18

PER CENT OF NATIVE-BORN AND SECOND-LANGUAGE FOREIGN-BORN[1] POPULATION AGED 16-65 AT EACH LITERACY LEVEL, DOCUMENT SCALE, 1994-1998

		Level 1		Level 2		Level 3		Level 4/5	
Canada	Native-born	14.8	(1.4)	25.6	(1.9)	35.4	(2.0)	24.2	(2.0)
	Second-language foreign-born	47.5	(5.9)	27.2	(5.2)	9.4*	(3.1)	15.9*	(10.0)
Ireland	Native-born	26.0	(1.7)	31.7	(1.2)	31.3	(1.4)	11.0	(1.3)
	Second-language foreign-born	9.4*	(7.3)	24.2*	(13.1)	41.3*	(12.4)	25.1*	(11.4)
Germany	Native-born	7.8	(0.7)	32.1	(1.3)	40.7	(1.2)	19.4	(0.8)
	Second-language foreign-born	23.3*	(2.9)	37.4	(5.6)	26.6	(4.8)	12.7*	(4.3)
Netherlands	Native-born	8.9	(0.6)	25.4	(0.8)	45.2	(1.0)	20.5	(0.8)
	Second-language foreign-born	33.2	(6.1)	31.7	(6.3)	27.5	(6.4)	7.5*	(2.9)
Poland	Native-born	45.0	(1.3)	30.8	(1.0)	18.3	(0.7)	5.9	(0.3)
	Second-language foreign-born	54.7*	(20.5)	45.3*	(20.5)	0.0*	(0.0)	0.0*	(0.0)
Sweden	Native-born	4.3	(0.2)	18.0	(0.9)	40.3	(0.8)	37.3	(0.6)
	Second-language foreign-born	26.6	(4.3)	27.6	(4.2)	32.0	(4.2)	13.7*	(2.6)
Switzerland[2]	Native-born	9.1	(0.8)	30.8	(1.1)	42.1	(0.7)	18.0	(0.9)
	Second-language foreign-born	63.0	(3.3)	19.5	(2.5)	13.4	(1.9)	4.1	(0.9)
United States	Native-born	17.5	(1.1)	27.4	(1.2)	34.0	(1.2)	21.2	(1.0)
	Second-language foreign-born	61.5	(2.5)	18.8	(2.1)	14.2	(1.8)	5.4*	(1.8)
Australia	Native-born	12.3	(0.5)	28.7	(0.7)	39.9	(0.8)	19.0	(0.7)
	Second-language foreign-born	47.7	(2.0)	21.6	(1.7)	24.7	(1.9)	5.9	(0.8)
Belgium (Flanders)	Native-born	14.5	(1.8)	24.0	(3.2)	44.0	(4.5)	17.6	(1.0)
	Second-language foreign-born	59.0*	(10.1)	30.5*	(8.8)	6.5*	(3.5)	4.0*	(3.6)
New Zealand	Native-born	19.8	(1.1)	29.8	(1.3)	32.7	(1.1)	17.7	(1.0)
	Second-language foreign-born	48.6	(3.7)	23.4	(3.5)	20.3	(3.2)	7.7*	(2.0)
United Kingdom	Native-born	21.5	(0.8)	27.6	(1.0)	31.4	(0.9)	19.4	(1.0)
	Second-language foreign-born	53.3	(7.2)	21.9	(3.7)	14.5	(4.6)	10.3*	(3.2)
Chile	Native-born	51.7	(1.7)	35.4	(1.0)	11.6	(0.8)	1.3	(0.5)
	Second-language foreign-born	33.1*	(44.5)	0.0*	(00)	66.9*	(44.5)	0.0*	(00)
Czech Republic	Native-born	14.1	(0.8)	27.9	(1.0)	38.4	(0.9)	19.6	(0.7)
	Second-language foreign-born	26.6*	(9.9)	39.9*	(8.6)	24.9*	(10.8)	8.6*	(5.2)
Denmark	Native-born	7.6	(0.5)	24.2	(0.8)	42.7	(0.9)	25.5	(0.7)
	Second-language foreign-born	32.2*	(9.4)	30.4*	(11.4)	28.2*	(9.9)	9.3*	(5.4)
Finland	Native-born	12.3	(0.5)	24.1	(0.9)	38.3	(0.9)	25.3	(0.6)
	Second-language foreign-born	39.4*	(7.1)	26.2*	(6.2)	26.4*	(7.2)	8.0*	(4.6)
Hungary	Native-born	32.9	(0.9)	34.3	(1.0)	24.9	(1.0)	8.0	(0.7)
	Second-language foreign-born	60.6*	(36.0)	0.0*	(0.0)	13.3*	(18.3)	26.2*	(33.3)
Norway	Native-born	7.6	(0.6)	21.1	(1.0)	41.9	(1.0)	29.4	(1.2)
	Second-language foreign-born	27.1	(3.2)	21.1	(2.6)	26.7	(3.1)	25.1	(3.7)
Portugal	Native-born	49.4	(2.5)	30.7	(2.3)	16.7	(0.9)	3.2	(0.4)
	Second-language foreign-born	55.3*	(26.7)	40.8*	(24.8)	3.9*	(2.9)	0.0*	(0.0)
Slovenia	Native-born	39.0	(1.2)	32.7	(1.0)	22.8	(1.0)	5.6	(0.5)
	Second-language foreign-born	64.0	(2.8)	21.5	(2.5)	13.4	(2.4)	1.1*	(0.8)

* Unreliable estimate.

1. Foreign-born persons whose mother tongue is the same as the language of test are excluded.

2. Combined estimate for whole country population, 1994 and 1998.

Note: Ireland, Poland, Belgium (Flanders), Chile, Czech Republic, Denmark, Finland, Hungary and Portugal are excluded from Figure 3.18 because the data are unreliable.

Source: International Adult Literacy Survey, 1994-1998.

TABLE 3.19

PER CENT OF ADULTS AGED 16-65 WHO RATE THEIR READING SKILLS AS EITHER POOR OR MODERATE BY LITERACY LEVEL, PROSE SCALE, 1994-1998

		Poor/moderate		Good/excellent	
Canada	Level 1	42.6	(6.6)	57.4	(6.6)
	Level 2	10.4	(4.2)	89.6	(4.2)
	Level 3	5.6	(1.9)	94.4	(1.9)
	Level 4/5	0.7*	(1.2)	99.3	(1.2)
Germany	Level 1	19.7	(2.9)	80.3	(2.9)
	Level 2	4.2	(0.7)	95.8	(0.7)
	Level 3	4.1*	(1.2)	95.9	(1.2)
	Level 4/5	0.6*	(0.4)	99.4	(0.4)
Ireland	Level 1	27.3	(4.5)	72.7	(4.5)
	Level 2	8.4	(1.8)	91.6	(1.8)
	Level 3	4.5*	(1.1)	95.5	(1.1)
	Level 4/5	1.3*	(0.8)	98.7	(0.8)
Netherlands	Level 1	49.3	(5.7)	50.7	(5.7)
	Level 2	31.9	(1.9)	68.1	(1.9)
	Level 3	15.8	(1.6)	84.2	(1.6)
	Level 4/5	7.3*	(1.8)	92.7	(1.8)
Poland	Level 1	24.2	(1.2)	75.8	(1.2)
	Level 2	9.1	(1.1)	90.9	(1.1)
	Level 3	3.3*	(1.1)	96.7	(1.1)
	Level 4/5	0.0*	(0.0)	100.0	(0.0)
Switzerland[1]	Level 1	34.1	(4.2)	65.9	(4.2)
	Level 2	5.5	(1.6)	94.5	(1.6)
	Level 3	2.2	(0.7)	97.8	(0.7)
	Level 4/5	0.8*	(0.4)	99.2	(0.4)
United States	Level 1	37.2	(2.1)	62.8	(2.1)
	Level 2	8.1	(1.5)	91.9	(1.5)
	Level 3	4.1*	(1.1)	95.9	(1.1)
	Level 4/5	1.5*	(0.5)	98.5	(0.5)
Australia	Level 1	28.2	(1.6)	71.8	(1.6)
	Level 2	11.0	(1.1)	89.0	(1.1)
	Level 3	3.6	(0.4)	96.4	(0.4)
	Level 4/5	1.4*	(0.3)	98.6	(0.3)
Belgium (Flanders)	Level 1	17.5*	(5.0)	82.5	(5.0)
	Level 2	6.9*	(2.3)	93.1	(2.3)
	Level 3	4.5*	(1.2)	95.5	(1.2)
	Level 4/5	3.5*	(1.5)	96.5	(1.5)
New Zealand	Level 1	31.4	(3.6)	68.6	(3.6)
	Level 2	12.6	(1.4)	87.4	(1.4)
	Level 3	6.3	(1.1)	93.7	(1.1)
	Level 4/5	1.5*	(0.5)	98.5	(0.5)
United Kingdom	Level 1	42.1	(3.2)	57.9	(3.2)
	Level 2	19.4	(1.8)	80.6	(1.8)
	Level 3	6.8	(0.9)	93.2	(0.9)
	Level 4/5	2.7*	(0.8)	97.3	(0.8)

TABLE 3.19 (concluded)

PER CENT OF ADULTS AGED **16-65** WHO RATE THEIR READING SKILLS AS EITHER POOR OR MODERATE BY LITERACY LEVEL, PROSE SCALE, **1994-1998**

		Poor/moderate		Good/excellent	
Chile	Level 1	52.9	(2.0)	47.1	(2.0)
	Level 2	16.1	(1.8)	83.9	(1.8)
	Level 3	6.3*	(1.9)	93.7	(1.9)
	Level 4/5	0.0*	(0.0)	100.0	(0.0)
Czech Republic	Level 1	1.5*	(0.7)	98.5	(0.7)
	Level 2	1.1*	(0.6)	98.9	(0.6)
	Level 3	0.7*	(0.3)	99.3	(0.3)
	Level 4/5	0.2*	(0.3)	99.8	(0.3)
Denmark	Level 1	10.7*	(2.1)	89.3	(2.1)
	Level 2	3.0*	(0.6)	97.0	(0.6)
	Level 3	1.0*	(0.3)	99.0	(0.3)
	Level 4/5	0.0*	(0.0)	100.0	(0.0)
Finland	Level 1	49.3	(4.8)	50.7	(4.8)
	Level 2	28.8	(1.8)	71.2	(1.8)
	Level 3	14.2	(1.2)	85.8	(1.2)
	Level 4/5	3.3*	(0.7)	96.7	(0.7)
Hungary	Level 1	28.3	(2.6)	71.7	(2.6)
	Level 2	16.7	(1.8)	83.3	(1.8)
	Level 3	8.2	(1.6)	91.8	(1.6)
	Level 4/5	4.0*	(3.0)	96.0	(3.0)
Norway	Level 1	48.0	(5.1)	52.0	(5.1)
	Level 2	19.4	(2.0)	80.6	(2.0)
	Level 3	8.4	(1.4)	91.6	(1.4)
	Level 4/5	2.8*	(0.9)	97.2	(0.9)
Portugal	Level 1	72.6	(4.5)	27.4	(4.5)
	Level 2	40.6	(4.7)	59.4	(4.7)
	Level 3	20.5	(4.5)	79.5	(4.5)
	Level 4/5	4.4*	(3.4)	95.6	(3.4)
Slovenia	Level 1	22.9	(2.1)	77.1	(2.1)
	Level 2	6.2	(1.0)	93.8	(1.0)
	Level 3	3.3*	(0.9)	96.7	(0.9)
	Level 4/5	2.9*	(2.2)	97.1	(2.2)

* Unreliable estimate.

1. Combined estimate for whole country population, 1994 and 1998.

Note: Sweden is excluded because the survey did not ask about respondents' self-assessment of skills. Belgium (Flanders), Czech Republic and Denmark are excluded from Figure 3.19 because the data are unreliable.

Source: International Adult Literacy Survey, 1994-1998.

TABLE 3.20

PER CENT OF POPULATION AGED **16-65** WHO REPORT THAT THEIR READING SKILLS LIMIT THEIR OPPORTUNITIES AT WORK
BY LITERACY LEVEL, DOCUMENT SCALE, **1994-1998**

		Not at all limiting		Greatly or moderately limiting	
Canada	Level 1	59.5	(7.6)	40.5	(7.6)
	Level 2	83.6	(4.4)	16.4	(4.4)
	Level 3	92.3	(3.0)	7.7	(3.0)
	Level 4/5	98.8	(0.5)	1.2*	(0.5)
Germany	Level 1	39.3*	(7.6)	60.7*	(7.6)
	Level 2	55.1*	(15.8)	44.9*	(15.8)
	Level 3	82.5*	(8.5)	17.5*	(8.5)
	Level 4/5	77.2*	(24.4)	22.8*	(24.4)
Ireland	Level 1	87.0	(2.7)	13.0	(2.7)
	Level 2	95.4	(1.0)	4.6*	(1.0)
	Level 3	96.6	(0.9)	3.4*	(0.9)
	Level 4/5	97.0	(1.3)	3.0*	(1.3)
Netherlands	Level 1	81.2	(4.2)	18.8*	(4.2)
	Level 2	89.9	(1.9)	10.1	(1.9)
	Level 3	91.1	(1.0)	8.9	(1.0)
	Level 4/5	94.0	(1.4)	6.0	(1.4)
Poland	Level 1	86.6	(0.8)	13.4	(0.8)
	Level 2	91.5	(1.1)	8.5	(1.1)
	Level 3	97.6	(1.0)	2.4*	(1.0)
	Level 4/5	97.2	(1.4)	2.8*	(1.4)
Switzerland[1]	Level 1	80.9	(2.8)	19.1	(2.8)
	Level 2	91.0	(1.5)	9.0	(1.5)
	Level 3	94.0	(0.7)	6.0	(0.7)
	Level 4/5	98.5	(0.9)	1.5*	(0.9)
United States	Level 1	65.9	(3.5)	34.1	(3.5)
	Level 2	89.2	(2.0)	10.8	(2.0)
	Level 3	95.2	(0.8)	4.8	(0.8)
	Level 4/5	96.5	(1.0)	3.5*	(1.0)
Australia	Level 1	76.6	(1.4)	23.4	(1.4)
	Level 2	95.0	(0.7)	5.0	(0.7)
	Level 3	98.7	(0.3)	1.3	(0.3)
	Level 4/5	99.0	(0.3)	1.0*	(0.3)
Belgium (Flanders)	Level 1	79.3	(5.4)	20.7*	(5.4)
	Level 2	94.9	(5.4)	5.1*	(5.4)
	Level 3	93.8	(1.2)	6.2	(1.2)
	Level 4/5	97.3	(1.1)	2.7*	(1.1)
New Zealand	Level 1	65.8	(4.0)	34.2	(4.0)
	Level 2	83.7	(1.6)	16.3	(1.6)
	Level 3	93.4	(1.2)	6.6	(1.2)
	Level 4/5	98.3	(0.6)	1.7*	(0.6)
United Kingdom	Level 1	73.4	(2.7)	26.6	(2.7)
	Level 2	85.1	(1.8)	14.9	(1.8)
	Level 3	93.4	(0.9)	6.6	(0.9)
	Level 4/5	95.4	(1.7)	4.6	(1.7)

TABLE 3.20 (concluded)

PER CENT OF POPULATION AGED **16-65** WHO REPORT THAT THEIR READING SKILLS LIMIT THEIR OPPORTUNITIES AT WORK
BY LITERACY LEVEL, DOCUMENT SCALE, **1994-1998**

		Not at all limiting		Greatly or moderately limiting	
Chile	Level 1	66.4	(2.2)	33.6	(2.2)
	Level 2	89.0	(1.3)	11.0	(1.3)
	Level 3	94.2	(1.7)	5.8*	(1.7)
	Level 4/5	94.9	(5.6)	5.1*	(5.6)
Czech Republic	Level 1	91.2	(2.3)	8.8*	(2.3)
	Level 2	96.1	(0.8)	3.9*	(0.8)
	Level 3	95.1	(0.9)	4.9	(0.9)
	Level 4/5	96.9	(1.0)	3.1*	(1.0)
Denmark	Level 1	67.9	(4.6)	32.1	(4.6)
	Level 2	85.8	(2.0)	14.2	(2.0)
	Level 3	94.2	(0.7)	5.8	(0.7)
	Level 4/5	97.6	(0.5)	2.4*	(0.5)
Finland	Level 1	88.0	(2.9)	12.0*	(2.9)
	Level 2	95.2	(0.9)	4.8*	(0.9)
	Level 3	97.5	(0.5)	2.5*	(0.5)
	Level 4/5	99.0	(0.3)	1.0*	(0.3)
Hungary	Level 1	94.4	(1.4)	5.6*	(1.4)
	Level 2	97.9	(0.6)	2.1*	(0.6)
	Level 3	97.7	(1.0)	2.3*	(1.0)
	Level 4/5	100.0	(0.0)	0.0*	(0.0)
Norway	Level 1	78.5	(4.0)	21.5	(4.0)
	Level 2	89.6	(2.2)	10.4	(2.2)
	Level 3	95.6	(0.6)	4.4	(0.6)
	Level 4/5	96.2	(0.8)	3.8	(0.8)
Portugal	Level 1	75.0	(3.1)	25.0	(3.1)
	Level 2	81.4	(3.8)	18.6	(3.8)
	Level 3	83.9	(4.2)	16.1*	(4.2)
	Level 4/5	94.4	(4.3)	5.6*	(4.3)
Slovenia	Level 1	87.3	(1.5)	12.7	(1.5)
	Level 2	94.8	(0.8)	5.2	(0.8)
	Level 3	96.9	(1.1)	3.1*	(1.1)
	Level 4/5	99.3	(0.7)	0.7*	(0.7)

* Unreliable estimate.

1. Combined estimate for whole country population, 1994 and 1998.

Note: Sweden is excluded because the survey did not ask about respondents' self-assessment of skills. Belgium (Flanders), Czech Republic, Finland, Germany, Hungary and Netherlands are excluded from Figure 3.20 because the data are unreliable.

Source: International Adult Literacy Survey, 1994-1998

TABLE 3.21

PER CENT OF VARIANCE (R²) IN LITERACY PROFICIENCY ACCOUNTED FOR BY 12 PREDICTOR VARIABLES
(STANDARDISED MAXIMUM LIKELIHOOD REGRESSION WEIGHTS) AND MEASURES OF MODEL FIT
(STANDARD ERRORS TIMES 100 IN BRACKETS), POPULATION AGED 25-65, 1994-1998

	Australia		Belgium (Flanders)		Canada		Chile		Czech Republic		Denmark		Finland	
Gender	0.017	(0.3)	0.042	(0.9)	-0.005	(0.6)	0.035	(0.6)	0.037	(0.6)	0.108	(0.6)	0.007	(0.7)
Age	-0.133	(0.6)	-0.148	(1.9)	-0.083	(1.2)	-0.012	(0.8)	-0.083	(1.8)	-0.238	(1.3)	-0.175	(1.2)
Native versus foreign language	0.299	(0.3)	0.151	(0.8)	0.179	(0.6)	0.072	(0.5)	0.014	(0.6)	0.047	(0.6)	0.113	(0.6)
Parents' education	0.052	(0.3)	0.037	(1.3)	0.057	(0.9)	0.097	(1.0)	0.073	(1.0)	0.082	(0.8)	0.159	(0.8)
Respondent's education	0.294	(0.5)	0.377	(1.3)	0.465	(0.9)	0.570	(0.9)	0.422	(1.0)	0.325	(0.9)	0.318	(1.0)
Labour force participation	0.112	(0.6)	0.072	(2.0)	0.064	(1.3)	0.011	(0.8)	0.023	(1.9)	0.043	(1.3)	0.103	(1.1)
Industrial sector	0.033	(0.3)	0.035	(0.9)	-0.042	(0.7)	0.058	(0.6)	-0.069	(0.6)	-0.038	(0.7)	0.019	(0.7)
Occupational category	0.164	(0.3)	0.062	(1.0)	0.145	(0.8)	0.011	(0.6)	0.012	(0.9)	0.175	(0.8)	0.138	(0.8)
Reading at work	0.033	(0.3)	0.078	(0.9)	0.026	(0.7)	0.083	(0.6)	-0.025	(0.7)	0.022	(0.6)	-0.042	(0.7)
Participation in adult education	0.090	(0.3)	0.048	(0.9)	0.071	(0.6)	0.004	(0.5)	0.051	(0.6)	0.063	(0.6)	0.091	(0.7)
Reading at home	0.093	(0.3)	0.133	(0.8)	0.068	(0.6)	0.016	(0.5)	0.018	(0.6)	0.051	(0.6)	0.019	(0.6)
Participation in voluntary activities	0.083	(0.3)	0.049	(0.9)	0.089	(0.6)	0.057	(0.5)	0.091	(0.6)	0.074	(0.6)	0.038	(0.6)
Literacy, explained variance	0.488	—	0.432	—	0.577	—	0.545	—	0.282	—	0.406	—	0.454	—
Root Mean Square Residual	0.014	—	0.013	—	0.015	—	0.012	—	0.015	—	0.023	—	0.020	—
Goodness of Fit Index	0.965	—	0.977	—	0.972	—	0.973	—	0.983	—	0.956	—	0.967	—

	Germany		Hungary		Ireland		Netherlands		New Zealand		Norway		Poland	
Gender	0.086	(0.8)	-0.041	(1.0)	0.040	(0.6)	0.028	(0.6)	0.049	(0.4)	0.051	(0.6)	0.130	(0.6)
Age	-0.166	(1.7)	-0.107	(2.4)	-0.044	(1.3)	-0.163	(1.1)	-0.063	(1.0)	-0.200	(1.3)	-0.156	(1.1)
Native versus foreign language	0.095	(0.8)	-0.013	(0.9)	-0.022	(0.6)	0.098	(0.6)	0.237	(0.4)	0.144	(0.6)	-0.003	(0.5)
Parents' education	0.044	(1.0)	0.073	(1.6)	0.000	(0.9)	0.081	(0.8)	0.066	(0.5)	0.070	(0.8)	0.030	(0.9)
Respondent's education	0.181	(1.1)	0.433	(1.2)	0.485	(1.0)	0.349	(0.9)	0.340	(0.7)	0.329	(0.9)	0.388	(0.9)
Labour force participation	0.086	(1.8)	0.080	(2.4)	0.102	(1.3)	0.112	(1.1)	0.112	(1.0)	0.082	(1.3)	0.042	(1.0)
Industrial sector	0.016	(0.8)	-0.055	(1.0)	-0.046	(0.7)	0.027	(0.6)	0.058	(0.5)	-0.007	(0.7)	0.044	(0.6)
Occupational category	0.201	(1.0)	0.020	(1.7)	0.071	(0.7)	0.110	(0.6)	0.141	(0.5)	0.139	(0.8)	0.091	(0.8)
Reading at work	0.018	(0.8)	-0.013	(1.1)	0.069	(0.7)	0.047	(0.5)	0.060	(0.5)	0.021	(0.7)	-0.021	(0.6)
Participation in adult education	0.077	(0.8)	0.048	(1.0)	0.054	(0.6)	0.058	(0.6)	0.077	(0.5)	0.065	(0.7)	-0.005	(0.5)
Reading at home	-0.018	(0.8)	-0.039	(0.9)	0.062	(0.6)	0.069	(0.6)	0.055	(0.4)	0.066	(0.6)	-0.012	(0.5)
Participation in voluntary activities	0.030	(0.9)	0.072	(1.0)	0.095	(0.6)	0.039	(0.6)	-0.002	(0.4)	0.094	(0.6)	0.115	(0.6)
Literacy, explained variance	0.248	—	0.352	—	0.441	—	0.402	—	0.388	—	0.392	—	0.368	—
Root Mean Square Residual	0.018	—	0.014	—	0.017	—	0.020	—	0.018	—	0.018	—	0.015	—
Goodness of Fit Index	0.975	—	0.980	—	0.965	—	0.959	—	0.960	—	0.966	—	0.978	—

	Portugal		Slovenia		Sweden		Switzerland[1]		United Kingdom		United States	
Gender	0.153	(1.4)	0.009	(0.5)	0.110	(0.6)	-0.033	(0.6)	0.080	(0.4)	-0.012	(0.6)
Age	0.012	(2.5)	-0.179	(1.1)	-0.123	(1.1)	-0.069	(1.2)	-0.064	(0.9)	0.001	(1.6)
Native versus foreign language	0.083	(1.4)	0.047	(0.5)	0.180	(0.5)	0.232	(0.5)	0.180	(0.3)	0.252	(0.6)
Parents' education	0.059	(2.4)	0.087	(0.8)	0.151	(0.7)	0.162	(0.7)	0.094	(0.5)	0.080	(1.0)
Respondent's education	0.797	(2.1)	0.395	(0.8)	0.240	(1.2)	0.195	(0.7)	0.290	(0.5)	0.389	(0.9)
Labour force participation	-0.015	(2.8)	0.080	(1.0)	0.048	(1.1)	0.139	(1.2)	0.132	(0.9)	0.095	(1.7)
Industrial sector	-0.090	(1.5)	0.069	(0.6)	-0.031	(0.6)	0.022	(0.5)	-0.013	(0.4)	-0.036	(0.6)
Occupational category	0.029	(1.7)	0.075	(0.8)	0.112	(0.7)	0.172	(0.6)	0.179	(0.4)	0.132	(0.7)
Reading at work	-0.024	(1.6)	0.044	(0.6)	0.030	(0.6)	0.070	(0.6)	-0.017	(0.4)	0.046	(0.7)
Participation in adult education	-0.018	(1.5)	0.044	(0.6)	0.045	(0.6)	0.060	(0.6)	0.105	(0.4)	0.065	(0.6)
Reading at home	0.049	(1.4)	0.017	(0.5)	0.033	(0.5)	0.102	(0.5)	0.082	(0.3)	0.079	(0.6)
Participation in voluntary activities	-0.042	(1.5)	0.047	(0.5)	0.030	(0.6)	0.032	(0.6)	0.114	(0.4)	-0.013	(0.6)
Literacy, explained variance	0.633	—	0.514	—	0.299	—	0.409	—	0.431	—	0.505	—
Root Mean Square Residual	0.016	—	0.011	—	0.022	—	0.012	—	0.015	—	0.013	—
Goodness of Fit Index	0.942	—	0.976	—	0.972	—	0.980	—	0.963	—	0.976	—

1. Combined estimate for whole country population, 1994 and 1998.
Source: International Adult Literacy Survey, 1994-1998.

TABLE 4.1

PER CENT OF EACH SOCIO-OCCUPATIONAL CATEGORY AT EACH LITERACY LEVEL,
PROSE SCALE, POPULATION AGED 16-65, 1994-1998

	Level 1		Level 2		Level 3		Level 4/5	
Blue-collar low-skilled workers	32.9	(1.7)	35.5	(1.7)	25.8	(1.4)	5.7	(0.8)
Blue-collar high-skilled workers	30.3	(1.5)	35.5	(1.7)	27.1	(1.1)	7.1	(0.9)
White-collar low-skilled workers	15.5	(0.9)	30.3	(1.5)	36.6	(1.6)	17.5	(0.9)
White-collar high-skilled workers	5.2	(0.5)	19.7	(0.9)	40.8	(1.4)	34.3	(1.3)
Students	15.6	(1.3)	26.7	(2.6)	39.2	(2.1)	18.5	(1.5)
Unemployed	33.1	(1.7)	30.6	(1.4)	27.7	(1.6)	8.5	(1.6)
Homemakers	31.8	(2.0)	28.7	(1.6)	28.6	(1.3)	11.0	(1.3)
Retired	36.0	(1.3)	36.4	(1.4)	21.2	(1.6)	6.4	(1.4)

Source: International Adult Literacy Survey, 1994-1998.

TABLE 4.2

AVERAGE ANNUAL HOURS WORKED PER PERSON IN EMPLOYMENT AND MEAN LITERACY PROFICIENCY,
DOCUMENT SCALE, POPULATION AGED 16-65, 1994-1998

	Labour volume per capita		Mean document literacy	
Canada	1,635.5	(32.3)	279.3	(3.0)
Germany	1,887.9	(35.6)	285.1	(1.0)
Ireland	1,908.0	(64.2)	259.3	(3.2)
Netherlands	1,670.9	(18.7)	286.9	(0.9)
Poland	2,174.8	(21.5)	223.9	(1.8)
Sweden[1]	—	—	305.6	(0.9)
Switzerland[2]	1,837.0	(22.7)	270.8	(1.3)
United States	1,895.4	(23.8)	267.9	(1.7)
Australia	1,766.3	(13.9)	273.3	(1.0)
Belgium (Flanders)	1,777.2	(197.4)	278.2	(3.2)
New Zealand	1,690.0	(26.2)	269.1	(1.3)
United Kingdom	1,686.8	(16.7)	267.5	(1.9)
Chile	2,085.6	(31.3)	218.9	(2.2)
Czech Republic	2,103.4	(15.2)	282.9	(0.9)
Denmark	1,705.1	(13.4)	293.8	(0.8)
Finland	1,696.8	(13.4)	289.2	(0.9)
Hungary	2,018.5	(21.4)	249.0	(1.2)
Norway	1,615.7	(10.2)	296.9	(1.2)
Portugal[1]	—	—	220.4	(3.7)
Slovenia	2,079.4	(19.6)	231.9	(1.7)

1. The Swedish and Portuguese surveys did not ask about hours worked in a comparable way.
2. Combined estimate for whole country population, 1994 and 1998.
Source: International Adult Literacy Survey, 1994-1998.

TABLE 4.3

PROBABILITY OF BEING UNEMPLOYED ACCORDING TO PROSE LITERACY SCORE FOR MEN AGED 16-25
WITH LESS THAN UPPER SECONDARY EDUCATION, 1994-1998

	Prose literacy score										
	0	50	100	150	200	250	300	350	400	450	500
Canada	0.55	0.46	0.36	0.28	0.21	0.15	0.11	0.08	0.05	0.04	0.02
Germany	0.59	0.48	0.37	0.27	0.19	0.13	0.09	0.06	0.04	0.02	0.02
Ireland	0.76	0.70	0.62	0.54	0.46	0.38	0.30	0.24	0.18	0.14	0.10
Netherlands	0.86	0.76	0.61	0.44	0.29	0.17	0.09	0.05	0.03	0.01	0.01
Poland	0.50*	0.50*	0.50*	0.50*	0.50*	0.50*	0.50*	0.50*	0.50*	0.50 *	0.50*
Sweden	0.72	0.65	0.57	0.49	0.41	0.34	0.27	0.21	0.17	0.13	0.10
Switzerland[1]	0.25	0.21	0.18	0.16	0.13	0.11	0.10	0.08	0.07	0.06	0.05
United States	0.60	0.53	0.47	0.41	0.35	0.30	0.25	0.20	0.17	0.13	0.11
Australia	0.77	0.68	0.57	0.45	0.34	0.24	0.16	0.11	0.07	0.05	0.03
Belgium (Flanders)	0.75	0.67	0.58	0.49	0.39	0.31	0.23	0.17	0.12	0.09	0.06
New Zealand	0.97	0.92	0.83	0.65	0.42	0.22	0.10	0.04	0.02	0.01	0.00
United Kingdom	0.72	0.64	0.54	0.45	0.35	0.27	0.20	0.15	0.11	0.07	0.05
Chile	0.52	0.46	0.41	0.35	0.30	0.26	0.22	0.18	0.15	0.12	0.10
Czech Republic	0.72	0.63	0.54	0.45	0.35	0.27	0.20	0.15	0.11	0.07	0.05
Denmark	0.39	0.33	0.27	0.22	0.17	0.13	0.10	0.08	0.06	0.05	0.04
Finland	0.93	0.89	0.82	0.72	0.59	0.45	0.32	0.21	0.13	0.08	0.05
Hungary	0.70	0.66	0.62	0.57	0.53	0.49	0.44	0.40	0.35	0.31	0.28
Norway	0.94	0.86	0.74	0.55	0.35	0.20	0.10	0.05	0.02	0.01	0.00
Portugal	0.10*	0.10*	0.10*	0.10*	0.10*	0.10*	0.10*	0.10*	0.10*	0.10 *	0.10*
Slovenia	0.65	0.58	0.51	0.44	0.37	0.30	0.25	0.20	0.16	0.12	0.10

See Box 4A in the text for further information on the logit model.

* Unreliable estimate.

1. Combined estimate for whole country population, 1994 and 1998.

Source: International Adult Literacy Survey, 1994-1998.

TABLE 4.4

PER CENT OF ADULTS AT PROSE LITERACY LEVELS 1 AND 2 BEING SHORT-TERM (LESS THAN 12 MONTHS)
AND LONG-TERM (MORE THAN 12 MONTHS) UNEMPLOYED, POPULATION AGED 16-65, 1994-1998

	Short-term unemployed		Long-term unemployed	
Canada	49.8	(8.0)	64.1	(15.1)
Germany	62.8*	(8.6)	59.8	(6.2)
Ireland	47.0*	(11.2)	72.6	(3.2)
Netherlands	29.9*	(6.9)	64.6	(4.8)
Poland	88.1	(3.8)	81.4	(2.6)
Sweden	29.6*	(4.0)	40.1*	(5.1)
Switzerland[1]	49.4	(11.9)	67.9*	(13.1)
United States	40.7	(10.3)	79.7	(8.1
Australia	53.2	(3.6)	62.5	(4.2)
Belgium (Flanders)	60.1*	(9.0)	68.3	(5.9)
New Zealand	66.0	(6.6)	84.8	(4.3)
United Kingdom	56.2	(5.3)	62.7	(3.8)
Chile	91.0	(2.4)	88.3	(8.2)
Czech Republic	66.3	(7.5)	66.0	(8.3)
Denmark	53.3	(5.7)	61.4	(6.1)
Finland	44.6	(4.8)	60.9	(4.2)
Hungary	67.8	(6.3)	80.2	(3.7)
Norway	37.1	(5.4)	57.6*	(8.3)
Portugal	87.1	(4.9)	84.3	(4.9)
Slovenia	82.6	(4.6)	86.5	(3.0)

* Unreliable estimate.

1. Combined estimate for whole country population, 1994 and 1998.

Source: International Adult Literacy Survey, 1994-1998.

TABLE 4.5

PER CENT OF WORKERS IN THE WHITE-COLLAR, HIGH-SKILLED OCCUPATIONAL CATEGORY[1]
AND MEAN PROSE LITERACY PROFICIENCY, EMPLOYED POPULATION **16-65, 1994-1998**

	White-collar high-skilled		Prose mean	
Canada	39.4	(3.7)	278.8	(3.2)
Germany	34.4	(2.0)	275.9	(1.0)
Ireland	31.5	(2.3)	265.7	(3.3)
Netherlands	51.7	(1.2)	282.7	(0.8)
Poland	28.7	(1.3)	229.5	(1.1)
Sweden	55.7	(1.6)	301.3	(0.8)
Switzerland[2]	44.7	(1.7)	270.8	(1.3)
United States	35.8	(1.4)	273.7	(1.6)
Australia	32.7	(0.6)	274.2	(1.0)
New Zealand	33.9	(1.4)	275.2	(1.3)
United Kingdom	36.9	(1.3)	266.7	(1.8)
Chile	16.5	(1.7)	220.8	(2.1)
Czech Republic	40.5	(1.5)	269.4	(0.8)
Denmark	41.7	(1.1)	275.0	(0.7)
Finland	46.6	(1.1)	288.6	(0.7)
Hungary	35.3	(1.8)	242.4	(1.1)
Norway	44.3	(1.3)	288.5	(1.0)
Portugal	25.6	(1.9)	222.6	(3.7)
Slovenia	29.4	(1.5)	229.7	(1.5)

1. White-collar high-skilled category, based on ISCO 1988 includes: legislators, senior officials and managers, professionals, technicians and associate professionals.

2. Combined estimate for whole country population, 1994 and 1998.

Note: Belgium (Flanders) excluded because the data are not comparable.

Source: International Adult Literacy Survey, 1994-1998.

TABLE 4.6a-b

PER CENT OF EACH OCCUPATIONAL CATEGORY AT EACH LITERACY LEVEL, DOCUMENT SCALE,
POPULATION AGED **16-65, 1994-1998**

		Level 1		Level 2		Level 3		Level 4/5	
Canada	Manager/Professional	2.6*	(0.9)	14.9	(4.3)	32.4	(4.4)	50.1	(5.0)
	Technician	3.5*	(4.0)	12.1	(5.3)	58.6	(15.9)	25.9	(9.1)
	Clerk	8.2	(2.4)	26.8	(7.5)	36.7	(7.7)	28.3	(6.7)
	Sales/Service	16.4	(3.7)	29.7	(5.2)	29.0	(2.5)	24.8	(3.9)
	Skilled craft workers	24.7	(6.9)	30.5	(4.9)	28.8	(5.2)	16.1	(3.6)
	Machine operator/Assembler	27.7	(7.5)	31.3	(7.1)	26.4	(8.0)	14.6	(2.6)
	Agriculture/Primary	17.5	(3.0)	31.4	(3.6)	32.7	(2.7)	18.4	(2.9)
Germany	Manager/Professional	1.5*	(0.8)	20.0	(3.8)	36.4	(3.4)	42.1	(3.4)
	Technician	2.3*	(1.3)	14.0	(2.9)	54.2	(3.2)	29.6	(4.9)
	Clerk	5.4*	(1.8)	31.1	(4.4)	44.2	(3.4)	19.3	(2.9)
	Sales/Service	5.5*	(2.2)	37.3	(5.1)	39.3	(5.0)	17.9	(3.8)
	Skilled craft workers	6.7*	(2.1)	33.0	(4.2)	46.5	(3.0)	13.7*	(3.3)
	Machine operator/Assembler	11.7*	(4.8)	48.3	(5.8)	32.1*	(6.5)	7.8*	(4.5)
	Agriculture/Primary	19.0*	(5.0)	39.1	(7.6)	28.7*	(5.4)	13.2*	(6.4)
Ireland	Manager/Professional	5.2*	(1.7)	21.7	(2.2)	43.8	(3.3)	29.4	(4.9)
	Technician	10.8*	(5.0)	24.6	(4.1)	42.7	(4.0)	21.9	(2.7)
	Clerk	8.8*	(2.5)	31.2	(4.2)	43.1	(2.3)	16.9	(3.9)
	Sales/Service	16.8	(2.4)	32.8	(3.1)	37.0	(3.5)	13.5*	(2.7)
	Skilled craft workers	19.5	(3.5)	35.3	(7.0)	35.9	(3.9)	9.3*	(2.9)
	Machine operator/Assembler	25.3	(6.5)	35.9	(5.3)	32.9	(5.8)	6.0*	(2.5)
	Agriculture/Primary	35.8	(4.4)	35.1	(5.4)	23.4	(2.4)	5.8*	(1.0)

TABLE 4.6a-b (continued)

PER CENT OF EACH OCCUPATIONAL CATEGORY AT EACH LITERACY LEVEL, DOCUMENT SCALE,
POPULATION AGED **16-65, 1994-1998**

		Level 1		Level 2		Level 3		Level 4/5	
Netherlands	Manager/Professional	2.3*	(0.9)	17.1	(1.2)	52.5	(2.0)	28.0	(2.1)
	Technician	2.6*	(1.0)	15.1	(1.7)	49.6	(2.6)	32.7	(2.1)
	Clerk	5.0*	(1.6)	20.3	(2.5)	55.1	(4.2)	19.5	(3.4)
	Sales/Service	7.1*	(2.1)	24.1	(3.1)	49.0	(4.1)	19.8	(3.2)
	Skilled craft workers	9.1*	(2.3)	36.2	(3.4)	39.1	(3.9)	15.6	(2.8)
	Machine operator/Assembler	12.8*	(3.1)	33.4	(5.2)	36.2	(5.3)	17.5*	(4.5)
	Agriculture/Primary	16.4*	(3.2)	24.2	(3.5)	43.7	(3.5)	15.7*	(3.3)
Poland	Manager/Professional	19.2	(3.4)	28.4	(3.1)	33.9	(3.7)	18.4	(2.7)
	Technician	22.2	(3.2)	39.2	(2.1)	29.8	(4.0)	8.8*	(2.4)
	Clerk	33.1	(6.9)	31.7	(4.2)	28.1	(5.0)	7.1*	(2.5)
	Sales/Service	34.3	(3.5)	32.9	(3.8)	25.8	(3.7)	6.9*	(2.0)
	Skilled craft workers	47.1	(2.6)	30.4	(2.5)	16.6	(2.6)	5.9*	(1.2)
	Machine operator/Assembler	57.7	(4.9)	27.3	(3.0)	12.7*	(2.3)	2.3*	(1.0)
	Agriculture/Primary	60.5	(2.9)	29.3	(2.8)	8.9	(1.5)	1.3*	(0.4)
Sweden	Manager/Professional	1.6*	(0.6)	13.7	(1.5)	38.2	(2.2)	46.4	(1.6)
	Technician	2.8*	(0.5)	14.8	(1.7)	41.7	(2.1)	40.8	(3.0)
	Clerk	2.2*	(1.7)	15.8*	(3.3)	41.1	(4.2)	40.9	(3.9)
	Sales/Service	5.9*	(1.3)	21.5	(1.8)	41.3	(1.0)	31.3	(1.4)
	Skilled craft workers	8.4*	(2.1)	17.3	(2.8)	44.5	(4.2)	29.8	(3.6)
	Machine operator/Assembler	7.3*	(1.8)	19.3*	(4.2)	45.3	(6.3)	28.1	(4.5)
	Agriculture/Primary	11.0*	(2.5)	25.5	(5.5)	37.8	(4.0)	25.8	(5.0)
Switzerland[1]	Manager/Professional	5.1	(1.3)	25.2	(3.6)	45.3	(2.7)	24.4	(2.2)
	Technician	4.9	(1.0)	24.3	(2.5)	48.0	(3.0)	22.7	(2.9)
	Clerk	7.0	(2.3)	31.6	(3.4)	43.9	(4.6)	17.4	(3.4)
	Sales/Service	19.4	(3.5)	38.1	(3.0)	35.8	(3.7)	6.7	(1.6)
	Skilled craft workers	22.3	(4.0)	34.7	(4.8)	32.4	(3.1)	10.6	(2.7)
	Machine operator/Assembler	30.4	(5.0)	28.9	(5.1)	29.6	(4.8)	11.1*	(4.8)
	Agriculture/Primary	28.9	(5.2)	35.0	(3.3)	25.2	(3.7)	10.9	(2.6)
United States	Manager/Professional	5.1	(0.9)	14.9	(1.9)	41.0	(2.1)	39.1	(2.8)
	Technician	4.2*	(2.3)	17.0*	(4.8)	48.8	(6.5)	30.1*	(6.2)
	Clerk	11.1	(2.0)	34.0	(2.9)	33.1	(3.1)	21.8	(2.2)
	Sales/Service	26.6	(2.0)	25.4	(2.6)	32.8	(3.0)	15.2	(1.9)
	Skilled craft workers	29.9	(3.3)	37.6	(4.0)	25.0	(3.4)	7.4*	(2.2)
	Machine operator/Assembler	35.4	(2.9)	32.2	(3.0)	25.8	(3.1)	6.6*	(1.4)
	Agriculture/Primary	36.4*	(5.6)	12.2*	(7.3)	27.3*	(4.7)	24.1*	(6.4)
Australia	Manager/Professional	3.6	(0.6)	13.9	(1.1)	44.1	(1.5)	38.4	(1.4)
	Technician	6.9	(1.1)	22.5	(2.5)	46.5	(2.7)	24.1	(1.8)
	Clerk	4.9	(0.6)	24.8	(1.5)	48.4	(1.1)	22.0	(1.2)
	Sales/Service	11.4	(1.3)	33.6	(2.0)	40.5	(1.9)	14.4	(1.4)
	Skilled craft workers	15.4	(2.1)	33.0	(2.4)	40.0	(2.3)	11.6	(1.8)
	Machine operator/Assembler	25.5	(2.6)	34.3	(2.2)	30.4	(2.5)	9.9	(1.6)
	Agriculture/Primary	22.9	(1.7)	34.9	(1.9)	34.2	(1.5)	8.0	(1.0)
Belgium (Flanders)	Manager/Professional	3.6*	(2.7)	16.5*	(5.6)	53.1	(5.1)	26.8	(4.1)
	Technician	5.6*	(4.0)	11.8*	(4.8)	47.3	(6.9)	35.3*	(6.2)
	Clerk	1.4*	(0.9)	17.5	(4.4)	57.3	(3.6)	23.7	(3.9)
	Sales/Service	4.4*	(2.3)	18.2	(2.6)	50.3	(5.2)	27.1	(2.3)
	Skilled craft workers	18.6	(2.6)	28.8	(3.9)	40.5	(4.0)	12.1	(2.6)
	Agriculture/Primary	30.4*	(12.1)	21.5*	(18.0)	38.6*	(18.5)	9.5*	(7.1)
New Zealand	Manager/Professional	7.6	(1.3)	18.2	(2.3)	42.2	(2.4)	31.9	(1.8)
	Technician	7.2*	(2.2)	14.9	(3.1)	44.9	(4.2)	33.1	(4.2)
	Clerk	8.8*	(1.9)	31.8	(3.2)	38.0	(3.4)	21.3	(2.4)
	Sales/Service	15.8	(2.4)	31.4	(3.1)	37.8	(2.5)	15.0	(1.9)
	Skilled craft workers	15.4	(3.7)	38.4	(4.9)	36.5	(4.6)	9.7*	(2.0)
	Machine operator/Assembler	28.5	(4.3)	33.9	(3.6)	25.3	(3.7)	12.3	(2.8)
	Agriculture/Primary	28.7	(3.6)	33.4	(2.8)	27.6	(2.8)	10.3	(1.9)

TABLE 4.6a-b (continued)

PER CENT OF EACH OCCUPATIONAL CATEGORY AT EACH LITERACY LEVEL, DOCUMENT SCALE,
POPULATION AGED 16-65, 1994-1998

		Level 1		Level 2		Level 3		Level 4/5	
United Kingdom	Manager/Professional	6.5	(1.2)	18.8	(1.3)	38.3	(2.2)	36.4	(2.4)
	Technician	12.4	(3.5)	16.6	(2.9)	39.6	(4.1)	31.4	(4.8)
	Clerk	13.1	(1.5)	26.4	(2.3)	35.4	(2.7)	25.1	(2.4)
	Sales/Service	17.3	(2.5)	28.1	(3.0)	36.3	(3.3)	18.3	(2.5)
	Skilled craft workers	23.7	(2.6)	35.9	(3.5)	28.1	(2.2)	12.3	(2.6)
	Machine operator/Assembler	22.1	(2.6)	41.6	(3.8)	28.3	(3.6)	7.9	(2.2)
	Agriculture/Primary	36.9	(3.3)	27.3	(3.6)	27.3	(2.7)	8.5*	(1.9)
Chile	Manager/Professional	21.1	(6.6)	37.7	(6.7)	31.4	(7.3)	9.7*	(3.8)
	Technician	12.7*	(3.4)	44.3	(5.2)	34.8	(4.3)	8.2*	(4.7)
	Clerk	22.8	(3.6)	61.9	(4.8)	14.1	(2.9)	1.2*	(0.7)
	Sales/Service	53.1	(2.2)	34.2	(2.9)	11.9	(2.2)	0.8*	(0.7)
	Skilled craft workers	55.1	(3.5)	34.8	(3.6)	9.9	(2.1)	0.2*	(0.2)
	Machine operator/Assembler	53.6	(5.6)	33.5	(4.5)	12.6*	(3.4)	0.3*	(0.3)
	Agriculture/Primary	67.4	(2.6)	27.0	(2.5)	5.5	(1.2)	0.1*	(0.1)
Czech Republic	Manager/Professional	3.4*	(1.0)	22.2	(2.0)	43.6	(1.9)	30.8	(1.4)
	Technician	5.1*	(0.8)	22.5	(1.8)	46.3	(2.3)	26.1	(1.8)
	Clerk	7.6*	(1.5)	28.2	(5.1)	41.7	(4.4)	22.6	(3.4)
	Sales/Service	20.5	(2.5)	28.8	(4.9)	32.1	(3.7)	18.7	(3.9)
	Skilled craft workers	18.5	(2.7)	26.2	(2.1)	41.5	(3.0)	13.8	(2.4)
	Machine operator/Assembler	19.0	(2.8)	38.3	(3.7)	30.5	(3.7)	12.2	(2.1)
	Agriculture/Primary	22.7	(3.2)	32.9	(3.7)	33.2	(4.0)	11.1*	(2.6)
Denmark	Manager/Professional	0.9*	(0.5)	11.7	(1.4)	45.1	(2.6)	42.2	(2.8)
	Technician	1.9*	(0.6)	13.8	(1.9)	44.3	(1.9)	40.0	(1.9)
	Clerk	3.2*	(1.4)	20.8	(2.5)	48.0	(3.4)	28.0	(3.3)
	Sales/Service	7.5	(1.4)	26.5	(2.4)	42.4	(2.8)	23.6	(2.2)
	Skilled craft workers	9.8*	(1.8)	28.6	(3.4)	46.2	(2.9)	15.3	(2.5)
	Machine operator/Assembler	10.4*	(2.3)	26.7	(3.8)	46.0	(3.5)	16.9	(2.6)
	Agriculture/Primary	11.4	(1.5)	32.3	(2.8)	37.6	(2.6)	18.7	(2.1)
Finland	Manager/Professional	1.1*	(0.4)	12.2	(1.3)	41.1	(1.5)	45.6	(1.5)
	Technician	4.1*	(1.0)	22.2	(3.0)	45.9	(3.4)	27.8	(2.8)
	Clerk	3.3*	(1.3)	16.7	(2.3)	49.2	(3.6)	30.8	(3.6)
	Sales/Service	9.4*	(1.9)	26.8	(2.9)	38.8	(2.6)	25.1	(2.0)
	Skilled craft workers	12.7	(2.1)	31.5	(3.2)	39.8	(2.8)	16.0	(2.1)
	Machine operator/Assembler	11.7*	(3.0)	24.5	(2.9)	46.0	(3.3)	17.9*	(3.4)
	Agriculture/Primary	18.4	(2.4)	34.3	(2.3)	29.5	(2.5)	17.8	(2.4)
Hungary	Manager/Professional	10.3*	(2.2)	33.6	(3.8)	34.6	(3.4)	21.5	(4.0)
	Technician	17.7	(2.8)	29.8	(2.5)	36.6	(3.2)	16.0	(2.8)
	Clerk	26.1*	(6.5)	39.4*	(7.4)	25.7*	(6.4)	8.8*	(3.1)
	Sales/Service	25.9	(3.0)	40.8	(3.0)	27.6	(2.7)	5.8*	(2.0)
	Skilled craft workers	30.7	(1.8)	36.6	(2.6)	27.1	(2.7)	5.7*	(1.1)
	Machine operator/Assembler	24.6*	(4.1)	40.1	(5.1)	32.0*	(4.6)	3.3*	(2.0)
	Agriculture/Primary	46.6	(3.0)	33.9	(3.6)	17.4	(2.6)	2.2*	(0.9)
Norway	Manager/Professional	1.8*	(0.6)	13.0	(1.9)	41.1	(2.5)	44.1	(2.6)
	Technician	0.9*	(0.4)	11.3	(1.7)	41.9	(2.0)	45.9	(2.4)
	Clerk	3.3*	(1.2)	15.2	(2.6)	46.7	(3.5)	34.8	(2.7)
	Sales/Service	9.2	(1.4)	23.9	(1.4)	44.0	(2.4)	22.9	(1.8)
	Skilled craft workers	6.5*	(2.1)	19.5	(2.4)	47.8	(4.3)	26.2	(3.4)
	Machine operator/Assembler	11.3*	(2.3)	25.6	(4.3)	41.6	(5.2)	21.4	(2.9)
	Agriculture/Primary	14.6	(1.7)	33.1	(2.8)	36.8	(2.1)	15.5	(2.5)
Portugal	Manager/Professional	38.3*	(8.4)	25.7	(7.4)	28.0	(5.6)	8.0*	(2.3)
	Technician	10.4*	(2.8)	45.3	(4.8)	34.4	(3.8)	9.9*	(2.6)
	Clerk	14.5*	(4.2)	47.2	(4.5)	36.5	(4.0)	1.8*	(1.0)
	Sales/Service	62.9	(8.1)	21.8	(6.5)	13.3*	(3.1)	2.0*	(1.2)
	Skilled craft workers	74.7	(4.8)	19.2*	(4.5)	4.8*	(2.1)	1.3*	(1.2)
	Machine operator/Assembler	52.5*	(14.9)	43.8*	(15.5)	3.7*	(2.1)	0.0*	(0.0)
	Agriculture/Primary	63.4	(8.4)	28.0*	(7.9)	8.6*	(4.1)	0.0*	(0.0)

TABLE 4.6a-b (concluded)

PER CENT OF EACH OCCUPATIONAL CATEGORY AT EACH LITERACY LEVEL, DOCUMENT SCALE,
POPULATION AGED 16-65, 1994-1998

		Level 1		Level 2		Level 3		Level 4/5	
Slovenia	Manager/Professional	13.8	(2.2)	27.4	(3.4)	47.2	(3.5)	11.7	(2.3)
	Technician	11.9	(2.3)	38.7	(3.9)	34.7	(3.6)	14.8	(2.3)
	Clerk	22.2	(2.6)	35.2	(3.3)	34.8	(2.7)	7.8*	(1.6)
	Sales/Service	29.8	(3.3)	39.8	(3.0)	25.6	(3.1)	4.8*	(1.1)
	Skilled craft workers	47.3	(4.0)	35.9	(3.2)	16.5	(3.4)	0.4*	(0.4)
	Machine operator/Assembler	51.0	(2.5)	34.7	(2.6)	13.5	(1.8)	0.8*	(0.4)
	Agriculture/Primary	66.7	(4.5)	23.9	(3.9)	7.5*	(1.9)	2.0*	(1.2)
Average	**Manager/Professional**	**5.6**	**(0.5)**	**17.5**	**(1.1)**	**40.0**	**(1.2)**	**36.9**	**(1.5)**
	Technician	**7.3**	**(0.6)**	**21.8**	**(1.3)**	**46.1**	**(1.4)**	**24.8**	**(1.4)**
	Clerk	**11.0**	**(1.0)**	**31.9**	**(1.6)**	**36.6**	**(1.3)**	**20.5**	**(1.2)**
	Sales/Service	**24.0**	**(1.2)**	**28.0**	**(1.4)**	**33.0**	**(1.6)**	**15.0**	**(1.0)**
	Skilled craft workers	**27.1**	**(1.2)**	**34.2**	**(1.3)**	**29.2**	**(1.4)**	**9.4**	**(0.8)**
	Machine operator/Assembler	**32.5**	**(2.0)**	**34.0**	**(1.5)**	**25.8**	**(2.2)**	**7.7**	**(1.1)**
	Agriculture/Primary	**39.5**	**(1.6)**	**28.5**	**(1.8)**	**22.8**	**(0.9)**	**9.2**	**(1.0)**

* Unreliable estimate.

1. Combined estimate for whole country population, 1994 and 1998.

Note: Chile, Poland, Portugal and the United States are excluded from Figure 4.6 because the data are unreliable. Belgium (Flanders) is excluded from Figure 4.6 because not all of the occupational categories are classified in a comparable way.

Source: International Adult Literacy Survey, 1994-1998.

TABLE 4.6c

PER CENT OF SKILLED CRAFT WORKERS AND MACHINE OPERATORS AT EACH LITERACY LEVEL,
DOCUMENT SCALE, POPULATION AGED 16-65, 1994-1998

	Level 1		Level 2		Level 3		Level 4/5	
Canada	26.2	(6.3)	30.9	(5.1)	27.6	(5.8)	15.3	(1.6)
Germany	8.1*	(2.6)	37.2	(3.5)	42.6	(3.5)	12.1	(2.5)
Ireland	21.7	(2.6)	35.5	(3.9)	34.8	(3.5)	8.0*	(2.4)
Netherlands	10.5	(1.9)	35.2	(3.0)	38.0	(3.3)	16.3	(2.8)
Poland	50.6	(1.9)	29.4	(2.1)	15.3	(2.1)	4.7*	(0.9)
Sweden	8.0	(1.3)	18.0	(2.7)	44.8	(4.7)	29.2	(3.3)
Switzerland[1]	24.2	(3.1)	33.3	(3.5)	31.7	(2.3)	10.7	(2.2)
United States	33.0	(1.9)	34.6	(2.5)	25.5	(2.2)	7.0	(1.3)
Australia	20.3	(1.5)	33.6	(1.3)	35.3	(1.6)	10.8	(1.3)
Belgium (Flanders)	18.6	(2.6)	28.8	(3.9)	40.5	(4.0)	12.1	(2.6)
New Zealand	23.1	(2.9)	35.8	(3.1)	29.9	(2.7)	11.2	(1.7)
United Kingdom	23.2	(2.0)	37.9	(2.3)	28.2	(2.0)	10.7	(1.7)
Chile	54.5	(2.7)	34.3	(2.7)	11.0	(1.6)	0.2*	(0.2)
Czech Republic	18.7	(1.9)	31.3	(2.0)	36.8	(2.2)	13.2	(1.3)
Denmark	10.1	(1.4)	27.8	(2.1)	46.1	(2.2)	16.0	(1.7)
Finland	12.4	(1.9)	28.9	(2.3)	42.1	(2.2)	16.7	(2.0)
Hungary	29.5	(1.5)	37.3	(2.0)	28.0	(2.4)	5.2*	(0.9)
Norway	8.8	(1.3)	22.4	(2.5)	44.9	(3.0)	23.9	(2.1)
Portugal	66.6	(6.1)	28.2	(6.2)	4.4*	(1.5)	0.8*	(0.8)
Slovenia	49.7	(1.9)	35.1	(2.1)	14.5	(1.7)	0.7*	(0.3)
Average	**29.5**	**(1.0)**	**34.1**	**(1.1)**	**27.7**	**(1.2)**	**8.7**	**(0.8)**

* Unreliable estimate.

1. Combined estimate for whole country population, 1994 and 1998.

Note: Chile, Ireland, Hungary, Poland, Portugal and Slovenia are excluded from Figure 4.6 because the data are unreliable.

Source: International Adult Literacy Survey, 1994-1998.

TABLE 4.7a-b

PROBABILITY OF BEING IN OCCUPATIONAL CATEGORY BY INCREASING LITERACY SCORES FOR MEN
WITH UPPER SECONDARY EDUCATION, WORKING IN ONE OF TWO INDUSTRIAL SECTORS
AND HAVING RECEIVED ADULT EDUCATION, PROSE SCALE, POPULATION AGED **36-45**, 1994-1998

	Prose literacy score										
	0	50	100	150	200	250	300	350	400	450	500
A. Community, social and personal services sector											
White-collar high-skilled[1]	0.15	0.22	0.31	0.41	0.52	0.63	0.72	0.80	0.86	0.91	0.94
White-collar low-skilled[2]	0.14	0.14	0.15	0.16	0.16	0.17	0.18	0.19	0.19	0.20	0.21
Blue-collar high-skilled[3]	0.21	0.19	0.17	0.14	0.13	0.11	0.09	0.08	0.07	0.06	0.05
Blue-collar low-skilled[4]	0.34	0.26	0.20	0.15	0.11	0.08	0.06	0.04	0.03	0.02	0.01
B. Manufacturing sector											
White-collar high-skilled[1]	0.04	0.07	0.10	0.15	0.21	0.30	0.39	0.50	0.61	0.71	0.79
White-collar low-skilled[2]	0.06	0.06	0.06	0.06	0.07	0.07	0.07	0.08	0.08	0.09	0.09
Blue-collar high-skilled[3]	0.55	0.51	0.47	0.43	0.39	0.35	0.32	0.28	0.25	0.22	0.20
Blue-collar low-skilled[4]	0.63	0.55	0.46	0.37	0.29	0.23	0.17	0.12	0.09	0.07	0.05

See Box 4A in the text for further information on the logit model.

1. White-collar high-skilled: Legislators, senior officials and managers and professionals, technicians and associate professionals.
2. White-collar low-skilled: Service workers and shop and market sales workers and clerks.
3. Blue-collar high-skilled: Skilled agricultural and fishery workers and craft and related trades workers.
4. Blue-collar low-skilled: Plant and machine operators and assemblers and elementary occupations.

Source: International Adult Literacy Survey, 1994-1998.

TABLE 4.8

PROBABILITY OF BEING WHITE-COLLAR HIGH-SKILLED BY INCREASING LITERACY SCORES FOR MEN
WORKING IN THE TRANSPORT, STORAGE AND COMMUNICATIONS SECTORS AND WHO HAVE NOT RECEIVED ADULT EDUCATION,
PROSE SCALE, POPULATION AGED **26-35**, 1994-1998

	Prose literacy score										
	0	50	100	150	200	250	300	350	400	450	500
With less than upper secondary education	0.05	0.07	0.11	0.16	0.22	0.31	0.41	0.52	0.63	0.73	0.81
Completed upper secondary education	0.09	0.13	0.19	0.27	0.37	0.48	0.59	0.69	0.77	0.84	0.89
Completed tertiary education	0.26	0.36	0.47	0.58	0.68	0.77	0.84	0.89	0.93	0.95	0.97

See Box 4A in the text for further information on the logit model.
Source: International Adult Literacy Survey, 1994-1998.

TABLE 4.9a-c

PER CENT OF POPULATION AGED 25-65 AT EACH LITERACY LEVEL WHO ARE IN THE TOP 60 PER CENT
OF EARNERS, 1994-1998

	Level 1		Level 2		Level 3		Level 4/5	
A. Prose								
Canada	23.5	(6.4)	44.9	(8.4)	56.9	(3.0)	68.9	(7.5)
Germany	35.4	(4.2)	43.7	(2.5)	49.9	(3.5)	55.8	(3.1)
Ireland	23.7	(2.6)	45.0	(3.8)	60.3	(3.0)	75.0	(4.0)
Netherlands	33.0	(4.3)	47.9	(1.7)	60.7	(1.6)	63.3	(3.1)
Poland	57.3	(2.1)	64.6	(1.5)	74.5	(2.6)	86.9	(4.2)
Sweden	72.3	(6.1)	78.8	(2.4)	81.3	(1.5)	82.6	(1.9)
Switzerland[1]	46.0	(6.0)	59.3	(4.3)	72.0	(3.9)	70.7	(5.1)
United States	13.4	(1.9)	31.6	(2.8)	47.4	(2.6)	60.3	(2.6)
Australia	26.4	(1.8)	43.8	(1.4)	50.8	(1.2)	57.9	(1.7)
Belgium (Flanders)	5.8*	(1.2)	13.0	(2.1)	23.0	(1.9)	33.7	(3.7)
New Zealand	34.0	(3.0)	53.7	(3.1)	62.9	(2.3)	73.4	(2.3)
United Kingdom	24.9	(1.9)	42.5	(2.2)	56.5	(1.7)	71.5	(3.0)
Chile	25.7	(1.8)	44.1	(2.0)	60.8	(3.2)	71.8*	(9.2)
Czech Republic	17.4	(2.6)	27.8	(2.0)	41.7	(2.7)	54.7	(4.1)
Denmark	36.5	(3.6)	56.9	(1.5)	70.1	(1.5)	67.3	(5.2)
Finland	25.7	(2.6)	52.1	(2.0)	66.7	(1.5)	73.7	(2.4)
Hungary	20.6	(1.4)	40.9	(2.2)	61.7	(3.7)	54.9*	(9.8)
Norway	37.8	(4.6)	57.3	(2.3)	73.6	(1.2)	69.6	(2.3)
Portugal	52.0	(3.8)	59.4	(4.3)	75.2	(4.4)	73.9	(6.1)
Slovenia	23.2	(1.3)	51.7	(2.6)	71.8	(2.8)	67.0*	(8.5)
Average	**25.6**	**(1.0)**	**41.2**	**(1.2)**	**52.5**	**(1.4)**	**62.2**	**(1.5)**
B. Document								
Canada	17.9	(3.7)	46.5	(8.5)	58.3	(5.6)	72.8	(8.2)
Germany	28.3	(2.7)	40.2	(3.6)	50.8	(2.1)	56.4	(5.2)
Ireland	24.6	(3.3)	46.5	(3.7)	63.6	(2.3)	74.4	(5.0)
Netherlands	27.7	(4.4)	45.8	(2.0)	59.9	(1.3)	68.0	(3.0)
Poland	57.6	(2.0)	66.5	(1.3)	70.6	(2.7)	81.2	(3.4)
Sweden	70.1	(4.2)	72.5	(2.6)	82.9	(1.5)	83.6	(1.4)
Switzerland[1]	42.4	(4.6)	60.9	(5.0)	68.5	(3.5)	74.0	(4.5)
United States	16.6	(1.8)	32.3	(2.6)	47.3	(2.7)	64.9	(2.7)
Australia	23.5	(1.5)	39.5	(1.2)	53.4	(1.3)	63.6	(1.7)
Belgium (Flanders)	3.1*	(1.1)	13.5	(2.2)	22.7	(2.1)	29.0	(2.9)
New Zealand	32.8	(2.9)	52.6	(3.0)	67.3	(2.0)	76.8	(2.6)
United Kingdom	22.6	(1.9)	42.1	(2.0)	55.7	(1.7)	75.0	(2.5)
Chile	26.0	(1.8)	42.4	(2.6)	68.2	(3.2)	59.0*	(11.6)
Czech Republic	13.2	(2.6)	26.5	(2.2)	40.7	(1.7)	44.5	(3.1)
Denmark	35.8	(4.3)	49.4	(2.1)	65.6	(1.5)	76.0	(2.0)
Finland	26.1	(2.1)	51.9	(2.2)	67.1	(1.4)	75.3	(1.9)
Hungary	20.6	(1.5)	38.0	(2.1)	52.5	(3.5)	70.3	(4.9)
Norway	31.4	(4.3)	54.1	(2.6)	69.0	(2.1)	80.0	(1.6)
Portugal	50.9	(3.2)	65.0	(4.0)	73.1	(5.3)	77.2	(7.3)
Slovenia	22.6	(1.4)	48.4	(2.3)	74.1	(2.5)	69.4	(7.7)
Average	**24.2**	**(0.9)**	**40.4**	**(1.0)**	**52.4**	**(1.2)**	**66.0**	**(1.3)**

TABLE 4.9a-c (concluded)

PER CENT OF POPULATION AGED 25-65 AT EACH LITERACY LEVEL WHO ARE IN THE TOP 60 PER CENT
OF EARNERS, 1994-1998

	Level 1		Level 2		Level 3		Level 4/5	
C. Quantitative								
Canada	20.2	(5.0)	43.1	(8.7)	55.3	(5.8)	75.7	(8.0)
Germany	33.8	(3.8)	36.6	(3.7)	48.9	(2.3)	56.1	(3.2)
Ireland	24.2	(2.8)	42.8	(3.7)	61.6	(3.4)	75.9	(4.0)
Netherlands	25.8	(3.7)	46.2	(2.3)	58.3	(1.3)	70.0	(2.8)
Poland	55.4	(2.0)	64.4	(1.9)	69.1	(1.9)	86.1	(3.4)
Sweden	63.5	(4.2)	76.0	(3.1)	81.9	(1.8)	83.9	(1.5)
Switzerland[1]	42.3	(6.6)	54.0	(4.3)	68.0	(4.0)	75.8	(3.5)
United States	12.2	(1.9)	29.7	(2.1)	44.9	(3.0)	65.9	(2.3)
Australia	21.0	(1.6)	38.8	(1.3)	51.8	(1.4)	65.8	(1.5)
Belgium (Flanders)	3.3*	(1.2)	12.8	(2.0)	18.6	(2.3)	34.9	(3.0)
New Zealand	31.2	(3.2)	53.5	(2.7)	65.0	(2.0)	78.2	(2.3)
United Kingdom	21.6	(1.9)	41.2	(1.7)	53.8	(2.2)	78.1	(1.9)
Chile	24.4	(1.6)	42.9	(2.9)	73.1	(3.5)	67.7	(9.1)
Czech Republic	13.3*	(3.4)	22.7	(1.7)	33.6	(2.0)	46.1	(2.0)
Denmark	37.8	(4.2)	44.2	(2.5)	63.4	(1.5)	76.9	(1.8)
Finland	26.6	(2.6)	53.9	(2.1)	63.8	(1.5)	77.4	(1.6)
Hungary	18.2	(1.5)	32.5	(2.2)	45.2	(3.0)	60.5	(3.4)
Norway	33.3	(3.1)	53.5	(2.2)	66.9	(1.5)	81.6	(2.1)
Portugal	49.9	(3.9)	56.6	(5.9)	76.6	(5.7)	74.4	(8.4)
Slovenia	20.7	(1.7)	43.7	(2.2)	64.6	(2.9)	72.9	(3.9)
Average	**22.3**	**(1.0)**	**37.8**	**(1.0)**	**50.7**	**(1.1)**	**66.5**	**(1.1)**

* Unreliable estimate.

1. Combined estimate for whole country population, 1994 and 1998.

Source: International Adult Literacy Survey, 1994-1998.

TABLE 4.10-4.11

PER CENT OF VARIANCE (R^2) IN EARNINGS ACCOUNTED FOR BY SIX PREDICTOR[1] VARIABLES
(STANDARDISED MAXIMUM LIKELIHOOD REGRESSION WEIGHT) AND MEASURES OF MODEL FIT
(STANDARD ERRORS TIMES 100 IN BRACKET), POPULATION AGED 25-55, 1994-1998

	Australia		Belgium (Flanders)		Canada		Chile		Czech Republic		Denmark		Finland	
Gender	0.410	(1.1)	0.484	(2.4)	0.515	(1.6)	0.545	(1.7)	0.465	(1.9)	0.442	(1.9)	0.259	(2.1)
Parents' education	-0.015	(1.4)	-0.035	(3.2)	-0.089	(2.2)	0.057	(2.5)	0.047	(2.4)	-0.022	(2.3)	0.046	(2.5)
Native versus foreign language	0.058	(1.2)	0.041	(2.4)	0.051	(1.6)	-0.012	(1.5)	0.062	(1.8)	-0.029	(1.8)	0.071	(2.1)
Respondent's education	0.284	(4.1)	0.441	(9.5)	0.278	(6.7)	0.403	(9.6)	0.375	(8.8)	0.330	(7.0)	0.306	(4.8)
Respondent's literacy proficiency	0.248	(4.3)	0.154	(11.2)	0.317	(7.7)	0.100	(10.5)	0.084	(10.4)	0.186	(8.0)	0.288	(5.3)
Experience	0.118	(1.2)	0.155	(2.7)	0.202	(1.8)	0.127	(2.0)	0.227	(2.1)	0.265	(2.0)	0.335	(2.3)
Earnings, explained variance	0.397	—	0.475	—	0.481	—	0.536	—	0.408	—	0.415	—	0.274	—
Root Mean Square Residual	0.029	—	0.021	—	0.020	—	0.017	—	0.019	—	0.034	—	0.042	—
Goodness of Fit Index	0.938	—	0.964	—	0.978	—	0.966	—	0.982	—	0.937	—	0.938	—

	Germany		Hungary		Ireland		Netherlands		New Zealand		Norway		Poland	
Gender	0.499	(2.4)	0.187	(2.3)	0.359	(2.2)	0.480	(1.9)	0.453	(1.7)	0.426	(1.8)	0.287	(2.0)
Parents' education	-0.212	(3.1)	0.078	(2.7)	0.051	(3.1)	-0.002	(2.4)	0.004	(1.8)	0.012	(2.1)	0.108	(9.1)
Native versus foreign language	0.064	(2.4)	0.005	(2.1)	0.025	(2.2)	0.055	(1.9)	0.136	(1.6)	0.020	(1.9)	0.010	(1.9)
Respondent's education	0.360	(9.1)	0.399	(8.4)	0.312	(10.7)	0.304	(4.2)	0.289	(10.0)	0.171	(6.4)	0.352	(7.9)
Respondent's literacy proficiency	0.078	(10.3)	0.192	(9.7)	0.212	(12.0)	0.164	(4.5)	0.259	(10.4)	0.283	(7.1)	0.001	(3.1)
Experience	0.196	(2.9)	0.084	(2.5)	0.107	(2.6)	0.206	(2.1)	0.161	(1.6)	0.217	(2.0)	0.164	(2.4)
Earnings, explained variance	0.389	—	0.333	—	0.349	—	0.411	—	0.467	—	0.354	—	0.224	—
Root Mean Square Residual	0.020	—	0.019	—	0.018	—	0.039	—	0.030	—	0.029	—	0.019	—
Goodness of Fit Index	0.969	—	0.976	—	0.964	—	0.922	—	0.948	—	0.956	—	0.975	—

	Portugal		Slovenia		Sweden		Switzerland[2]		United Kingdom		United States	
Gender	0.346	(3.6)	0.239	(2.0)	0.409	(2.2)	0.387	(1.6)	0.373	(1.3)	0.360	(1.9)
Parents' education	0.213	(11.6)	-0.008	(2.9)	0.067	(2.5)	-0.063	(1.9)	-0.062	(1.5)	-0.019	(2.6)
Native versus foreign language	0.062	(3.6)	-0.033	(2.0)	0.017	(2.3)	0.008	(1.6)	0.030	(1.2)	-0.041	(2.2)
Respondent's education	0.231	(8.8)	0.462	(12.8)	0.228	(7.5)	0.402	(3.7)	0.383	(6.6)	0.384	(8.7)
Respondent's literacy proficiency	0.197	(8.4)	0.184	(14.6)	0.103	(8.8)	0.115	(4.0)	0.287	(6.5)	0.241	(9.7)
Experience	0.346	(4.3)	0.051	(2.4)	0.370	(2.5)	0.286	(1.8)	0.166	(1.3)	0.113	(2.2)
Earnings, explained variance	0.408	—	0.374	—	0.299	—	0.388	—	0.482	—	0.432	—
Root Mean Square Residual	0.027	—	0.016	—	0.035	—	0.037	—	0.036	—	0.016	—
Goodness of Fit Index	0.932	—	0.972	—	0.948	—	0.949	—	0.933	—	0.974	—

1. Education is measured as a latent construct with the variables "years of schooling" and "completed levels of education" in the models specified for Australia, Finland, Netherlands, New Zealand, Sweden, Switzerland and United Kingdom.
   Due to the very high correlations between "years of schooling" and "completed levels of education", the education construct is measured by either one of these variables in the models specified for the other countries.
2. Combined estimate for whole country population, 1994 and 1998.
Source: International Adult Literacy Survey, 1994-1998.

TABLE 4.12

RELATIONSHIP BETWEEN GDP PER CAPITA (IN CURRENT PRICES, EQUIVALENT US DOLLARS CONVERTED USING PPPS),
LIFE EXPECTANCY AT BIRTH (1997) AND PER CENT OF ADULTS AT LITERACY LEVELS 1 AND 2 AND LEVEL 4/5,
PROSE SCALE, POPULATION AGED 16-65, 1994-1998

	Per cent at Levels 1 and 2		Per cent at Level 4/5		GDP per capita[1]	Life expectancy at birth
Canada	42.2	(1.9)	22.7	(2.3)	22 735	79.0
Germany	48.6	(0.6)	13.4	(1.0)	21 221	77.2
Ireland	52.4	(2.5)	13.5	(1.4)	18 484	76.3
Netherlands	40.6	(0.9)	15.3	(0.6)	21 089	77.9
Poland	77.2	(0.7)	3.1	(0.3)	6 884	72.5
Sweden	27.8	(0.7)	32.4	(0.5)	19 730	78.5
Switzerland[2]	54.1	(1.0)	9.2	(0.7)	25 088	78.6
United States	46.5	(1.2)	21.1	(1.2)	27 936	76.7
Australia	44.2	(0.6)	18.9	(0.5)	21 223	78.2
Belgium (Flanders)	46.6	(3.2)	14.3	(1.2)	22 205	77.2
New Zealand	45.8	(1.0)	19.2	(0.7)	17 345	76.9
United Kingdom	52.1	(1.3)	16.6	(0.7)	19 521	77.2
Chile	85.1	(1.5)	1.6	(0.4)	12 730	74.9
Czech Republic	53.8	(0.9)	8.4	(0.4)	12 902	73.9
Denmark	46.0	(0.9)	6.5	(0.4)	24 872	75.7
Finland	36.7	(0.7)	22.4	(0.6)	20 032	76.8
Hungary	76.6	(1.1)	2.6	(0.4)	9 735	70.9
Norway	33.2	(1.1)	17.6	(0.9)	26 428	78.1
Portugal	77.0	(1.2)	4.4	(0.5)	14 607	75.3
Slovenia	76.7	(1.0)	3.2	(0.3)	11 800	74.4

1. GDP per capita in Purchasing Power Parity (PPP) using 1996 prices and exchange rates for first and interim wave of data collection and 1998 prices and exchange rates for second wave of data collection.
2. Combined estimate for whole country population, 1994 and 1998.
Sources: International Adult Literacy Survey, 1994-1998; OECD database; UNDP, *Human Development Report, 1999.*

TABLE 4.13

RELATIONSHIP BETWEEN ECONOMIC INEQUALITY (GINI COEFFICIENT) AND INEQUALITY IN THE DISTRIBUTION
OF LITERACY (9th DECILE/1st DECILE) WITHIN COUNTRIES, PROSE SCALE, 1994-1998

	Literacy inequality	Economic inequality
Canada	1.78	28.5
Germany	1.51	28.2
Ireland	1.71	32.4
Netherlands	1.48	25.5
Sweden	1.51	23.0
Switzerland[1]	1.72	26.9
United States	1.90	34.4
Australia	1.69	30.5
Belgium (Flanders)	1.68	27.2
United Kingdom	1.75	32.4
Denmark	1.39	21.7
Finland	1.54	22.8
Norway	1.44	25.6

See Box 4D in text for definition and scale of economic inequality.
1. Combined estimate for whole country population, 1994 and 1998.
Note: Poland, New Zealand, Chile, Czech Republic, Hungary, Portugal, Slovenia are excluded because comparable data are unavailable.
Sources: International Adult Literacy Survey, 1994-1998; OECD, *Trends in Income Distribution and Poverty in OECD Area,* 1999.

TABLE 4.14 For data values for FIGURE 4.14, see TABLE 4.12

TABLE 4.15

RELATIONSHIP BETWEEN THE PROPORTION OF SEATS IN PARLIAMENT HELD BY WOMEN AND MEAN LITERACY PROFICIENCY,
PROSE SCALE, POPULATION AGED **16-65, 1994-1998**

	Mean		Seats in parliament held by women
Canada	278.8	(3.2)	23.3
Germany	275.9	(1.0)	29.8
Ireland	265.7	(3.3)	13.7
Netherlands	282.7	(0.8)	31.6
Poland	229.5	(1.1)	12.9
Sweden	301.3	(0.8)	42.7
Switzerland[1]	270.5	(1.3)	20.3
United States	273.7	(1.6)	12.5
Australia	274.2	(1.0)	25.9
Belgium (Flanders)	271.8	(3.9)	15.8
New Zealand	275.2	(1.3)	29.2
United Kingdom	266.7	(1.8)	12.3
Chile	220.8	(2.1)	9.0
Czech Republic	269.4	(0.8)	13.9
Denmark	275.0	(0.7)	37.4
Finland	288.6	(0.7)	33.5
Hungary	242.4	(1.1)	8.3
Norway	288.5	(1.0)	36.4
Portugal	222.6	(3.7)	13.0
Slovenia	229.7	(1.5)	7.8

1. Combined estimate for whole country population, 1994 and 1998.

Sources: International Adult Literacy Survey, 1994-1998; UNDP, *Human Development Report,* 1999.

ANNEX E

Source Database for the International Adult Literacy Survey[*]

AUSTRALIAN BUREAU OF STATISTICS (1997a*), Aspects of Literacy: Profiles and Perceptions, Australia, 1996*, ABS Catalogue No. 4226.0, Australian Bureau of Statistics, Canberra.

AUSTRALIAN BUREAU OF STATISTICS (1997b), *Aspects of Literacy: Assessed Skill Levels, Australia, 1996*, ABS Catalogue No. 4228.0, Australian Bureau of Statistics, Canberra.

BETCHERMAN, G., McMULLEN, K., and DAVIDMAN, K. (1998), *Training for the New Economy: A Synthesis Report*, CPRN, Ottawa.

BINKLEY, M., MATHESON, N., and WILLIAMS, T. (1997), "Adult literacy: An international perspective", Working paper No. 97-33, US Department of Education, Washington, DC.

BLOOM, M., BURROWS, M., LAFLEUR, B., and SQUIRES, R. (1997), *The Economic Benefits of Improving Literacy Skills in the Workplace*, Report 206-97, The Conference Board of Canada, Ottawa.

CAREY, S., LOW, S., and HANSBRO, J. (1997), *Adult Literacy in Britain*, J0024129, C15, 9/97, 5673, The Stationery Office, London.

DECKER, P.T., RICE, J.K., MOORE, M.T., and ROLLEFSON, M.R. (1997), *Education and the Economy: An Indicators Report*, NCES 97-269, U.S. Department of Education, Washington, DC.

DEPARTMENT FOR EDUCATION AND EMPLOYMENT (1996), *The Skills Audit: A Report from an Interdepartmental Group*, DfEE and Cabinet Office, London.

DEPARTMENT FOR EDUCATION AND EMPLOYMENT (1999), *Improving Literacy and Numeracy: A Fresh Start,* The Report of the Working Group Chaired by Sir Claus Moser, DfEE Publications, London.

ECONOMIST (1996), "Learning to cope", in "Training and jobs, What works?", *The Economist,* April 6, 1996, Vol. 339, No. 7960, pp. 19-21, The Economist Newspaper Limited, New York.

FREEMAN, R.B., and SCHETTKAT, R. (2000), "The role of wage and skill differences in US-German employment differences", NBER Working Paper No. 7474, National Bureau of Economic Research, Cambridge, MA.

FUNDAÇÃO CALOUSTE GULBENKIAN (1996), *A Literacia em Portugal: Resultados de uma pesquisa extensiva e monográfica*, Conselho nacional de Educação, Berna, Lisboa.

GARCEAU, M.-L. (1998), *Alphabétisme des adultes en Ontario français : Résultats de l'Enquête internationale sur l'alphabétisation des adultes*, Centre FORA, Sudbury, Ontario.

---

* This annex contains selected references to academic work and policy documents that build on the data collected as part of the International Adult Literacy Survey. Due to limitations of space the bibliography provided here is not exhaustive. Readers may contact Statistics Canada for information about the source database. Additional reference materials can be accessed at site: http://www.nald.ca/nls/ials/introduc.htm

GOUVERNEMENT DU QUÉBEC (1997), *Education Indicators*, Edition 1996 and 1997, Ministère de l'Éducation, Québec.

GUSTAVSSON, A.-L. (1997), *Reading: A need, a requirement, a necessity,* FiF Report, Linköping University, Department of Education and Psychology, Linköping.

HOUTKOOP, W. (1996), "De lees- en rekenvaardigheid van de Nederlanders internationaal bezien", *Kwartaalschrift Onderwijsstatistieken*, Vol. 3 (2).

HOUTKOOP, W. (1999), *De "geletterdheid" van de Nederlandse beroepsbevolking*, Max Goote Kenniscentrum, Amsterdam.

HOUTKOOP, W., and OOSTERBEEK, H. (1997), "Supply and demand of adult education and training", in P. Bélanger and A. Tuijnman (Eds.), *New Patterns of Adult Learning: A Six-country Comparative Study*, Elsevier Science and Pergamon Press, Oxford.

HUMAN RESOURCES DEVELOPMENT CANADA (1998), "Literacy skills of Canadian youth", *Applied Research Bulletin*, Vol. 4 (1), pp. 3-5, HRDC, Applied Research Branch, Ottawa.

HUMAN RESOURCES DEVELOPMENT CANADA and NATIONAL LITERACY SECRETARIAT (1998), *Policy Strategies for Improving Literacy Skills,* HRDC, Ottawa.

JENSEN, T.P., HOLM, A., ANDERSEN, A., HASTRUP, S., HEINSKOV, M.B., and JACOBSEN, J.E. (2000), *Danskernes læse-regnefærdigheder: Udvalgte resultater*, AKF Förlaget, Copenhaguen.

KAPSALIS, C. (1998), "The connection between literacy and work: Implications for social assistance recipients", Working paper W-98-1E, HRDC, Applied Research Branch, Ottawa.

LAFLAMME, S., and BERNIER, C. (1998), *Vivre dans l'alternance linguistique : Médias, langue et littératie en Ontario français*, Centre FORA, Sudbury, Ontario.

LEHMANN, R.H. (1997), "Alfabetismo em Países Industrializados – Mudanças de Perspectiva e Abordagens de Pesquisa", in Instituto Brasileiro de Estudos e Apoio Comunitário (Ed.), *Educação e Escolarização de Jovens e Adultos, Vol. 1: Experiências Internacionais*, pp. 104-124, Ministério da Educação e do Desporto, Brasília.

LEHMANN, R.H. and PEEK, R. (1995), "Zur Anwendung eines kognitiven Tests im Rahmen einer Haushaltsbefragung. Methodische Probleme bei der Erhebung von Grundqualifikationen Erwachsener", in R. Arbinger and R.S. Jäger (Eds.), *Empirische Pädagogik. Zeitschrift zu Theorie und Praxis erziehungswissenschaftlicher Forschung, Beiheft 4*, pp. 469-481, Zentrum für empirische pädagogische Forschung, Landau.

LURIN, J. and SOUSSI, A. (1998), *La littératie à Genève : Enquête sur les compétences des adultes dans la vie quotidienne,* Cahier 2, septembre, Service de la Recherche en Éducation, Geneva.

MARTIN, J.P. (1998), "Education and economic performance in the OECD countries: An elusive relationship?", *Journal of the Statistical and Social Inquiry Society of Ireland,* 1997/1998, pp. 99-128.

MORGAN, M., HICKEY, B., and KELLAGHAN, T. (1997), *International Adult Literacy Survey: Results for Ireland,* M25372, The Stationery Office, Dublin.

MOSENTHAL, P.B. (1998), "Defining prose task characteristics for use in computer-adaptive testing and instruction", *American Educational Research Journal,* Vol. 35 (2), pp. 269-307, American Educational Research Association, Washington, DC.

MOZINA, E., KNAFLIC, I., and EMERSIC, B. (1998), *Nacionalna raziskava pismenosti in udelezbe odraslih v izobrazevanju, Tehnicno porocilo*, Slovenian Institute for Adult Education, Slovenia.

MYRBERG, M. (1997), "To learn or not to learn from everyday experience", in M. Matsberg (Ed.), *Bridging the Gap*, CEDEFOP, Tessaloniki.

MYRBERG, M. (2000), *Invandrares läs-, skriv- och räkneförmåga*, Skolverket, Stockholm, February.

NATIONAL CENTER FOR EDUCATION STATISTICS (1998), *Adult Literacy in OECD Countries: Technical Report on the First International Adult Literacy Survey*, NCES Report No. 98-053, US Department of Education, Washington, DC.

NIER (1997), *Study on Adult Learning Corresponding to the OECD International Adult Literacy Survey*, National Institute for Educational Research, Tokyo.

NOTTER, Ph. (1997), "Ausbildung und Lesekompetenz. Eine Analyse aufgrund der Schweizer Daten der 'International Adult Literacy Survey'", *Bildungsforschung und Bildungspraxis*, Band 19, Heft 3, pp. 292-314.

NOTTER, Ph., BONERAD, E.-M., and STOLL, F. (Hrsg.) (1999), *Lesen – eine Selbstverständlichkeit? Schweizer Bericht zum "International Adult Literacy Survey"*, Rüegger, Chur.

OECD (1996), *Education at a Glance: Analysis*, Paris.

OECD (1996), *Education at a Glance: OECD Indicators 1996*, Paris.

OECD (1996), *Lifelong Learning for All*, Paris.

OECD (1997), *Education at a Glance: OECD Indicators 1997*, Paris.

OECD (1997), *Education Policy Analysis 1997*, Paris.

OECD (1998), *Education at a Glance: OECD Indicators 1998*, Paris.

OECD (1998), *Education Policy Analysis 1998*, Paris.

OECD (1998), *Employment Outlook,* June, Paris.

OECD (1998), *Human Capital Investment: An International Comparison*, Paris.

OECD (1999), *Education Policy Analysis 1999*, Paris.

OECD (1999), *Employment Outlook,* June, Paris.

OECD and HUMAN RESOURCES DEVELOPMENT CANADA (1997), *Literacy Skills for the Knowledge Society: Further Results from the International Adult Literacy Survey*, Paris.

OECD and STATISTICS CANADA (1995), *Literacy, Economy and Society: Results of the First International Adult Literacy Survey*, Paris and Ottawa.

ONS (2000), *Measuring Adult Literacy: The International Adult Literacy Survey in the European Context*, Office for National Statistics, London.

OOSTERBEEK, H. (1998), "Unravelling supply and demand factors in work-related training*", Oxford Economic Papers,* Vol. 50, pp. 266-283.

QUÉBEC, MINISTÈRE DE L'ÉDUCATION DU (1996), *Making Choices Together: The Cost and Results of Education*, Les publications du Québec, Québec.

RAUDENBUSH, S.W., and KASIM, R.M. (1998), "Cognitive skill and economic inequality", *Harvard Educational Review,* Vol. 68, No. 1, pp. 33-79.

ROY, S. (1997), *L'alphabétisme et l'alphabétisation des groupes minoritaires du Canada*, Secrétariat national à l'alphabétisation, Ottawa.

RUBENSON, K. (1997), "Adult education and training: The poor cousin - An analysis of national policies for education", WRNET Working Paper 97.02, University of British Columbia, Vancouver.

SKOLVERKET (1996), *Grunden för fortsatt lärande: En internationell jämförande studie av vuxnas förmåga att förstå och använda tryckt och skriven information*, Rapport 96:265, Liber Distribution, Stockholm.

STATISTICS CANADA (1996), "Reading between the lines: Some other results from the International Adult Literacy Survey", *Focus on Culture*, Statistics Canada Catalogue No. 87-004-XPB, Vol. 8, No. 3, Autumn, 5, Minister of Industry, Ottawa.

STATISTICS CANADA (1997), *A Portrait of Seniors in Canada,* Second Edition, Statistics Canada Catalogue No. 89-519-XPE, Minister of Industry, Ottawa.

STATISTICS CANADA and HUMAN RESOURCES DEVELOPMENT CANADA (1997), *Literacy Skills of Canadian Youth*, Statistics Canada Catalogue No. 89-552-MPE, No. 1, Minister of Industry, Ottawa.

STATISTICS CANADA and HUMAN RESOURCES DEVELOPMENT CANADA (1997), *Employee Training: An International Perspective*, Statistics Canada Catalogue No. 89-552-MPE, Minister of Industry, Ottawa.

STATISTICS CANADA and HUMAN RESOURCES DEVELOPMENT CANADA (1998a), *The Value of Words: Literacy and Economic Security in Canada*, Statistics Canada Catalogue No. 89-552-MPE, Minister of Industry, Ottawa.

STATISTICS CANADA and HUMAN RESOURCES DEVELOPMENT CANADA (1998b), *Literacy Utilization in Canadian Workplaces*, Statistics Canada Catalogue No. 89-552-MPE, Minister of Industry, Ottawa.

STATISTICS CANADA and HUMAN RESOURCES DEVELOPMENT CANADA (1998c), *At Risk: A Socio-economic Analysis of Health and Literacy Among Seniors*, Statistics Canada Catalogue No. 89-552-MPE, Minister of Industry, Ottawa.

STATISTICS CANADA and HUMAN RESOURCES DEVELOPMENT CANADA (1999), *Inequalities in Literacy Skills Among Youth in Canada and the United States*, Statistics Canada Catalogue No. 89-552-MPE, Minister of Industry, Ottawa.

STATISTICS CANADA, HUMAN RESOURCES DEVELOPMENT CANADA and NATIONAL LITERACY SECRETARIAT (1996), *Reading the Future: A Portrait of Literacy in Canada*, Statistics Canada Catalogue No. 89-551-XPE, Minister of Industry, Ottawa.

STOLL, F., and NOTTER, Ph. (1999), *Lesekompetenzen der Erwachsenen in der Schweiz. Umsetzungsbericht zum Nationalen Forschungsprogramm 33: Wirksamkeit unserer Bildungssysteme*, Programmleitung NFP 33 in Zusamenarbeit mit der Schweizerischen Koordinationsstelle für Bildungsforschung, Bern.

SWEENEY, K., MORGAN, B., and DONNELLY, D. (1998), *Adult Literacy in Northern Ireland*, Northern Ireland Statistics and Research Agency, The Stationery Office Limited, London.

TUIJNMAN, A.C. (1998), "Schriftkundigkeit in vergleichender perspektive aus sicht der OECD", in W. Stark, T. Fitzner, and C. Schubert (Eds.), *Wer Schreibt, Der Bleibt! Und Wer Nicht Schreibt?*, Ernst Klett Verlag, Stuttgart.

TUIJNMAN, A.C. (1998), "Nödvändiga basfärdigheter för vuxna i kunskapssamhället", in A. Mäkitalo and L.-E. Olsson (Eds.), *Vuxenpedagogik i teori och praktik: Kunskapslyftet i focus,* Statens Offentliga Utredningar, SOU 1997:158, Stockholm.

UNDP (1998), *Human Development Report*, Oxford University Press, New York.

van DAMME, D. (1998), "Wat leert ons de International Adult Literacy Survey? Beleidsaanbevelingen op basis van de internationale en Vlaamse IALS-resultaten", *Tijdschrift voor Onderwijsrecht en Onderwijsbeleid 1998-1999*, Vol. 3-4, pp. 248-261.

van DAMME, D., van de POELE, L., and VERHASSELT, E. (1997), *Hoe geletterd/gecijferd is Vlaanderen? Functionele taal- en rekenvaardigheden van Vlamingen in internationaal perspectief*, NUGI:722, Garant Uitgevers, Brussels.

van der KAMP, M. (1997), "European Traditions in Literacy Research and Measurement", in A. Tuijnman, I. Kirsch, and D.A. Wagner (Eds.), *Adult Basic Skills: Innovations in Measurement and Policy Analysis*, Hampton Press, Cresskil, NJ.

van der KAMP, M., and SCHEEREN, J. (1996), *Functionele taal- en rekenvaardigheden van oudere volwassenen in Nederland*, Max Goote Kenniscentrum, Amsterdam.

van der KAMP, M., and SCHEEREN, J. (1997), "New Trajectories of Learning Across the Lifespan", in P. Bélanger and A. Tuijnman (Eds*.), New Patterns of Adult Learning: A Six-country Comparative Study*, pp. 131-154, Elsevier Science and Pergamon Press, Oxford.

van WIERINGEN, F., and ATTWELL, G. (Eds) (1999), *Vocational and Adult Education in Europe*, Kluwer Academic Publishers, Dordrecht.

ANNEX F

Principal Participants in the Project

International Direction and Co-ordination

Ms. Nancy Darcovich
International Study Director for SIALS, Statistics Canada, Ottawa

Mr. T. Scott Murray
International Study Director for IALS, Statistics Canada, Ottawa

Mr. Albert Tuijnman
International Study Co-ordinator, National Agency for Education, Stockholm, and Institute of International Education, Stockholm

Mr. Abrar Hasan
International Study Co-ordinator, OECD, Paris

International Scoring and Scaling

Mr. Irwin Kirsch
Educational Testing Service, Princeton

Mr. Kentaro Yamamoto
Educational Testing Service, Princeton

Ms. Minh-Wei Wang,
Educational Testing Service, Princeton

National Study Managers

Australia	Mr. Mel Butler *Australian Bureau of Statistics, Canberra*
Chile	Mr. David Bravo *Universidad de Chile, Santiago*
Czech Republic	Mr. Petr Mateju *Academy of Sciences, Prague*
Belgium	Mr. Luc van de Poele *University of Ghent, Ghent*

National Study Managers

Canada	Mr. Jean Pignal *Statistics Canada, Ottawa*
Denmark	Mr. Torben Pilegaard Jensen *Danish Institute of Local Government Studies, Copenhagen*
Finland	Ms. Pirjo Linnakylä *University of Jyväskylä, Jyväskylä*
Germany	Mr. Rainer Lehmann *Humboldt University, Berlin*
Great Britain	Ms. Siobhàn Carey *Office for National Statistics, London*
Hungary	Ms. Judit Krolopp *National Institute of Public Education, Budapest*
Italy	Ms. Vittoria Gallina *Centro Europeao Dell'Educazione, Frascati*
Ireland	Mr. Mark Morgan *St. Patrick's College, Dublin*
Netherlands	Mr. Willem Houtkoop *Max Goote Expert Center, Amsterdam*
New Zealand	Mr. Hans Wagemaker *IEA Secretariat, Amsterdam, formerly Ministry of Education, Wellington*
Northern Ireland	Mr. Kevin Sweeney *Central Survey Unit, Belfast*
Norway	Mr. Egil Gabrielsen *Centre for Reading Research, Stavanger*
Poland	Mr. Ireneusz Bialecki *Warsaw University, Warsaw*
Portugal	João Sebastião *Centro de Investigação e Estudos de Sociologia, Lisbon*
Slovenia	Ms. Ester Mozina *Slovene Adult Education Centre, Ljubljana*
Sweden	Mr. Mats Myrberg *Linköping University, Linköping*
Switzerland	Mr. Philipp Notter *University of Zurich, Zurich*
	Ms. Francesca Pedrazzini-Pesce *Ufficio Studi e Ricerche, Bellinzona*
	Mr. François Stoll *University of Zurich, Zurich*
United States	Ms. Marilyn Binkley *National Center for Education Statistics, Washington, DC*

Survey Team, Analysts and Production Team

Ms. Danielle Baum
Statistics Canada, Ottawa

Mr. Yves Bélanger
Statistics Canada, Ottawa

Mr. Emmanuel Boudard
Institute of International Education, Stockholm

Mr. Richard Desjardins
Statistics Canada, Ottawa

Ms. Marlène Mohier
Organisation for Economic Co-operation and Development, Paris

Mr. Richard Porzuczek
Statistics Canada, Ottawa

Ms. Cindy Sceviour
Statistics Canada, Ottawa

Ms. Sophie Vayssettes
Organisation for Economic Co-operation and Development, Paris

Mr. Kentaro Yamamoto
Educational Testing Service, Princeton

Ms. Minh-Wei Wang
Educational Testing Service, Princeton

Authors

Ms. Nancy Darcovich
Statistics Canada, Ottawa

Mr. Abrar Hasan
Organisation for Economic Co-operation and Development, Paris

Mr. Stan Jones
Statistics Canada, Yarmouth

Mr. Irwin Kirsch
Educational Testing Service, Princeton

Mr. T. Scott Murray
Statistics Canada, Ottawa

Ms. Beatriz Pont
Organisation for Economic Co-operation and Development, Paris

Mr. Kjell Rubenson
University of British Columbia, Vancouver

Mr. Albert Tuijnman (Editor)
National Agency for Education, Stockholm and
Institute of International Education, Stockholm

Mr. Patrick Werquin
Organisation for Economic Co-operation and Development, Paris

Mr. J. Douglas Willms
University of New Brunswick, Fredericton

OECD PUBLICATIONS, 2 rue André-Pascal, 75775 PARIS CEDEX 16
PRINTED IN FRANCE
(81 2000 051 P) ISBN 92-64-17654-3 - No. 50551 2000